Bibliotheca Britannica Philosophica

The Works of George Berkeley Bishop of Cloyne

Volume Four

The Works of George Berkeley
Bishop of Cloyne

Edited by

A A Luce and T E Jessop

Volume Four

De Motu with an English Translation
The Analyst
A Defence of Free-thinking in Mathematics
Reasons for not replying to Mr. Walton's *Full Answer*
Arithmetica and Miscellanea Mathematica
Of Infinites
Letters on Vesuvius, on Petrifactions, and on Earthquakes
Description of the Cave of Dunmore

Edited by

A A Luce DD Litt D
Senior Fellow Trinity College Dublin

NELSON

THOMAS NELSON AND SONS LTD
36 Park Street London W1
Parkside Works Edinburgh 9
117 Latrobe Street Melbourne C1
10 Warehouse Road Apapa Lagos

THOMAS NELSON AND SONS (AFRICA) (Pty) LTD
P.O. Box 9881 Johannesburg

THOMAS NELSON AND SONS (CANADA) LTD
81 Curlew Drive Don Mills Ontario

THOMAS NELSON AND SONS
Copewood and Davis Streets Camden 3, N.J.

SOCIÉTÉ FRANÇAISE D'ÉDITIONS NELSON
97 rue Monge Paris 5

———

First published 1951
Reprinted 1964

EDITOR'S PREFACE

THE contents of this volume are somewhat miscellaneous, and they differ widely *inter se* both in date and in degree of importance. You have here Berkeley's publications and other writings on mathematics, physics, and natural history. The more important pieces, namely, the *De Motu*, and the *Analyst* with its mathematical sequels, are given in chronological order. The very early writings, the *Of Infinites* and the *Description of the Cave of Dunmore*, and the first publication, the *Arithmetica* and *Miscellanea Mathematica*, being mainly of biographical interest, have been grouped according to subject-matter.

My acknowledgments are due to my colleagues, Mr. F. La T. Godfrey and Professor E. J. Furlong, who have read the proof-sheets and have made valuable suggestions. I am obliged to the Representative Church Body, St. Stephen's Green, Dublin, for the loan of their copy of that very rare book, the original edition of the *De Motu*.   A. A. L.

LIST OF ABBREVIATIONS

BERKELEY'S WRITINGS

PC   the *Philosophical Commentaries* (by A. C. Fraser misnamed 'Commonplace Book of occasional metaphysical thoughts'). Sometimes, too, I refer to *PC* as *Commentaries*. The entry numbers are those of my (1944) edition.

TV   *An Essay towards a New Theory of Vision* I also refer to it as *Essay on Vision*.

Princ. *A Treatise concerning the Principles of Human Knowledge* (which I sometimes refer to simply as *Principles*).

Defence *A Defence of free-thinking in mathematics*

LL   *Life and Letters of George Berkeley, D.D.*, by A. C. Fraser, Volume IV of his edition of Berkeley's Works (1871)

CONTENTS

De Motu

Sive de motus principio & natura
et de causa communicationis motuum

First printed in 1721

EDITOR'S INTRODUCTION

BERKELEY's *De motu sive de motus principio & natura, et de causa communicationis motuum* was published in 1721. The title-page gives the author as ' G.B.' and bears the imprint, ' Londini : Impensis Jacobi Tonson MDCCXXI.' Berkeley refers to the tract in his *Analyst* (Qu. 9) and in *Siris* (S. 249), and in a letter of 25 November 1729, to his American friend, Samuel Johnson, he writes, ' As for absolute space and motion. . . . I refer you to what I have already published ; particularly in a Latin treatise, *De Motu*, which I shall take care to send you.' He republished it in 1752 in his *Miscellany* a few months before his death.

Our only information about the occasion of the work is a remarkably precise statement, furnished no doubt by Dr. Robert Berkeley, the Bishop's brother, in Stock's Life—' On his way homeward [*i.e.* from the Continent] he drew up at Lyons a curious tract *De Motu* which he sent to the Royal Academy of Sciences at Paris, the subject being proposed by that assembly and committed it to the press shortly after his arrival in London in 1721.' Fraser adds that a prize for an essay on the ' cause of Motion ' was offered in 1720 by the Paris Academy of Sciences, and that the prize was awarded to Crousaz, the logician and professor of philosophy at Lausanne.

The *De Motu* is written in good, correct Latin, but in construction and balance the workmanship falls below Berkeley's usual standards. The title is ambitious for so brief a tract, and may lead the reader to expect a more sustained argument than he will find. A more modest title, say *Motion without Matter*, would fitly describe its scope and content. Regarded as a treatise on motion in general, it is a slight and disappointing work ; but viewed from a narrower angle, it is of absorbing interest and high importance. It is the application of immaterialism to contemporary problems of motion, and should be read as such. It is clear proof, if proof were needed, that Berkeley never abandoned the philosophy of his youth. In early middle life Berkeley wrote and published the *De Motu*, and he brought out a second edition in the last year of his life, thus placing the seal of his mature

DE MOTU

approval upon the argument of the *Principles* : for apart from the *Principles* the *De Motu* would be nonsense. The tract was no sudden incursion into physics. The French prize, if it was the occasion, was not the motive. Berkeley had the work in mind some fifteen years before he wrote it ; it is a sequel to the great works of his youth, and must be read in conjunction with them. On the third page of his *Philosophical Commentaries* we find the entries :

> [13]×   Motion, figure & extension perceivable by sight are different from those ideas perceived by touch wch goe by the same name.   (28)
>
> N   Qu: how to reconcile Newton's 2 sorts of motion with my doctrine.   (30)

The marginal signs connect the entries, respectively, with the Essay on Vision and the intended book on Natural Philosophy, and these entries together with the many other entries on motion show that the young immaterialist habitually considered motion in connection with his creed. He could not banish material substance from the world at rest, and allow it back into the world in motion. In the Essay on Vision (SS. 137–8) he discusses visible motion and tangible motion, and shows their heterogeneity, adding ' The consideration of motion may furnish a new field for inquiry.' That inquiry is to some extent represented in the *Principles* (SS. 97, 102–5, 110–16), but the promise of an inquiry was not fully redeemed till the *De Motu* was published, and as a redemption of that promise the tract should to-day be read. It arose directly from the discussions in the *Commentaries*, and it treats of those problems and aspects of motion which are of significance for immaterialism or create difficulties for the immaterialist. Newton's doctrine of gravitation, as popularly understood, and his absolute space, time, and motion were utterly at variance with Berkeley's conception of nature, and in the *De Motu* Berkeley examines and refutes them, and substitutes his own world of passive, significant realities *in* the mind of God and *for* the mind of man. The spirit of the Introduction to the *Principles* presides over the argument of the *De Motu*, the spirit of concrete thinking with the rejection of abstract ideas.

ANALYSIS

The sub-title of the work is threefold and promises to treat of the principle of motion, of the nature of motion, and of the cause of the communication of motions. There are three corresponding divisions, SS. 1–42, SS. 43–66, and SS. 67–72. Here is a brief analysis of the three divisions :

The Principle of Motion. Obscure and abstract terms used in contemporary physics must be criticized ; such are *solicitation of gravity, urge,* and *dead forces.* The first two terms characterize the animate, and if applied to the inanimate are only metaphorical. Gravity known by sense is real, but gravity, a supposed occult quality with the power of the cause, is a mere abstract idea. Sensible gravity is accelerated motion towards the centre of the earth, and if we are supporting a body so moving we feel the corresponding muscular effort. The same is true of other forces and of force in general. What is known of them by sense is the sensible effect, the visible and tangible motions ; but when the mind goes further and reads into the force the cause of the motions, it turns the force into an occult quality. Torricelli and Leibniz have used the term *force* in such a way as to occasion absurd notions (like the small force of percussion, infinitely great) and idle controversies like that between Newton, Leibniz and Borelli on *impetus.* Terms like *hylarchic principle, natural appetite,* or *instinct* are non-explanatory.

For the true principle of motion we must turn to the true philosophy ; and here (SS. 21*ff*) Berkeley touches on his own metaphysic, using Cartesian terms, as was proper in an essay to be submitted, apparently, to French *savants,* but giving those terms a turn which brings them into line with his own technique. There are two supreme classes of things, body and soul, and these are heterogeneous. Then comes a passage which is pure Berkeley, which converts the Cartesian ' body and soul ' into, respectively, Berkeleian ' sensible idea and spirit,' thus indissolubly binding the *De Motu* to the *Principles.* Both these ultimate categories are, he says, categories of the *known.* Body is known by sense, and soul by consciousness. ' Loquor autem de rebus cognitis, de incognitis enim disserere nil juvat.' That statement puts a world of difference between Berkeleian ' body ' known by its sensible qualities, and the unknown and unknowable matter which Descartes taught and tried in vain to prove.

To seek the principle of motion in the former category is useless ; for all body is passive and inert ; there is nothing in body which could make a movement begin to be, and we may not postulate occult virtues and qualities. Minds or thinking things, on the other hand, can cause motion. We know it by experience. The mind, therefore, is a principle of motion, depending on the first and universal principle.

Anaxagoras was the first to express this truth, which was accepted by Plato and Aristotle and, in later days, by the Schoolmen, the Cartesians, and Newton.

Attraction, resistance, persistence, and vitality are not principles of motion ; they may be principles of science, primary laws, proved by experiment and developed by reason, and a thing is explained mechanically when it is reduced to one such principle ; but in the precise sense of the term *the principle of motion* must be the true, efficient, and conserving cause of all things.

The Nature of Motion (SS. 43–66). The division begins and ends on a positive note ; the central portion refutes false opinions. We know motion by our senses, and we never meet it apart from bodily mass, space, and time. The nature of motion is, therefore, what *in concreto* we see and touch it to be ; if we wish to know what motion is we must watch things that move. There are three maxims for determining its nature : (1) distinguish mathematical hypotheses from the nature of things ; (2) distinguish abstractions from reality ; (3) consider *sensible,* or at least *imaginable,* motion.

Those who try to consider motion as a simple and abstract idea create difficulties, as happened both with Aristotle and with Newton. Some have even pushed abstraction into the constituent parts of motion, forming abstract ideas of movement, velocity, urge, force, and impetus, thus increasing the confusion and multiplying paradox. The Cartesian view that the same quantity of motion is conserved and the Peripatetic doctrine that motion is the act of both mover and moved are to be rejected ; they fail by insufficiently distinguishing cause from effect.

Sections 52–65 cover much the same ground as the *Principles* (SS. 110–16), and make reference to that work. Their chief concern is Newton's doctrine of absolute space and motion. Absolute space is defined entirely in negative terms and is indistinguishable from nothing. Space and motion in space are essentially relative, the very notion of motion implying two bodies and the relation between them. Circular motion is no exception, and there is nothing in Newton's experiment of the rotating bucket of water to justify belief in absolute circular motion.

The Cause of the Communication of Motions (SS. 67–72). This last division is a mere sketch, outlining theories of Newton and Torricelli, suggesting that the latter is rather closer to the facts, but that both theories are adequate for the purposes of physics. Physics aims at bringing a given motion under rule, and at connecting it with a wide mechanical principle, but does not attempt to give the metaphysical explanation or to assign the truly active and incorporeal cause. The universal Mind which causes motion communicates it.

THE TEXT AND TRANSLATION

The present text has been printed from that of the *Miscellany*, which is virtually identical with that of the original edition. Berkeley carefully prepared both his editions, correcting in 1752 half a dozen small blunders which had crept into the previous edition. I have removed the accents from the Latin words, and have corrected without remark two or three obvious blunders, and have noted in footnotes two or three unimportant alternatives which my collation revealed. Of variants proper there are none.

The translation is my own, but I have consulted and used G. N. Wright's version of 1843. I have tried to avoid the extremes of free rendering and literalness, and have aimed at presenting a version which can be read with ease and yet is faithful to the sense of the original.

De Motu

The Text

DE MOTU

SIVE

DE MOTUS PRINCIPIO & NATURA, ET DE CAUSA
COMMUNICATIONIS MOTUUM

1 Ad veritatem inveniendam præcipuum est cavisse ne voces
male intellectæ nobis officiant : quod omnes fere monent philosophi, pauci observant. Quanquam id quidem haud adeo difficile
videtur, in rebus præsertim Physicis tractandis, ubi locum habent
sensus, experientia, & ratiocinium geometricum. Seposito
igitur, quantum licet, omni præjudicio, tam a loquendi consuetudine, quam a philosophorum auctoritate nato, ipsa rerum natura
diligenter inspicienda. Neque enim cujusquam auctoritatem
usque adeo valere oportet, ut verba ejus & voces in pretio sint,
dummodo nihil clari & certi iis subesse comperiatur.

2 Motus contemplatio mire torsit veterum philosophorum
mentes, unde natæ sunt variæ opiniones supra modum difficiles, ne
dicam absurdæ, quæ quum jam fere in desuetudinem abierint,
haud merentur ut iis discutiendis nimio studio immoremur. Apud
recentiores autem & saniores hujus ævi Philosophos, ubi de motu
agitur, vocabula haud pauca abstractæ nimium & obscuræ
significationis occurrunt, cujusmodi sunt *solicitatio gravitatis,
conatus, vires mortuæ,* &c. quæ scriptis alioqui doctissimis tenebras
offundunt, sententiisque, non minus a vero quam a sensu hominum
communi abhorrentibus ortum præbent. Hæc vero necesse est
ut, veritatis gratia, non alios refellendi studio, accurate discu-
tiantur.

3 Solicitatio & nisus sive conatus rebus solummodo animatis
revera competunt. Cum aliis rebus tribuuntur, sensu meta-
phorico accipiantur necesse est. A metaphoris autem abstinen-
dum philosopho. Porro seclusa omni tam animæ affectione quam
corporis motione, nihil clari ac distincti iis vocibus significari
cuilibet constabit, qui modo rem serio perpenderit.

4 Quamdiu corpora gravia a nobis sustinentur, sentimus in
nobismet ipsis nisum, fatigationem, & molestiam. Percipimus
etiam in gravibus cadentibus motum acceleratum versus centrum

11

telluris : ope sensuum præterea nihil. Ratione tamen colligitur causam esse aliquam vel principium horum phænomenon, illud autem *gravitas* vulgo nuncupatur. Quoniam vero causa descensus gravium cæca sit & incognita : gravitas ea acceptione proprie dici nequit qualitas sensibilis : est igitur qualitas occulta. Sed vix, & ne vix quidem, concipere licet quid sit qualitas occulta, aut qua ratione qualitas ulla agere aut operari quidquam possit. Melius itaque foret, si, missa qualitate occulta, homines attenderent solummodo ad effectus sensibiles, vocibusque abstractis, (quantumvis illæ ad disserendum utiles sint) in meditatione omissis, mens in particularibus & concretis, hoc est in ipsis rebus, defigeretur.

5 *Vis* similiter corporibus tribuitur ; usurpatur autem vocabulum illud, tanquam significaret qualitatem cognitam, distinctamque tam a motu, figura, omnique alia re sensibili, quam ab omni animalis affectione, id vero nihil aliud esse quam qualitatem occultam rem acrius rimanti constabit. Nisus animalis & motus corporeus vulgo spectantur tanquam symptomata & mensuræ hujus qualitatis occultæ.

6 Patet igitur gravitatem aut vim frustra poni pro principio motus : nunquid enim principium illud clarius cognosci potest ex eo quod dicatur qualitas occulta ? Quod ipsum occultum est nihil explicat. Ut omittamus causam agentem incognitam rectius dici posse substantiam quam qualitatem. Porro, *vis*, *gravitas*, & istiusmodi voces fæpius, nec inepte, in concreto usurpantur, ita ut connotent corpus motum, difficultatem resistendi, *&c.* Ubi vero a Philosophis adhibentur ad significandas naturas quasdam ab hisce omnibus præcisas & abstractas, quæ nec sensibus subjiciuntur nec ulla mentis vi intelligi nec imaginatione effingi possunt, tum demum errores & confusionem pariunt.

7 Multos autem in errorem ducit, quod voces generales & abstractas in disserendo utiles esse videant, nec tamen earum vim satis capiant. Partim vero a consuetudine vulgari inventæ sunt illæ ad sermonem abbreviandum, partim, a Philosophis ad docendum excogitatæ : non, quod ad naturas rerum accommodatæ sint, quæ quidem singulares, & concretæ existunt, fed quod idoneæ ad tradendas disciplinas, propterea quod faciant notiones vel saltem propositiones universales.

8 Vim corpoream esse aliquid conceptu facile plerumque existimamus : ii tamen qui rem accuratius inspexerunt in diversa sunt opinione, uti apparet ex mira verborum obscuritate qua laborant, ubi illam explicare conantur. Torricellius ait vim &

impetum esse res quasdam abstractas subtilesque, & quintessentias
quæ includuntur in substantia corporea, tanquam in vase magico
Circes [1]. Leibnitius item in natura vis explicanda hæc habet.
Vis activa, primitiva, quæ est ἐντελέχεια ἡ πρώτη, *animæ vel
formæ substantiali respondet. vid. Acta erudit. Lips.* Usque adeo
necesse est ut vel summi viri quamdiu abstractionibus indulgent,
voces nulla certa significatione præditas & meras scholasticorum
umbras sectentur. Alia ex neotericorum scriptis, nec pauca
quidem ea, producere liceret, quibus abunde constaret, metaphysicas abstractiones non usquequaque cessisse mechanicæ &
experimentis, sed negotium inane philosophis etiamnum facessere.

9 Ex illo fonte derivantur varia absurda cujus generis est
illud, *vim percussionis utcunque exiguæ esse infinite magnam.* Quod sane
supponit, gravitatem esse qualitatem quandam realem ab aliis
omnibus diversam : & gravitationem esse quasi actum hujus
qualitatis a motu realiter distinctum ; minima autem percussio
producit effectum majorem quam maxima gravitatio sine motu.
Illa scilicet motum aliquem edit, hæc nullum. Unde sequitur,
vim percussionis ratione infinita excedere vim gravitationis, hoc
est esse infinite magnam. Videantur experimenta Galilæi & quæ
de definita vi percussionis scripserunt Torricellius, Borellus & alii.

10 Veruntamen fatendum est vim nullam per se immediate
sentiri, neque aliter quam per effectum cognosci & mensurari ;
sed vis mortuæ seu gravitationis simplicis, in corpore quiescente
subjecto nulla facta mutatione, effectus nullus est. Percussionis
autem, effectus aliquis. Quoniam ergo vires sunt effectibus proportionales : concludere licet vim mortuam esse nullam : neque
tamen propterea vim percussionis esse infinitam : non enim
oportet quantitatem ullam positivam habere pro infinita, propterea quod ratione infinita superet quantitatem nullam sive nihil.

11 Vis gravitationis a momento secerni nequit, momentum
autem sine celeritate nullum est, quum sit moles in celeritatem
ducta, porro celeritas sine motu intelligi non potest, ergo nec vis
gravitationis. Deinde, vis nulla nisi per actionem innotescit &
per eandem mensuratur, actionem autem corporis a motu præ-
scindere non possumus, ergo, quamdiu corpus grave plumbi
subjecti vel chordæ figuram mutat, tamdiu movetur : ubi vero

---

[1] La materia altro non e che un vaso di Circe incantato, il quale serve per
ricettacolo della forza & de momenti dell' impeto. La forza & l'impeti sono
astratti tanto sottili, sono quintessenze tanto spiritose, che in altre ampolle
non si possono racchiudere, fuor che nell' intima corpulenza de solidi naturali.
Vid. *Lezioni Academiche.*

quiescit, nihil agit, vel, quod idem est, agere prohibetur. Breviter, voces istæ *vis mortua* & *gravitatio*, etsi per abstractionem metaphysicam aliquid significare supponuntur diversum a movente, moto, motu & quiete, revera tamen id totum nihil est.

12 Siquis diceret pondus appensum vel impositum agere in chordam, quoniam impedit quominus se restituat vi elastica : dico, pari ratione corpus quodvis inferum agere in superius incumbens, quoniam illud descendere prohibet : dici vero non potest actio corporis, quod prohibeat aliud corpus existere in eo loco quem occupat.

13 Pressionem corporis gravitantis quandoque sentimus. Verum sentio ista molesta oritur ex motu corporis istius gravis fibris nervisque nostri corporis communicato, & eorundem situm immutante, adeoque percussioni accepta referri debet. In hisce rebus multis & gravibus præjudiciis laboramus, sed illa acri atque iterata meditatione subigenda sunt, vel potius penitus averruncanda.

14 Quo probetur, quantitatem ullam esse infinitam, ostendi oportet partem aliquam finitam homogeneam in ea infinities contineri. Sed vis mortua se habet ad vim percussionis non ut pars ad totum, sed ut punctum ad lineam, juxta ipsos vis infinitæ percussionis auctores. Multa in hanc rem adjicere liceret sed vereor ne prolixus sim.

15 Ex principiis præmissis lites insignes solvi possunt, quæ viros doctos multum exercuerunt. Hujus rei exemplum sit controversia illa de proportione virium. Una pars dum concedit, momenta, motus, impetus, data mole, esse simpliciter ut velocitates, affirmat vires esse ut quadrata velocitatum. Hanc autem sententiam supponere, vim corporis distingui a momento, motu, & impetu, eaque suppositione sublata corruere, nemo non videt.

16 Quo clarius adhuc appareat, confusionem quandam miram per abstractiones metaphysicas in doctrinam de motu introductam esse, videamus quantum intersit inter notiones virorum celebrium de vi & impetu. Leibnitius impetum cum motu confundit. Juxta Newtonum impetus revera idem est cum vi inertiæ. Borellus asserit impetum non aliud esse quam gradum velocitatis. Alii impetum & conatum inter se differre, alii non differre volunt. Plerique vim motricem motui proportionalem intelligunt, nonnulli aliam aliquam vim præter motricem, & diversimode mensurandam, utpote per quadrata velocitatum in moles, intelligere præ se ferunt. Sed infinitum esset hæc prosequi.

17 *Vis, gravitas, attractio*, & hujusmodi voces utiles sunt ad

ratiocinia, & computationes de motu & corporibus motis : fed
non ad intelligendam simplicem ipsius motus naturam, vel ad
qualitates totidem distinctas designandas. Attractionem certe
quod attinet, patet illam ab Newtono adhiberi, non tanquam
qualitatem veram & physicam, sed solummodo ut hypothesin
mathematicam. Quin & Leibnitius, nisum elementarem seu
solicitationem ab impetu distinguens, fatetur illa entia non re
ipsa inveniri in rerum natura, sed abstractione facienda esse.

18 Similis ratio est compositionis & resolutionis virium qua-
rumcunque directarum in quascunque obliquas, per diagonalem
& latera parallelogrammi. Hæc mechanicæ & computationi
inserviunt : sed aliud est computationi & demonstrationibus
mathematicis inservire, aliud, rerum naturam exhibere.

19 Ex recentioribus multi sunt in ea opinione, ut putent
motum neque destrui nec de novo gigni, sed eandem semper
motus quantitatem permanere. Aristoteles etiam dubium illud
olim proposuit, utrum motus factus sit & corruptus, an vero ab
æterno ? *Phys.* l. 8. Quod vero motus sensibilis pereat, patet
sensibus, illi autem eundem impetum, nisum, aut summam virium
eandem manere velle videntur. Unde affirmat Borellus, vim in
percussione, non imminui sed expandi, impetus etiam contrarios
suscipi & retineri in eodem corpore. Item Leibnitius nisum ubique
& semper esse in materia, &, ubi non patet sensibus, ratione
intelligi contendit. Hæc autem nimis abstracta esse & obscura,
ejusdemque fere generis cum formis substantialibus & Entelechiis,
fatendum.

20 Quotquot ad explicandam motus causam atque originem
vel principio Hylarchico, vel naturæ indigentia, vel appetitu, aut
denique instinctu naturali utuntur, dixisse aliquid potius quam
cogitasse censendi sunt. Neque ab hisce multum absunt qui
supposuerint [1] *partes terræ esse se moventes, aut etiam spiritus iis im-
plantatos ad instar formæ,* ut assignent causam accelerationis gravium·
cadentium. Aut qui dixerit [2] *in corpore præter solidam extensionem
debere etiam poni aliquid unde virium consideratio oriatur.* Siquidem hi
omnes vel nihil particulare & determinatum enuntiant : vel, si
quid sit, tam difficile erit illud explicare, quam id ipsum cujus
explicandi causa adducitur.

21 Frustra ad naturam illustrandam adhibentur ea quæ nec
sensibus patent, nec ratione intelligi possunt. Videndum ergo
quid sensus, quid experientia, quid demum ratio iis innixa suadeat.
Duo sunt summa rerum genera, corpus & anima. Rem extensam,

[1] Borellus.   [2] Leibnitius.

solidam, mobilem, figuratam, aliisque qualitatibus quæ sensibus occurrunt præditam, ope sensuum, rem vero sentientem, percipientem, intelligentem, conscientia quadam interna cognovimus. Porro, res istas plane inter se diversas esse, longeque heterogeneas, cernimus. Loquor autem de rebus cognitis, de incognitis enim disserere nil juvat.

22 Totum id quod novimus, cui nomen *corpus* indidimus, nihil in se continet quod motus principium seu causa efficiens esse possit ; etenim impenetrabilitas, extensio, figura nullam includunt vel connotant potentiam producendi motum : quinimo e contrario non modo illas verum etiam alias, quotquot sint, corporis qualitates singillatim percurrentes, videbimus omnes esse revera passivas, nihilque iis activum inesse, quod ullo modo intelligi possit tanquam fons & principium motus. Gravitatem quod attinet, voce illa nihil cognitum & ab ipso effectu sensibili, cujus causa quæritur, diversum significari jam ante ostendimus. Et sane quando corpus grave dicimus nihil aliud intelligimus, nisi quod feratur deorsum, de causa hujus effectus sensibilis nihil omnino cogitantes.

23 De corpore itaque audacter pronunciare licet, utpote de re comperta, quod non sit principium motus. Quod si quisquam, præter solidam extensionem ejusque modificationes, vocem *corpus* qualitatem etiam occultam, virtutem, formam, essentiam complecti sua significatione contendat ; licet quidem illi inutili negotio sine ideis disputare, & nominibus nihil distincte exprimentibus abuti. Cæterum sanior philosophandi ratio videtur ab notionibus abstractis & generalibus (si modo notiones dici debent quæ intelligi nequeunt) quantum fieri potest abstinuisse.

24 Quicquid continetur in idea corporis novimus : quod vero novimus in corpore id non esse principium motus constat. Qui præterea aliquid incognitum in corpore, cujus ideam nullam habent, comminiscuntur, quod motus principium dicant : ii revera nihil aliud quam principium motus esse incognitum dicunt. Sed hujusmodi subtilitatibus diutius immorari piget.

25 Præter res corporeas alterum est genus rerum cogitantium, in iis autem potentiam inesse corpora movendi, propria experientia didicimus, quandoquidem anima nostra pro lubitu possit ciere & sistere membrorum motus, quacunque tandem ratione id fiat. Hoc certe constat, corpora moveri ad nutum animæ, eamque proinde haud inepte dici posse principium motus ; particulare quidem & subordinatum, quodque ipsum dependeat a primo & universali principio.

26 Corpora gravia feruntur deorsum, etsi nullo impulsu

apparente agitata, non tamen existimandum propterea in iis contineri principium motus : cujus rei hanc rationem assignat Aristoteles, *gravia & levia*, inquit, *non moventur a seipsis, id enim vitale esset, & se sistere possent*. Gravia omnia una eademque certa & constanti lege centrum telluris petunt, neque in ipsis animadvertitur principium vel facultas ulla motum istum sistendi, minuendi vel, nisi pro rata proportione, augendi, aut denique ullo modo immutandi : habent adeo se passive. Porro idem, stricte & accurate loquendo, dicendum de corporibus percussivis. Corpora ista quamdiu moventur, ut & in ipso percussionis momento, se gerunt passive, perinde scilicet atque cum quiescunt. Corpus iners tam agit quam corpus motum, si res ad verum exigatur : id quod agnoscit Newtonus, ubi ait, vim inertiæ esse eandem cum impetu. Corpus autem iners & quietum nihil agit, ergo nec motum.

27 Revera corpus æque perseverat in utrovis statu, vel motus vel quietis. Ista vero perseverantia non magis dicenda est actio corporis, quam existentia ejusdem actio diceretur. Perseverantia nihil aliud est quam continuatio in eodem modo existendi, quæ proprie dici actio non potest. Cæterum resistentiam, quam experimur in sistendo corpore moto, ejus actionem esse fingimus vana specie delusi. Revera enim ista resistentia quam sentimus, passio est in nobis, neque arguit corpus agere, sed nos pati : constat utique nos idem passuros fuisse, sive corpus illud a se moveatur, sive ab alio principio impellatur.

28 Actio & reactio dicuntur esse in corporibus ; nec incommode ad demonstrationes mechanicas. Sed cavendum, ne propterea supponamus virtutem aliquam realem quæ motus causa, sive principium sit, esse in iis. Etenim voces illæ eodem modo intelligendæ sunt ac vox *attractio*, & quemadmodum hæc est hypothesis solummodo mathematica non autem qualitas physica ; idem etiam de illis intelligi debet, & ob eandem rationem. Nam sicut veritas & usus theorematum de mutua corporum attractione in philosophia mechanica stabiles manent, utpote unice fundati in motu corporum, sive motus iste causari supponatur per actionem corporum se mutuo attrahentium, sive per actionem agentis alicujus a corporibus diversi impellentis & moderantis corpora ; pari ratione, quæcunque tradita sunt de regulis & legibus motuum, simul ac theoremata inde deducta, manent inconcussa, dummodo concedantur effectus sensibiles, & ratiocinia iis innixa ; sive supponamus actionem ipsam, aut vim horum effectuum causatricem, esse in corpore, sive in agente incorporeo.

29 Auferantur ex idea corporis extensio, soliditas, figura, remanebit nihil. Sed qualitates istæ sunt ad motum indifferentes, nec in se quidquam habent, quod motus principium dici possit. Hoc ex ipsis ideis nostris perspicuum est. Si igitur voce *corpus* significatur, id quod concipimus : plane constat inde non peti posse principium motus : pars scilicet nulla aut attributum illius causa efficiens vera est, quæ motum producat. Vocem autem proferre, & nihil concipere, id demum indignum esset philosopho.

30 Datur res cogitans activa quam principium motus esse in nobis experimur. Hanc *animam, mentem, spiritum* dicimus ; datur etiam res extensa, iners, impenetrabilis, mobilis, quæ a priori toto cœlo differt, novumque genus constituit. Quantum intersit inter res cogitantes & extensas, primus omnium deprehendens Anaxagoras vir longe sapientissimus, asserebat mentem nihil habere cum corporibus commune, id quod constat ex primo libro Aristotelis de anima. Ex neotericis idem optime animadvertit Cartesius. Ab eo alii rem satis claram vocibus obscuris impeditam ac difficilem reddiderunt.

31 Ex dictis manifestum est eos qui vim activam, actionem, motus principium, in corporibus revera inesse affirmant, sententiam nulla experientia fundatam amplecti, eamque terminis obscuris & generalibus adstruere, nec quid sibi velint satis intelligere. E contrario, qui mentem esse principium motus volunt, sententiam propria experientia munitam proferent,[1] hominumque omni ævo doctissimorum suffragiis comprobatam.

32 Primus Anaxagoras τὸν νοῦν introduxit, qui motum inerti materiæ imprimeret, quam quidem sententiam probat etiam Aristoteles pluribusque confirmat, aperte pronuncians primum movens esse immobile, indivisibile, & nullam habens magnitudinem. Dicere autem, omne motivum esse mobile, recte animadvertit idem esse ac siquis diceret, omne ædificativum esse ædificabile, *Phys.* l. 8. Plato insuper in Timæo tradit machinam hanc corpoream, seu mundum visibilem agitari & animari a mente, quæ sensum omnem fugiat. Quinetiam hodie, philosophi Cartesiani principium motuum naturalium Deum agnoscunt. Et Newtonus passim nec obscure innuit, non solummodo motum ab initio a numine profectum esse, verum adhuc systema mundanum ab eodem actu moveri. Hoc sacris literis consonum est : hoc scholasticorum calculo comprobatur. Nam etsi peripatetici naturam tradant esse principium motus & quietis, interpretantur tamen naturam naturantem esse Deum. Intelligunt nimirum

---

[1] [Probably an error for ' proferunt,' which the first edition reads.—Ed.]

corpora omnia systematis hujusce mundani a mente præpotenti, juxta certam & constantem rationem moveri.

33 Cæterum qui principium vitale corporibus tribuunt, obscurum aliquid & rebus parum conveniens fingunt. Quid enim aliud est vitali principio præditum esse quam vivere? aut vivere quam se movere, sistere, & statum suum mutare? Philosophi autem hujus saeculi doctissimi pro principio indubitato ponunt, omne corpus perseverare in statu suo, vel quietis vel motus uniformis in directum, nisi quatenus aliunde cogitur statum illum mutare; e contrario, in anima sentimus esse facultatem tam statum suum quam aliarum rerum mutandi; id quod proprie dicitur vitale, animamque a corporibus longe discriminat.

34 Motum & quietem in corporibus recentiores considerant velut duos status existendi, in quorum utrovis corpus omne sua natura iners permaneret, nulla vi externa urgente. Unde colligere licet, eandem esse causam motus & quietis, quæ est existentiæ corporum. Neque enim quærenda videtur alia causa existentiæ corporis successivæ in diversis partibus spatii, quam illa unde derivatur existentia ejusdem corporis successiva in diversis partibus temporis. De Deo autem optimo maximo rerum omnium conditore & conservatore tractare: & qua ratione res cunctæ a summo & vero ente pendeant demonstrare, quamvis pars sit scientiæ humanæ præcellentissima, spectat tamen potius ad philosophiam primam seu metaphysicam & theologiam, quam ad philosophiam naturalem, quæ hodie fere omnis continetur in experimentis & mechanica. Itaque cognitionem de Deo vel supponit philosophia naturalis, vel mutuatur ab aliqua scientia superiori. Quanquam verissimum sit, naturæ investigationem scientiis altioribus argumenta egregia ad sapientiam, bonitatem & potentiam Dei illustrandam & probandam undequaque subministrare.

35 Quod hæc minus intelligantur, in causa est, cur nonnulli immerito repudient physicæ principia mathematica, eo scilicet nomine quod illa causas rerum efficientes non assignant. Quum tamen revera ad physicam aut mechanicam spectet regulas solummodo, non causas efficientes, impulsionum attractionumve &, ut verbo dicam, motuum leges tradere: ex iis vero positis phænomenon particularium solutionem, non autem, causam efficientem assignare.

36 Multum intererit considerasse quid proprie sit principium & quo sensu intelligenda sit vox illa apud philosophos. Causa quidem vera efficiens, & conservatrix rerum omnium jure optimo

appellatur fons & principium earundem. Principia vero philosophiæ experimentalis proprie dicenda sunt fundamenta, quibus illa innititur, seu fontes unde derivatur, (non dico existentia, sed) cognitio rerum corporearum, sensus utique & experientia. Similiter, in philosophia mechanica, principia dicenda sunt, in quibus fundatur & continetur universa disciplina, leges illae motuum primariæ, quæ experimentis comprobatæ, ratiocinio etiam excultæ sunt & redditæ universales. Hæ motuum leges commode dicuntur principia, quoniam ab iis tam theoremata mechanica [1] generalia quam particulares τῶν Φαινομένων explicationes derivantur.

37 Tum nimirum dici potest quidpiam explicari mechanice, cum reducitur ad ista principia simplicissima & universalissima, & per accuratum ratiocinium, cum iis consentaneum & connexum esse ostenditur. Nam, inventis semel naturæ legibus, deinceps monstrandum est philosopho, ex constanti harum legum observatione, hoc est, ex iis principiis phænomenon quodvis necessario consequi : id quod est phænomena explicare & solvere, causamque, id est rationem cur fiant, assignare.

38 Mens humana gaudet scientiam suam extendere & dilatare. Ad hoc autem notiones & propositiones generales efformandæ sunt, in quibus quodam modo continentur propositiones & cognitiones particulares, quæ tum demum intelligi creduntur. Hoc geometris notissimum est. In mechanica etiam præmittuntur notiones, hoc est definitiones, et enunciationes de motu primæ & generales, ex quibus postmodum methodo mathematica conclusiones magis remotæ, & minus generales colliguntur. Et sicut per applicationem theorematum geometricorum, corporum particularium magnitudines mensurantur ; ita etiam per applicationem theorematum mechanices universalium, systematis mundani partium quarumvis motus, & phænomena inde pendentia innotescunt & determinantur : ad quem scopum unice collineandum physico.

39 Et quemadmodum geometræ disciplinæ causa, multa comminiscuntur, quæ nec ipsi describere possunt, nec in rerum natura invenire : simili prorsus ratione mechanicus voces quasdam abstractas & generales adhibet, fingitque in corporibus vim, actionem, attractionem, solicitationem, &c. quæ ad theorias & enunciationes, ut & computationes de motu apprime utiles sunt, etiamsi in ipsa rerum veritate & corporibus actu existentibus frustra quærerentur, non minus quam quæ a geometris per abstractionem mathematicam finguntur.

[1] [The first edition reads ' mechanicae ' ; but note ' mechanices ' in S. 38.—Ed.]

40 Revera, ope sensuum nihil [1] nisi effectus seu qualitates sensibiles, & res corporeas omnino passivas, sive in motu sint sive in quiete, percipimus : ratioque & experientia activum nihil præter mentem aut animam esse suadet. Quid quid ultra fingitur, id ejusdem generis esse cum aliis hypothesibus & abstractionibus mathematicis existimandum ; quod penitus animo infigere oportet. Hoc ni fiat, facile in obscuram scholasticorum subtilitatem, quæ per tot sæcula, tanquam dira quædam pestis, philosophiam corrupit, relabi possumus.

41 Principia mechanica legesque motuum aut naturæ universales, sæculo ultimo feliciter inventæ, & subsidio geometriæ tractatæ & applicatæ, miram lucem in philosophiam intulerunt. Principia vero metaphysica causæque reales efficientes motus & existentiæ corporum attributorumve corporeorum nullo modo ad mechanicam aut experimenta pertinent, neque eis lucem dare possunt, nisi quatenus, velut præcognita inserviant ad limites physicæ præfiniendos, eaque ratione ad tollendas difficultates quæstionesque peregrinas.

42 Qui a spiritibus motus principium petunt, ii vel rem corpoream vel incorpoream voce *spiritus* intelligunt : si rem corpoream, quantumvis tenuem, tamen redit difficultas : si incorpoream, quantumvis id verum sit, attamen ad physicam non proprie pertinet. Quod si quis philosophiam naturalem ultra limites experimentorum & mechanicæ extenderit, ita ut rerum etiam incorporearum, & inextensarum cognitionem complectatur : latior quidem illa vocis acceptio tractationem de anima, mente, seu principio vitali admittit. Cæterum commodius erit, juxta usum jam fere receptum, ita distinguere inter scientias, ut singulæ propriis circumscribantur cancellis, & philosophus naturalis totus sit in experimentis, legibusque motuum, & principiis mechanicis, indeque depromptis ratiociniis ; quidquid autem de aliis rebus protulerit id superiori alicui scientiæ acceptum referat. Etenim ex cognitis naturæ legibus pulcherrimæ theoriæ, praxes etiam mechanicæ ad vitam utiles consequuntur. Ex cognitione autem ipsius naturæ auctoris considerationes, longe præstantissimæ quidem illæ, sed metaphysicæ, theologicæ, morales oriuntur.

43 De principiis hactenus : nunc dicendum de natura motus, atque is quidem, cum sensibus clare percipiatur non tam natura sua, quam doctis philosophorum commentis obscuratus est. Motus nunquam in sensus nostros incurrit sine mole corporea,

---

[1] [The first edition reads ' nil.'—Ed.]

spatio, & tempore. Sunt tamen qui motum, tanquam ideam quandam simplicem & abstractam, atque ab omnibus aliis rebus sejunctam, contemplari student. Verum idea illa tenuissima & subtilissima intellectus aciem eludit : id quod quilibet secum meditando experiri potest. Hinc nascuntur magnæ difficultates de natura motus, & definitiones, ipsa re quam illustrare debent, longe obscuriores. Hujusmodi sunt definitiones illæ Aristotelis & Scholasticorum, qui motum dicunt esse actum *mobilis, quatenus est mobile, vel actum entis in potentia quatenus in potentia.* Hujusmodi etiam est illud, viri inter recentiores celebris, qui asserit *nihil in motu esse reale præter momentaneum illud quod in vi ad mutationem nitente constitui debet.*[1] Porro, constat, horum & similium definitionum auctores in animo habuisse abstractam motus naturam, seclusa omni temporis & spatii consideratione, explicare, sed qua ratione abstracta illa motus quintessentia (ut ita dicam) intelligi possit non video.

44 Neque hoc contenti, ulterius pergunt partesque ipsius motus a se invicem dividunt & secernunt, quarum ideas distinctas, tanquam entium revera distinctorum, efformare conantur. Etenim sunt qui motionem a motu distinguant, illam velut instantaneum motus elementum spectantes. Velocitatem insuper, conatum, vim, impetum totidem res essentia diversas esse volunt, quarum quæque per propriam atque ab aliis omnibus segregatam & abstractam ideam intellectui objiciatur. Sed in hisce rebus discutiendis, stantibus iis quæ supra disseruimus, non est cur diutius immoremur.

45 Multi etiam per *transitum* motum definiunt, obliti scilicet transitum ipsum sine motu intelligi non posse, & per motum definiri oportere. Verissimum adeo est definitiones, sicut nonnullis rebus lucem, ita vicissim aliis tenebras afferre. Et profecto, quascumque res sensu percipimus, eas clariores aut notiores definiendo efficere vix quisquam potuerit. Cujus rei vana spe allecti res faciles difficillimas reddiderunt philosophi, mentesque suas difficultatibus, quas ut plurimum ipsi peperissent, implicavere. Ex hocce definiendi, simulac abstrahendi studio, multæ, tam de motu, quam de aliis rebus natæ subtilissimæ quæstiones, eædemque nullius utilitatis, hominum ingenia frustra torserunt, adeo ut Aristoteles ultro & sæpius fateatur motum esse *actum*

---

[1] [Editors attribute this assertion to Newton, but they give no reference. I have looked in vain for the words or their substance in the *Principia*. The Preface sharply distinguishes true motion from apparent, but Newton does not, so far as I can find, resolve all motion into change.—Ed.]

quendam cognitu difficilem, & nonnulli ex veteribus usque eo nugis exercitati deveniebant, ut motum omnino esse negarent.

46 Sed hujusmodi minutiis distineri piget. Satis sit fontes solutionum indicasse : ad quos etiam illud adjungere libet : quod ea quæ de infinita divisione temporis & spatii in mathesi traduntur, ob congenitam rerum naturam paradoxa & theorias spinosas (quales sunt illæ omnes in quibus agitur de infinito) in speculationes de motu intulerunt. Quidquid autem hujus generis sit, id omne motus commune habet cum spatio & tempore, vel potius ad ea refert acceptum.

47 Et quemadmodum, ex una parte nimia abstractio seu divisio rerum vere inseparabilium, ita, ab altera parte, compositio seu potius confusio rerum diversissimarum motus naturam perplexam reddidit. Usitatum enim est motum cum causa motus efficiente confundere. Unde accidit ut motus sit quasi biformis, unam faciem sensibus obviam, alteram caliginosa nocte obvolutam habens. Inde obscuritas & confusio, & varia de motu paradoxa originem trahunt, dum effectui perperam tribuitur id quod revera causæ solummodo competit.

48 Hinc oritur opinio illa, eandem semper motus quantitatem conservari ; quod, nisi intelligatur de vi & potentia causæ, sive causa illa dicatur natura, sive *νοῦς*, vel quodcunque tandem agens sit, falsum esse cuivis facile constabit. Aristoteles quidem l. 8. *Physicorum,* ubi quærit *utrum motus factus sit & corruptus, an vero ab æterno tanquam vita immortalis insit rebus omnibus,* vitale principium potius, quam effectum externum, sive mutationem loci intellexisse videtur.

49 Hinc etiam est, quod multi suspicantur motum non esse meram passionem in corporibus. Quod si intelligamus id quod, in motu corporis, sensibus objicitur, quin omnino passivum sit nemo dubitare potest. Ecquid enim in se habet successiva corporis existentia in diversis locis, quod actionem referat, aut aliud sit quam nudus & iners effectus ?

50 Peripatetici, qui dicunt motum esse actum unum utriusque, moventis & moti, non satis discriminant causam ab effectu. Similiter, qui nisum aut conatum in motu fingunt, aut idem corpus simul in contrarias partes ferri putant, eadem idearum confusione, eadem vocum ambiguitate ludificari videntur.

51 Juvat multum, sicut in aliis omnibus, ita in scientia de motu accuratam diligentiam adhibere, tam ad aliorum conceptus intelligendos quam ad suos enunciandos : in qua re nisi peccatum esset, vix credo in disputationem trahi potuisse, utrum corpus

indifferens sit ad motum & ad quietem necne. Quoniam enim experientia constat, esse legem naturæ primariam, ut corpus perinde perseveret in *statu motus ac quietis, quamdiu aliunde nihil accidat ad statum istum mutandum.* Et propterea vim inertiæ sub diverso respectu esse vel resistentiam, vel impetum, colligitur. Hoc sensu, profecto corpus dici potest sua natura indifferens ad motum vel quietem. Nimirum, tam difficile est quietem in corpus motum, quam motum in quiescens inducere ; cum vero corpus pariter conservet statum utrumvis, quid ni dicatur ad utrumvis se habere indifferenter ?

52 Peripatetici pro varietate mutationum, quas res aliqua subire potest, varia motus genera distinguebant. Hodie de motu agentes intelligunt solummodo motum localem. Motus autem localis intelligi nequit nisi simul intelligatur quid sit *locus* ; is vero a neotericis definitur *pars spatii quam corpus occupat,* unde dividitur in relativum & absolutum pro ratione spatii. Distinguunt enim inter spatium absolutum sive verum, ac relativum sive apparens. Volunt scilicet dari spatium undequaque immensum, immobile, insensibile, corpora universa permeans & continens, quod vocant spatium absolutum. Spatium, autem, a corporibus comprehensum, vel definitum, sensibusque adeo subjectum, dicitur spatium relativum, apparens, vulgare.

53 Fingamus itaque corpora cuncta destrui & in nihilum redigi. Quod reliquum est vocant spatium absolutum, omni relatione quæ a situ & distantiis corporum oriebatur, simul cum ipsis corporibus, sublata. Porro spatium illud est infinitum, immobile, indivisible, insensibile, sine relatione & sine distinctione. Hoc est, omnia ejus attributa sunt privativa vel negativa : videtur igitur esse merum nihil. Parit solummodo difficultatem aliquam quod extensum sit. Extensio autem est qualitas positiva. Verum qualis tandem extensio est illa, quæ nec dividi potest, nec mensurari, cujus nullam partem, nec sensu percipere, nec imaginatione depingere possumus ? Etenim nihil in imaginationem cadit, quod, ex natura rei, non possibile est ut sensu percipiatur, siquidem imaginatio nihil aliud est quam facultas representatrix rerum sensibilium, vel actu existentium, vel saltem possibilium. Fugit insuper intellectum purum, quum facultas illa versetur tantum circa res spirituales & inextensas, cujusmodi sunt mentes nostræ, earumque habitus, passiones, virtutes & similia. Ex spatio igitur absoluto, auferamus modo vocabula, & nihil remanebit in sensu, imaginatione aut intellectu ; nihil aliud ergo iis designatur, quam pura privatio aut negatio, hoc est, merum nihil.

54 Confitendum omnino est nos circa hanc rem gravissimis praejudiciis teneri, a quibus ut liberemur, omnis animi vis exerenda. Etenim multi, tantum abest quod spatium absolutum pro nihilo ducant ut rem esse ex omnibus (Deo excepto) unicam existiment, quae annihilari non possit : statuantque illud suapte natura necessario existere, aeternumque esse & increatum, atque adeo attributorum divinorum particeps. Verum enimvero quum certissimum sit, res omnes, quas nominibus designamus, per qualitates aut relationes, vel aliqua saltem ex parte, cognosci, (ineptum enim foret vocabulis uti quibus cogniti nihil, nihil notionis, ideae vel conceptus subjiceretur.) Inquiramus diligenter, utrum formare liceat ideam ullam spatii illius puri, realis, absoluti, post omnium corporum annihilationem perseverantis existere. Ideam porro talem paulo acrius intuens, reperio ideam esse nihili purissimam, si modo idea appellanda sit. Hoc ipse summa adhibita diligentia expertus sum : hoc alios pari adhibita diligentia experturos reor.

55 Decipere nos nonnunquam solet, quod aliis omnibus corporibus imaginatione sublatis, nostrum tamen manere supponimus. Quo supposito, motum membrorum ab omni parte liberrimum imaginamur. Motus autem sine spatio concipi non potest. Nihilominus si rem attento animo recolamus, constabit primo concipi spatium relativum partibus nostri corporis definitum : 2°. movendi membra potestatem liberrimam nullo obstaculo retusam : & praeter haec duo nihil. Falso tamen credimus tertium aliquod, spatium, videlicet, immensum realiter existere, quod liberam potestatem nobis faciat movendi corpus nostrum : ad hoc enim requiritur absentia solummodo aliorum corporum. Quam absentiam, sive privationem corporum, nihil esse positivum fateamur necesse est.[1]

56 Caeterum hasce res nisi quis libero & acri examine perspexerit, verba & voces parum valent. Meditanti vero, & rationes secum reputanti, ni fallor, manifestum erit, quaecunque de spatio puro & absoluto praedicantur, ea omnia de nihilo praedicari posse. Qua ratione mens humana facillime liberatur a magnis difficultatibus, simulque ab ea absurditate tribuendi existentiam necessariam ulli rei praeterquam soli Deo optimo maximo.

57 In proclivi esset sententiam nostram argumentis a posteriori (ut loquuntur) ductis confirmare, quaestiones de spatio absoluto proponendo, exempli gratia, utrum sit substantia vel

[1] Vide quae contra spatium absolutum disseruntur in libro de principiis cognitionis humanae, idiomate anglicano, decem abhinc annis edito.

accidens ? Utrum creatum vel increatum ? & absurditates ex
utravis parte consequentes demonstrando. Sed brevitati con-
sulendum. Illud tamen omitti non debet, quod sententiam hancce
Democritus olim calculo suo comprobavit, uti auctor est Aristoteles
l. 1. *Phys.* ubi hæc habet ; *Democritus solidum & inane ponit principia,
quarum aliud quidem ut quod est, aliud ut quod non est esse dicit.* Scrupulum si forte injiciat, quod distinctio illa inter spatium absolutum
& relativum a magni nominis philosophis usurpetur, eique quasi
fundamento inædificentur multa præclara theoremata, scrupulum
istum vanum esse, ex iis, quæ secutura sunt, apparebit.

58 Ex præmissis patet, non convenire, ut definiamus locum
verum corporis, esse partem spatii absoluti quam occupat corpus,
motumque verum seu absolutum esse mutationem loci veri &
absoluti. Siquidem omnis locus est relativus, ut et omnis motus.
Veruntamen ut hoc clarius appareat, animadvertendum est,
motum nullum intelligi posse sine determinatione aliqua seu
directione, quæ quidem intelligi nequit, nisi præter corpus motum,
nostrum etiam corpus, aut aliud aliquod, simul intelligatur
existere. Nam sursum, deorsum, sinistrorsum, dextrorsum om-
nesque plagæ & regiones in relatione aliqua fundantur, &, necessario, corpus a moto diversum connotant & supponunt. Adeo
ut, si reliquis corporibus in nihilum redactis, globus, exempli
gratia, unicus existere supponatur ; in illo motus nullus concipi
possit ; usque adeo necesse est, ut detur aliud corpus, cujus situ
motus determinari intelligatur. Hujus sententiæ veritas clarissime
elucebit, modo corporum omnium tam nostri quam aliorum
præter globum istum unicum, annihilationem recte supposue-
rimus.

59 Concipiantur porro duo globi, & præterea nil corporeum,
existere. Concipiantur deinde vires quomodocunque applicari,
quicquid tandem per applicationem virium intelligamus, motus
circularis duorum globorum circa commune centrum nequit per
imaginationem concipi. Supponamus deinde cœlum fixarum
creari : subito ex concepto appulsu globorum ad diversas cœli
istius partes motus concipietur. Scilicet cum motus natura sua
sit relativus, concipi non potuit priusquam darentur corpora
correlata. Quemadmodum nec ulla alia relatio sine correlatis
concipi potest.

60 Ad motum circularem quod attinet, putant multi, cres-
cente motu vero circulari, corpus necessario magis semper magisque
ab axe niti. Hoc autem ex eo provenit, quod, cum motus circularis spectari possit tanquam in omni momento a duabus direc-

tionibus ortum trahens, una secundum radium, altera secundum tangentem ; si in hac ultima tantum directione impetus augeatur, tum a centro recedet corpus motum, orbita vero desinet esse circularis. Quod si æqualiter augeantur vires in utraque directione, manebit motus circularis, sed acceleratus conatu, qui non magis arguet vires recedendi ab axe, quam accedendi ad eundem, auctas esse. Dicendum igitur, aquam in situla circumactam ascendere ad latera vasis, propterea quod, applicatis novis viribus in directione tangentis ad quamvis particulam aquæ, eodem instanti non applicentur novæ vires æquales centripetæ. Ex quo experimento nullo modo sequitur, motum absolutum circularem per vires recedendi ab axe motus necessario dignosci. Porro, qua ratione intelligendæ sunt voces istæ, *vires corporum & conatus*, ex præmissis satis superque innotescit.

61 Quo modo curva considerari potest tanquam constans ex rectis infinitis, etiamsi revera ex illis non constet, sed quod ea hypothesis ad geometriam utilis sit, eodem motus circularis spectari potest, tanquam a directionibus rectilineis infinitis ortum ducens, quæ suppositio utilis est in philosophia mechanica. Non tamen ideo affirmandum, impossibile esse, ut centrum gravitatis corporis cujusvis successive existat in singulis punctis peripheriæ circularis, nulla ratione habita directionis ullius rectilineæ, sive in tangente, sive in radio.

62 Haud omittendum est, motum lapidis in funda, aut aquæ in situla circumacta dici non posse motum vere circularem, juxta mentem eorum qui per partes spatii absoluti definiunt loca vera corporum ; cum sit mire compositus ex motibus non solum situlæ vel fundæ, sed etiam telluris diurno circa proprium axem, menstruo circa commune centrum gravitatis terræ & lunæ, & annuo circa solem. Et propterea, particula quævis lapidis vel aquæ describat lineam a circulari longe abhorrentem. Neque revera est, qui creditur, conatus axifugus, quoniam non respicit unum aliquem axem ratione spatii absoluti, supposito quod detur tale spatium : proinde non video quomodo appellari possit conatus unicus, cui motus vere circularis tanquam proprio & adæquato effectui respondet.

63 Motus nullus dignosci potest, aut mensurari, nisi per res sensibiles. Cum ergo spatium absolutum nullo modo in sensus incurrat, necesse est ut inutile prorsus sit ad distinctionem motuum. Præterea, determinatio sive directio motui essentialis est, illa vero in relatione consistit. Ergo impossibile est ut motus absolutus concipiatur.

64 Porro, quoniam pro diversitate loci relativi, varius sit motus ejusdem corporis, quinimo, uno respectu moveri, altero quiescere dici quidpiam possit : ad determinandum motum verum & quietem veram, quo scilicet tollatur ambiguitas, & consulatur mechanicæ philosophorum, qui systema rerum latius contemplantur, satis fuerit spatium relativum fixarum cœlo, tanquam quiescente spectato, conclusum adhibere, loco spatii absoluti. Motus autem & quies tali spatio relativo definiti, commode adhiberi possunt loco absolutorum, qui ab illis nullo symptomate discerni possunt. Etenim imprimantur utcunque vires : sint quicunque conatus ; concedamus motum distingui per actiones in corpora exercitas ; nunquam tamen inde sequetur, dari spatium illud, & locum absolutum, ejusque mutationem esse locum verum.

65 Leges motuum, effectusque, & theoremata eorundem proportiones & calculos continentia, pro diversis viarum figuris, accelerationibus itidem & directionibus diversis, mediisque plus minusve resistentibus, hæc omnia constant sine calculatione motus absoluti. Uti vel ex eo patet quod, quum secundum illorum principia qui motum absolutum inducunt, nullo symptomate scire liceat, utrum integra rerum compages quiescat, an moveatur uniformiter in directum, perspicuum sit motum absolutum nullius corporis cognosci posse.

66 Ex dictis patet ad veram motus naturam perspiciendam summopere juvaturum : 1°. Distinguere inter hypotheses mathematicas & naturas rerum. 2°. Cavere ab abstractionibus. 3°. Considerare motum tanquam aliquid sensible, vel saltem imaginabile : mensurisque relativis esse contentos. Quæ si fecerimus, simul clarissima quæque philosophiæ mechanicæ theoremata, quibus reserantur naturæ recessus, mundique systema calculis humanis subjicitur, manebunt intemerata : et motus contemplatio a mille minutiis, subtilitatibus, ideisque abstractis libera evadet. Atque hæc de natura motus dicta sufficiant.

67 Restat, ut disseramus de causa communicationis motuum. Esse autem vim impressam in corpus mobile, causam motus in eo plerique existimant. Veruntamen, illos non assignare causam motus cognitam, & a corpore motuque distinctam, ex præmissis constat. Patet insuper vim non esse rem certam & determinatam, ex eo quod viri summi de illa multum diversa, immo contraria, proferant, salva tamen in consequentiis veritate. Siquidem Newtonus ait vim impressam consistere in actione sola, esseque actionem exercitam in corpus ad statum ejus mutandum, nec post

actionem manere. Torricellius cumulum quendam sive aggregatum virium impressarum per percussionem in corpus mobile recipi, ibidemque manere atque impetum constituere contendit. Idem fere Borellus aliique prædicant. At vero, tametsi inter se pugnare videantur Newtonus & Torricellius, nihilominus, quum dum singuli sibi consentanea proferunt, res satis commode ab utrisque explicatur. Quippe vires omnes corporibus attributæ, tam sunt hypotheses mathematicæ quam vires attractivæ in planetis & sole. Cæterum entia mathematica in rerum natura stabilem essentiam non habent : pendent autem a notione definientis : unde eadem res diversimode explicari potest.

68 Statuamus motum novum in corpore percusso conservari, sive per vim insitam, qua corpus quodlibet perseverat in statu suo, vel motus, vel quietis uniformis in directum : sive per vim impressam, durante percussione in corpus percussum receptam ibidemque permanentem, idem erit quoad rem, differentia existente in nominibus tantum. Similiter, ubi mobile percutiens perdit & percussum acquirit motum, parum refert disputare, utrum motus acquisitus sit idem numero cum motu perdito, ducit enim in minutias metaphysicas, & prorsus nominales de identitate. Itaque sive dicamus motum transire a percutiente in percussum, sive in percusso motum de novo generari, destrui autem in percutiente, res eodem recidit. Utrobique intelligitur unum corpus motum perdere, alterum acquirere, & præterea nihil.

69 Mentem, quæ agitat & continet universam hancce molem corpoream, estque causa vera efficiens motus, eandem esse, proprie & stricte loquendo, causam communicationis ejusdem haud negaverim. In philosophia tamen physica, causas & solutiones phænomenon a principiis mechanicis petere oportet. Physice igitur res explicatur non assignando ejus causam vere agentem & incopoream, sed demonstrando ejus connexionem cum principiis mechanicis : cujusmodi est illud, *actionem & reactionem esse semper contrarias & æquales*, a quo, tanquam fonte & principio primario, eruuntur regulæ de motuum communicatione, quæ a neotericis, magno scientiarum bono, jam ante repertæ sunt & demonstratæ.

70 Nobis satis fuerit, si innuamus principium illud alio modo declarari potuisse. Nam si vera rerum natura, potius quam abstracta mathesis spectetur, videbitur rectius dici, in attractione vel percussione passionem corporum, quam actionem, esse utrobique æqualem. Exempli gratia, lapis fune equo alligatus tantum trahitur versus equum, quantum equus versus lapidem : corpus

etiam motum in aliud quiescens impactum, patitur eandem
mutationem cum corpore quiescente. Et quoad effectum realem,
percutiens est item percussum, percussumque percutiens. Mutatio
autem illa est utrobique, tam in corpore equi quam in lapide,
tam in moto quam in quiescente, passio mera. Esse autem vim,
virtutem, aut actionem corpoream talium effectuum vere &
proprie causatricem non constat. Corpus motum in quiescens
impingitur, loquimur tamen active, dicentes illud hoc impellere :
nec absurde in mechanicis, ubi ideæ mathematicæ potius quam
veræ rerum naturæ spectantur.

71 In physica, sensus & experientia, quæ ad effectus appa-
rentes solummodo pertingunt, locum habent ; in mechanica,
notiones abstractæ mathematicorum admittuntur. In philosophia prima seu metaphysica agitur de rebus incorporeis, de
causis, veritate, & existentia rerum. Physicus series sive succes-
siones rerum sensibilium contemplatur, quibus legibus connectuntur, & quo ordine, quid præcedit tanquam causa, quid sequitur
tanquam effectus animadvertens. Atque hac ratione dicimus
corpus motum esse causam motus in altero, vel ei motum im-
primere, trahere etiam, aut impellere. Quo sensu causæ secundæ
corporeæ intelligi debent, nulla ratione habita veræ sedis virium,
vel potentiarum actricum, aut causæ realis cui insunt. Porro,
dici possunt causæ vel principia mechanica, ultra corpus, figuram,
motum, etiam axiomata scientiæ mechanicæ primaria, tanquam
causæ consequentium spectata.

72 Causæ vere activæ meditatione tantum, & ratiocinio e
tenebris erui quibus involvuntur possunt, & aliquatenus cognosci.
Spectat autem ad philosophiam primam, seu metaphysicam, de
iis agere. Quod si cuique scientiæ provincia sua tribuatur, limites
assignentur, principia & objecta accurate distinguantur, quæ ad
singulas pertinent, tractare licuerit majore, cum facilitate, tum
perspicuitate.

OF MOTION

OR

THE PRINCIPLE AND NATURE OF MOTION AND THE CAUSE OF THE COMMUNICATION OF MOTIONS

Editor's Translation

1 In the pursuit of truth we must beware of being misled by terms which we do not rightly understand. That is the chief point. Almost all philosophers utter the caution ; few observe it. Yet it is not so difficult to observe, where sense, experience, and geometrical reasoning obtain, as is especially the case in physics. Laying aside, then, as far as possible, all prejudice, whether rooted in linguistic usage or in philosophical authority, let us fix our gaze on the very nature of things. For no one's authority ought to rank so high as to set a value on his words and terms unless they are found to be based on clear and certain fact.

2 The consideration of motion greatly troubled the minds of the ancient philosophers, giving rise to various exceedingly difficult opinions (not to say absurd) which have almost entirely gone out of fashion, and not being worth a detailed discussion need not delay us long. In works on motion by the more recent and sober thinkers of our age, not a few terms of somewhat abstract and obscure signification are used, such as *solicitation of gravity, urge, dead forces,* etc., terms which darken writings in other respects very learned, and beget opinions at variance with truth and the commonsense of men. These terms must be examined with great care, not from a desire to prove other people wrong, but in the interest of truth.

3 *Solicitation* and *effort* or *conation* belong properly to animate beings alone. When they are attributed to other things, they must be taken in a metaphorical sense ; but a philosopher should abstain from metaphor. Besides, anyone who has seriously considered the matter will agree that those terms have no clear and distinct meaning apart from all affection of the mind and motion of the body.

4 While we support heavy bodies we feel in ourselves effort, fatigue, and discomfort. We perceive also in heavy bodies falling an accelerated motion towards the centre of the earth ; and that is all the senses tell us. By reason, however, we infer that there is some cause or principle of these phenomena, and that is popularly called *gravity*. But since the cause of the fall of heavy bodies is unseen and unknown, gravity in that usage cannot properly be styled a sensible quality. It is, therefore, an occult quality. But what an occult quality is, or how any quality can act or do anything, we can scarcely conceive—indeed we cannot conceive. And so men would do better to let the occult quality go, and attend only to the sensible effects. Abstract terms (however useful they may be in argument) should be discarded in meditation, and the mind should be fixed on the particular and the concrete, that is, on the things themselves.

5 *Force* likewise is attributed to bodies ; and that word is used as if it meant a known quality, and one distinct from motion, figure, and every other sensible thing and also from every affection of the living thing. But examine the matter more carefully and you will agree that such force is nothing but an occult quality. Animal effort and corporeal motion are commonly regarded as symptoms and measures of this occult quality.

6 Obviously then it is idle to lay down gravity or force as the principle of motion ; for how could that principle be known more clearly by being styled an occult quality ? What is itself occult explains nothing. And I need not say that an unknown acting cause could be more correctly styled substance than quality. Again, *force, gravity*, and terms of that sort are more often used in the concrete (and rightly so) so as to connote the body in motion, the effort of resisting, *etc.* But when they are used by philosophers to signify certain natures carved out and abstracted from all these things, natures which are not objects of sense, nor can be grasped by any force of intellect, nor pictured by the imagination, then indeed they breed errors and confusion.

7 About general and abstract terms many men make mistakes ; they see their value in argument, but they do not appreciate their purpose. In part the terms have been invented by common habit to abbreviate speech, and in part they have been thought out by philosophers for instructional purposes, not that they are adapted to the natures of things which are in fact singulars and concrete, but they come in useful for handing on received opinions by making the notions or at least the propositions universal.

8 We generally suppose that corporeal force is something easy to conceive. Those, however, who have studied the matter more carefully are of a different opinion, as appears from the strange obscurity of their language when they try to explain it. Torricelli says that force and impetus are abstract and subtle things and quintessences which are included in corporeal substance as in the magic vase of Circe.[1] Leibniz likewise in explaining the nature of force has this : ' Active primitive force which is ἐντελέχεια ἡ πρώτη corresponds to the soul or substantial form.' See *Acta Erudit. Lips.* Thus even the greatest men when they give way to abstractions are bound to pursue terms which have no certain significance and are mere shadows of scholastic things. Other passages in plenty from the writings of the younger men could be produced which give abundant proof that metaphysical abstractions have not in all quarters given place to mechanical science and experiment, but still make useless trouble for philosophers.

9 From that source derive various absurdities, such as that dictum : ' The force of percussion, however small, is infinitely great '—which indeed supposes that gravity is a certain real quality different from all others, and that gravitation is, as it were, an act of this quality, really distinct from motion. But a very small percussion produces a greater effect than the greatest gravitation without motion. The former gives out some motion indeed, the latter none. Whence it follows that the force of percussion exceeds the force of gravitation by an infinite ratio, *i.e.* is infinitely great. See the experiments of Galileo, and the writings of Torricelli, Borelli, and others on the definite force of percussion.

10 We must, however, admit that no force is immediately felt by itself, nor known or measured otherwise than by its effect ; but of a dead force or of simple gravitation in a body at rest, no change taking place, there is no effect ; of percussion there is some effect. Since, then, forces are proportional to effects, we may conclude that there is no dead force, but we must not on that account infer that the force of percussion is infinite ; for we cannot regard as infinite any positive quantity on the ground that it exceeds by an infinite ratio a zero-quantity or nothing.

---

[1] Matter is nothing else than a magic vase of Circe, which serves as a receptacle of force and of the moments of the impetus. Force and the impetus are such subtle abstractions and such volatile quintessences that they cannot be shut up in any vessel except in the innermost substance of natural solids. See *Academic Lectures.*

11 The force of gravitation is not to be separated from momentum ; but there is no momentum without velocity, since it is mass multiplied by velocity ; again, velocity cannot be understood without motion, and the same holds therefore of the force of gravitation. Then no force makes itself known except through action, and through action it is measured ; but we are not able to separate the action of a body from its motion ; therefore as long as a heavy body changes the shape of a piece of lead put under it, or of a cord, so long is it moved ; but when it is at rest, it does nothing, or (which is the same thing) it is prevented from acting. In brief, those terms *dead force* and *gravitation* by the aid of metaphysical abstraction are supposed to mean something different from moving, moved, motion, and rest, but, in point of fact, the supposed difference in meaning amounts to nothing at all.

12 If anyone were to say that a weight hung or placed on the cord acts on it, since it prevents it from restoring itself by elastic force, I reply that by parity of reasoning any lower body acts on the higher body which rests on it, since it prevents it from coming down. But for one body to prevent another from existing in that space which *it* occupies cannot be styled the action of that body.

13 We feel at times the pressure of a gravitating body. But that unpleasant sensation arises from the motion of the heavy body communicated to the fibres and nerves of our body and changing their situation, and therefore it ought to be referred to percussion. In these matters we are afflicted by a number of serious prejudices, which should be subdued, or rather entirely exorcised by keen and continued reflection.

14 In order to prove that any quantity is infinite, we have to show that some, finite, homogeneous part is contained in it an infinite number of times. But dead force is to the force of percussion, not as part to the whole, but as the point to the line, according to the very writers who maintain the infinite force of percussion. Much might be added on this matter, but I am afraid of being prolix.

15 By the foregoing principles famous controversies which have greatly exercised the minds of learned men can be solved ; for instance, that controversy about the proportion of forces. One side conceding that momenta, motions, and impetus, given the mass, are simply as the velocities, affirms that the forces are as the squares of the velocities. Everyone sees that this opinion supposes that the force of the body is distinguished from momentum, motion, and impetus, and without that supposition it collapses.

16 To make it still clearer that a certain strange confusion has been introduced into the theory of motion by metaphysical abstractions, let us watch the conflict of opinion about force and impetus among famous men. Leibniz confuses impetus with motion. According to Newton impetus is in fact the same as the force of inertia. Borelli asserts that impetus is only the degree of velocity. Some would make impetus and effort different, others identical. Most regard the motive force as proportional to the motion ; but a few prefer to suppose some other force besides the motive, to be measured differently, for instance by the squares of the velocities into the masses. But it would be an endless task to follow out this line of thought.

17 *Force, gravity, attraction,* and terms of this sort are useful for reasonings and reckonings about motion and bodies in motion, but not for understanding the simple nature of motion itself or for indicating so many distinct qualities. As for attraction, it was certainly introduced by Newton, not as a true, physical quality, but only as a mathematical hypothesis. Indeed Leibniz when distinguishing elementary effort or solicitation from impetus, admits that those entities are not really found in nature, but have to be formed by abstraction.

18 A similar account must be given of the composition and resolution of any direct forces into any oblique ones by means of the diagonal and sides of the parallelogram. They serve the purpose of mechanical science and reckoning ; but to be of service to reckoning and mathematical demonstrations is one thing, to set forth the nature of things is another.

19 Of the moderns many are of the opinion that motion is neither destroyed nor generated anew, but that the quantity of motion remains for ever constant. Aristotle indeed propounded that problem long ago, Does motion come into being and pass away, or is it eternal ? *Phys.* Bk. 8. That sensible motion perishes is clear to the senses, but apparently they will have it that the same impetus and effort remains, or the same sum of forces. Borelli affirms that force in percussion is not lessened, but expanded, that even contrary impetus are received and retained in the same body. Likewise Leibniz contends that effort exists everywhere and always in matter, and that it is understood by reason where it is not evident to the senses. But these points, we must admit, are too abstract and obscure, and of much the same sort as substantial forms and entelechies.

20 All those who, to explain the cause and origin of motion,

make use of the hylarchic principle, or of a nature's want or
appetite, or indeed of a natural instinct, are to be considered as
having said something, rather than thought it. And from these
they [1] are not far removed who have supposed ' that the parts
of the earth are self-moving, or even that spirits are implanted in
them like a form ' in order to assign the cause of the acceleration
of heavy bodies falling. So too with him [2] who said ' that in the
body besides solid extension, there must be something posited
to serve as starting-point for the consideration of forces.' All
these indeed either say nothing particular and determinate, or if
there is anything in what they say, it will be as difficult to explain
as that very thing it was brought forward to explain.

21 To throw light on nature it is idle to adduce things which
are neither evident to the senses, nor intelligible to reason. Let
us see then what sense and experience tell us, and reason that
rests upon them. There are two supreme classes of things, body
and soul. By the help of sense we know the extended thing,
solid, mobile, figured, and endowed with other qualities which
meet the senses, but the sentient, percipient, thinking thing we
know by a certain internal consciousness. Further we see that
those things are plainly different from one another, and quite
heterogeneous. I speak of things known ; for of the unknown
it is profitless to speak.

22 All that which we know to which we have given the name
body contains nothing in itself which could be the principle of
motion or its efficient cause ; for impenetrability, extension, and
figure neither include nor connote any power of producing
motion ; nay, on the contrary, if we review singly those qualities
of body, and whatever other qualities there may be, we shall see
that they are all in fact passive and that there is nothing active
in them which can in any way be understood as the source and
principle of motion. As for gravity we have already shown above
that by that term is meant nothing we know, nothing other than
the sensible effect, the cause of which we seek. And indeed when
we call a body heavy we understand nothing else except that it is
borne downwards, and we are not thinking at all about the cause
of this sensible effect.

23 And so about body we can boldly state as established fact
that it is not the principle of motion. But if anyone maintains
that the term *body* covers in its meaning occult quality, virtue,
form, and essence, besides solid extension and its modes, we must

just leave him to his useless disputation with no ideas behind it, and to his abuse of names which express nothing distinctly. But the sounder philosophical method, it would seem, abstains as far as possible from abstract and general notions (if *notions* is the right term for things which cannot be understood).

24 The contents of the idea of body we know ; but what we know in body is agreed not to be the principle of motion. But those who as well maintain something unknown in body of which they have no idea and which they call the principle of motion, are in fact simply stating that the principle of motion is unknown, and one would be ashamed to linger long on subtleties of this sort.

25 Besides corporeal things there is the other class, *viz.* thinking things, and that there is in them the power of moving bodies we have learned by personal experience, since our mind at will can stir and stay the movements of our limbs, whatever be the ultimate explanation of the fact. This is certain that bodies are moved at the will of the mind, and accordingly the mind can be called, correctly enough, a principle of motion, a particular and sub-ordinate principle indeed, and one which itself depends on the first and universal principle.

26 Heavy bodies are borne downwards, although they are not affected by any apparent impulse ; but we must not think on that account that the principle of motion is contained in them. Aristotle gives this account of the matter, ' Heavy and light things are not moved by themselves ; for that would be a char-acteristic of life, and they would be able to stop themselves.' All heavy things by one and the same certain and constant law seek the centre of the earth, and we do not observe in them a principle or any faculty of halting that motion, of diminishing it or increasing it except in fixed proportion, or finally of altering it in any way. They behave quite passively. Again, in strict and accurate speech, the same must be said of percussive bodies. Those bodies as long as they are being moved, as also in the very moment of percussion, behave passively, exactly as when they are at rest. Inert body so acts as body moved acts, if the truth be told. Newton recognizes that fact when he says that the force of inertia is the same as impetus. But body, inert and at rest, does nothing ; therefore body moved does nothing.

27 Body in fact persists equally in either state, whether of motion or of rest. Its existence is not called its action ; nor

should its persistence be called its action. Persistence is only continuance in the same way of existing which cannot properly be called action. Resistance which we experience in stopping a body in motion we falsely imagine to be its action, deluded by empty appearance. For that resistance which we feel is in fact passion in ourselves, and does not prove that body acts, but that we are affected ; it is quite certain that we should be affected in the same way, whether that body were to be moved by itself, or impelled by another principle.

28 Action and reaction are said to be in bodies, and that way of speaking suits the purposes of mechanical demonstrations ; but we must not on that account suppose that there is some real virtue in them which is the cause or principle of motion. For those terms are to be understood in the same way as the term *attraction* ; and just as attraction is only a mathematical hypothesis, and not a physical quality, the same must be understood also about action and reaction, and for the same reason. For in mechanical philosophy the truth and the use of theorems about the mutual attraction of bodies remain firm, as founded solely in the motion of bodies, whether that motion be supposed to be caused by the action of bodies mutually attracting each other, or by the action of some agent different from the bodies, impelling and controlling them. Similarly the traditional formulations of rules and laws of motions, along with the theorems thence deduced remain unshaken, provided that sensible effects and the reasonings grounded in them are granted, whether we suppose the action itself or the force that causes these effects to be in the body or in the incorporeal agent.

29 Take away from the idea of body extension, solidity, and figure, and nothing will remain. But those qualities are indifferent to motion, nor do they contain anything which could be called the principle of motion. This is clear from our very ideas. If therefore by the term *body* be meant that which we conceive, obviously the principle of motion cannot be sought therein, that is, no part or attribute thereof is the true, efficient cause of the production of motion. But to employ a term, and conceive nothing by it is quite unworthy of a philosopher.

30 A thinking, active thing is given which we experience as the principle of motion in ourselves. This we call *soul, mind,* and *spirit.* Extended thing also is given, inert, impenetrable, moveable, totally different from the former and constituting a new genus. Anaxagoras, wisest of men, was the first to grasp the great

difference between thinking things and extended things, and he asserted that the mind has nothing in common with bodies, as is established from the first book of Aristotle's *De Anima*. Of the moderns Descartes has put the same point most forcibly. What was left clear by him others have rendered involved and difficult by their obscure terms.

31 From what has been said it is clear that those who affirm that active force, action, and the principle of motion are really in bodies are adopting an opinion not based on experience, are supporting it with obscure and general terms, and do not well understand their own meaning. On the contrary those who will have mind to be the principle of motion are advancing an opinion fortified by personal experience, and one approved by the suffrages of the most learned men in every age.

32 Anaxagoras was the first to introduce *nous* to impress motion on inert matter. Aristotle, too, approves that opinion and confirms it in many ways, openly stating that the first mover is immoveable, indivisible, and has no magnitude. And he rightly notes that to say that every mover must be moveable is the same as to say that every builder must be capable of being built. *Phys.* Bk. 8. Plato, moreover, in the Timaeus records that this corporeal machine, or visible world, is moved and animated by mind which eludes all sense. To-day indeed Cartesian philosophers recognize God as the principle of natural motions. And Newton everywhere frankly intimates that not only did motion originate from God, but that still the mundane system is moved by the same actus. This is agreeable to Holy Scripture; this is approved by the opinion of the schoolmen; for though the Peripatetics tell us that nature is the principle of motion and rest, yet they interpret *natura naturans* to be God. They understand of course that all the bodies of this mundane system are moved by Almighty Mind according to certain and constant reason.

33 But those who attribute a vital principle to bodies are imagining an obscure notion and one ill suited to the facts. For what is meant by being endowed with the vital principle, except to live? And to live, what is it but to move oneself, to stop, and to change one's state? But the most learned philosophers of this age lay it down for an indubitable principle that every body persists in its own state, whether of rest or of uniform movement in a straight line, except in so far as it is compelled from without to alter that state. The contrary is the case with mind; we feel it as a faculty of altering both our own state and that of other

things, and that is properly called vital, and puts a wide distinction between soul and bodies.

34 Modern thinkers consider motion and rest in bodies as two states of existence in either of which every body, without pressure from external force, would naturally remain passive ; whence one might gather that the cause of the existence of bodies is also the cause of their motion and rest. For no other cause of the successive existence of the body in different parts of space should be sought, it would seem, than that cause whence is derived the successive existence of the same body in different parts of time. But to treat of the good and great God, creator and preserver of all things, and to show how all things depend on supreme and true being, although it is the most excellent part of human knowledge, is, however, rather the province of first philosophy or metaphysics and theology than of natural philosophy which to-day is almost entirely confined to experiments and mechanics. And so natural philosophy either presupposes the knowledge of God or borrows it from some superior science. Although it is most true that the investigation of nature everywhere supplies the higher sciences with notable arguments to illustrate and prove the wisdom, the goodness, and the power of God.

35 The imperfect understanding of this situation has caused some to make the mistake of rejecting the mathematical principles of physics on the ground that they do not assign the efficient causes of things. It is not, however, in fact the business of physics or mechanics to establish efficient causes, but only the rules of impulsions or attractions, and, in a word, the laws of motions, and from the established laws to assign the solution, not the efficient cause, of particular phenomena.

36 It will be of great importance to consider what properly a principle is, and how that term is to be understood by philosophers. The true, efficient and conserving cause of all things by supreme right is called their fount and principle. But the principles of experimental philosophy are properly to be called foundations and springs, not of their existence but of our knowledge of corporeal things, both knowledge by sense and knowledge by experience, foundations on which that knowledge rests and springs from which it flows. Similarly in mechanical philosophy those are to be called principles, in which the whole discipline is grounded and contained, those primary laws of motions which have been proved by experiments, elaborated by reason and rendered universal. These laws of motion are conveniently called

principles, since from them are derived both general mechanical theorems and particular explanations of the phenomena.

37 A thing can be said to be explained mechanically then indeed when it is reduced to those most simple and universal principles, and shown by accurate reasoning to be in agreement and connection with them. For once the laws of nature have been found out, then it is the philosopher's task to show that each phenomenon is in constant conformity with those laws, that is, necessarily follows from those principles. In that consist the explanation and solution of phenomena and the assigning their cause, *i.e.* the reason why they take place.

38 The human mind delights in extending and expanding its knowledge ; and for this purpose general notions and propositions have to be formed in which particular propositions and cognitions are in some way comprised, which then, and not till then, are believed to be understood. Geometers know this well. In mechanics also notions are premised, *i.e.* definitions and first and general statements about motion from which afterwards by mathematical method conclusions more remote and less general are deduced. And just as by the application of geometrical theorems, the sizes of particular bodies are measured, so also by the application of the universal theorems of mechanics, the movements of any parts of the mundane system, and the phenomena thereon depending, become known and are determined. And that is the sole mark at which the physicist must aim.

39 And just as geometers for the sake of their art make use of many devices which they themselves cannot describe nor find in the nature of things, even so the mechanician makes use of certain abstract and general terms, imagining in bodies force, action, attraction, solicitation, *etc.* which are of first utility for theories and formulations, as also for computations about motion, even if in the truth of things, and in bodies actually existing, they would be looked for in vain, just like the geometers' fictions made by mathematical abstraction.

40 We actually perceive by the aid of the senses nothing except the effects or sensible qualities and corporeal things entirely passive, whether in motion or at rest ; and reason and experience advise us that there is nothing active except mind or soul. Whatever else is imagined must be considered to be of a kind with other hypotheses and mathematical abstractions. This ought to be laid to heart ; otherwise we are in danger of sliding back into the obscure subtlety of the schoolmen,

which for so many ages like some dread plague, has corrupted philosophy.

41 Mechanical principles and universal laws of motions or of nature, happy discoveries of the last century, treated and applied by aid of geometry, have thrown a remarkable light upon philosophy. But metaphysical principles and real efficient causes of the motion and existence of bodies or of corporeal attributes in no way belong to mechanics or experiment, nor throw light on them, except in so far as by being known beforehand they may serve to define the limits of physics, and in that way to remove imported difficulties and problems.

42 Those who derive the principle of motion from spirits mean by *spirit* either a corporeal thing or an incorporeal ; if a corporeal thing, however tenuous, yet the difficulty recurs ; if an incorporeal thing, however true it may be, yet it does not properly belong to physics. But if anyone were to extend natural philosophy beyond the limits of experiments and mechanics, so as to cover a knowledge of incorporeal and inextended things, that broader interpretation of the term permits a discussion of soul, mind, or vital principle. But it will be more convenient to follow the usage which is fairly well accepted, and so to distinguish between the sciences as to confine each to its own bounds ; thus the natural philosopher should concern himself entirely with experiments, laws of motions, mechanical principles, and reasonings thence deduced ; but if he shall advance views on other matters, let him refer them for acceptance to some superior science. For from the known laws of nature very elegant theories and mechanical devices of practical utility follow ; but from the knowledge of the Author of nature Himself by far the most excellent considerations arise, but they are metaphysical, theological, and moral.

43 So far about principles ; now we must speak of the nature of motion. Motion though it is clearly perceived by the senses has been rendered obscure rather by the learned comments of philosophers than by its own nature. Motion never meets our senses apart from corporeal mass, space, and time. There are indeed those who desire to contemplate motion as a certain simple and abstract idea, and separated from all other things. But that very fine-drawn and subtle idea eludes the keen edge of intellect, as anyone can find for himself by meditation. Hence arise great difficulties about the nature of motion, and definitions far more obscure than the thing they are meant to illustrate. Such are those definitions of Aristotle and the school-men, who say that

motion is the act ' of the moveable in so far as it is moveable, or the act of a being in potentiality in so far as it is in potentiality.' Such is the saying of a famous man [1] of modern times, who asserts that ' there is nothing real in motion except that momentary thing which must be constituted when a force is striving towards a change.' Again, it is agreed that the authors of these and similar definitions had it in mind to explain the abstract nature of motion, apart from every consideration of time and space ; but how that abstract quintessence, so to speak, of motion, can be understood I do not see.

44 Not content with this they go further and divide and separate from one another the parts of motion itself, of which parts they try to make distinct ideas, as if of entities in fact distinct. For there are those who distinguish movement from motion, looking on the movement as an instantaneous element in the motion. Moreover, they would have velocity, conation, force, and impetus to be so many things differing in essence, each of which is presented to the intellect through its own abstract idea separated from all the rest. But we need not spend any more time on these discussions if the principles laid down above hold good.

45 Many also define motion by *passage*, forgetting indeed that passage itself cannot be understood without motion, and through motion ought to be defined. So very true is it that definitions throw light on some things, and darkness again on others. And certainly hardly anyone could by defining them make clearer or better known the things we perceive by sense. Enticed by the vain hope of doing so, philosophers have rendered easy things very difficult, and have ensnared their own minds in difficulties which for the most part they themselves produced. From this desire of defining and abstracting many very subtle questions both about motion and other things take their rise. Those useless questions have tortured the minds of men to no purpose ; so that Aristotle often actually confesses that motion is ' a certain act difficult to know,' and some of the ancients became such pastmasters in trifling as to deny the existence of motion altogether.

46 But one is ashamed to linger on minutiæ of this sort ; let it suffice to have indicated the sources of the solutions ; but this, too, I must add. The traditional mathematical doctrines of the infinite division of time and space have, from the very nature of the case, introduced paradoxes and thorny theories (as are all those that involve the infinite) into speculations about motion.

[1] [On the authorship of this assertion see above, p. 22n.—Ed.]

All such difficulties motion shares with space and time, or rather has taken them over from that source.

47 Too much abstraction, on the one hand, or the division of things truly inseparable, and on the other hand composition or rather confusion of very different things have perplexed the nature of motion. For it has become usual to confuse motion with the efficient cause of motion. Whence it comes about that motion appears, as it were, in two forms, presenting one aspect to the senses, and keeping the other aspect covered in dark night. Thence obscurity, confusion, and various paradoxes of motion take their rise, while what belongs in truth to the cause alone is falsely attributed to the effect.

48 This is the source of the opinion that the same quantity of motion is always conserved ; anyone will easily satisfy himself of its falsity unless it be understood of the force and power of the cause, whether that cause be called nature or *nous*, or whatever be the ultimate agent. Aristotle indeed (*Phys.* Bk. 8) when he asks whether motion be generated and destroyed, or is truly present in all things from eternity like life immortal, seems to have understood the vital principle rather than the external effect or change of place.

49 Hence it is that many suspect that motion is not mere passivity in bodies. But if we understand by it that which in the movement of a body is an object to the senses, no one can doubt that it is entirely passive. For what is there in the successive existence of body in different places which could relate to action, or be other than bare, lifeless effect ?

50 The Peripatetics who say that motion is the one act of both the mover and the moved do not sufficiently divide cause from effect. Similarly those who imagine effort or conation in motion, or think that the same body at the same time is borne in opposite directions, seem to be the sport of the same confusion of ideas, and the same ambiguity of terms.

51 Diligent attention in grasping the concepts of others and in formulating one's own is of great service in the science of motion as in all other things ; and unless there had been a failing in this respect I do not think that matter for dispute could have come from the query, Whether a body is indifferent to motion and to rest, or not. For since experience shows that it is a primary law of nature that a body persists exactly in ' a state of motion and rest as long as nothing happens from elsewhere to change that state,' and on that account it is inferred that the force of inertia

is under different aspects either resistance or impetus, in this sense assuredly a body can be called indifferent in its own nature to motion or rest. Of course it is as difficult to induce rest in a moving body as motion in a resting body ; but since the body conserves equally either state, why should it not be said to be indifferent to both ?

52 The Peripatetics used to distinguish various kinds of motion corresponding to the variety of changes which a thing could undergo. To-day those who discuss motion understand by the term only local motion. But local motion cannot be understood without understanding the meaning of *locus*. Now *locus* is defined by moderns as ' the part of space which a body occupies,' whence it is divided into relative and absolute corresponding to space. For they distinguish between absolute or true space and relative or apparent space. That is they postulate space on all sides measureless, immoveable, insensible, permeating and containing all bodies, which they call absolute space. But space comprehended or defined by bodies, and therefore an object of sense, is called relative, apparent, vulgar space.

53 And so let us suppose that all bodies were destroyed and brought to nothing. What is left they call absolute space, all relation arising from the situation and distances of bodies being removed together with the bodies. Again, that space is infinite, immoveable, indivisible, insensible, without relation and without distinction. That is, all its attributes are privative or negative. It seems therefore to be mere nothing. The only slight difficulty arising is that it is extended, and extension is a positive quality. But what sort of extension, I ask, is that which cannot be divided nor measured, no part of which can be perceived by sense or pictured by the imagination ? For nothing enters the imagination which from the nature of the thing cannot be perceived by sense, since indeed the imagination is nothing else than the faculty which represents sensible things either actually existing or at least possible. Pure intellect, too, knows nothing of absolute space. That faculty is concerned only with spiritual and inextended things, such as our minds, their states, passions, virtues, and such like. From absolute space then let us take away now the words of the name, and nothing will remain in sense, imagination, or intellect. Nothing else then is denoted by those words than pure privation or negation, *i.e.* mere nothing.

54 It must be admitted that in this matter we are in the grip of serious prejudices, and to win free we must exert the whole

force of our minds. For many, so far from regarding absolute space as nothing, regard it as the only thing (God excepted) which cannot be annihilated ; and they lay down that it necessarily exists of its own nature, that it is eternal and uncreate, and is actually a participant in the divine attributes. But in very truth since it is most certain that all things which we designate by names are known by qualities or relations, at least in part (for it would be stupid, to use words to which nothing known, no notion, idea or concept, were attached), let us diligently inquire whether it is possible to form any idea of that pure, real, and absolute space continuing to exist after the annihilation of all bodies. Such an idea, moreover, when I watch it somewhat more intently, I find to be the purest idea of nothing, if indeed it can be called an idea. This I myself have found on giving the matter my closest attention ; this, I think, others will find on doing likewise.

55 We are sometimes deceived by the fact that when we imagine the removal of all other bodies, yet we suppose our own body to remain. On this supposition we imagine the movement of our limbs fully free on every side ; but motion without space cannot be conceived. None the less if we consider the matter again we shall find, 1st, relative space conceived defined by the parts of our body ; 2nd, a fully free power of moving our limbs obstructed by no obstacle ; and besides these two things nothing. It is false to believe that some third thing really exists, *viz.* immense space which confers on us the free power of moving our body ; for this purpose the absence of other bodies is sufficient. And we must admit that this absence or privation of bodies is nothing positive.[1]

56 But unless a man has examined these points with a free and keen mind, words and terms avail little. To one who meditates, however, and reflects, it will be manifest, I think, that predications about pure and absolute space can all be predicated about nothing. By this argument the human mind is easily freed from great difficulties, and at the same time from the absurdity of attributing necessary existence to any being except to the good and great God alone.

57 It would be easy to confirm our opinion by arguments drawn, as they say *a posteriori*, by proposing questions about absolute space, *e.g.* Is it substance or accidents ? Is it created or uncreated ?

[1] See the arguments against absolute space in my book on *The Principles of Human Knowledge* in the English tongue published ten years ago [1710—Ed.].

and showing the absurdities which follow from either answer. But I must be brief. I must not omit, however, to state that Democritus of old supported this opinion with his vote. Aristotle is our authority for the statement, *Phys.* Bk. 1, where he has these words, ' Democritus lays down as principles the solid and the void, of which the one, he says, is as what is, the other as what is not.' That the distinction between absolute and relative space has been used by philosophers of great name, and that on it as on a foundation many fine theorems have been built, may make us scruple to accept the argument, but those are empty scruples as will appear from what follows.

58 From the foregoing it is clear that we ought not to define the true place of the body as the part of absolute space which the body occupies, and true or absolute motion as the change of true or absolute place ; for all place is relative just as all motion is relative. But to make this appear more clearly we must point out that no motion can be understood without some determination or direction, which in turn cannot be understood unless besides the body in motion our own body also, or some other body, be understood to exist at the same time. For *up, down, left,* and *right* and all places and regions are founded in some relation, and necessarily connote and suppose a body different from the body moved. So that if we suppose the other bodies were annihilated and, for example, a globe were to exist alone, no motion could be conceived in it ; so necessary is it that another body should be given by whose situation the motion should be understood to be determined. The truth of this opinion will be very clearly seen if we shall have carried out thoroughly the supposed annihilation of all bodies, our own and that of others, except that solitary globe.

59 Then let two globes be conceived to exist and nothing corporeal besides them. Let forces then be conceived to be applied in some way ; whatever we may understand by the application of forces, a circular motion of the two globes round a common centre cannot be conceived by the imagination. Then let us suppose that the sky of the fixed stars is created ; suddenly from the conception of the approach of the globes to different parts of that sky the motion will be conceived. That is to say that since motion is relative in its own nature, it could not be conceived before the correlated bodies were given. Similarly no other relation can be conceived without correlates.

60 As regards circular motion many think that, as motion truly circular increases, the body necessarily tends ever more and

more away from its axis. This belief arises from the fact that
circular motion can be seen taking its origin, as it were, at every
moment from two directions, one along the radius and the other
along the tangent, and if in this latter direction only the impetus
be increased, then the body in motion will retire from the centre,
and its orbit will cease to be circular. But if the forces be increased
equally in both directions the motion will remain circular though
accelerated—which will not argue an increase in the forces of
retirement from the axis, any more than in the forces of approach
to it. Therefore we must say that the water forced round in the
bucket rises to the sides of the vessel, because when new forces
are applied in the direction of the tangent to any particle of
water, in the same instant new equal centripetal forces are not
applied. From which experiment it in no way follows that
absolute circular motion is necessarily recognized by the forces
of retirement from the axis of motion. Again, how those terms
corporeal forces and *conation* are to be understood is more than sufficiently shown in the foregoing discussion.

61 A curve can be considered as consisting of an infinite
number of straight lines, though in fact it does not consist of them.
That hypothesis is useful in geometry ; and just so circular motion
can be regarded as arising from an infinite number of rectilinear
directions—which supposition is useful in mechanics. Not, however, on that account must it be affirmed that it is impossible
that the centre of gravity of each body should exist successively
in single points of the circular periphery, no account being taken
of any rectilineal direction in the tangent or the radius.

62 We must not omit to point out that the motion of a stone
in a sling or of water in a whirled bucket cannot be called truly
circular motion as that term is conceived by those who define the
true places of bodies by the parts of absolute space, since it is
strangely compounded of the motions, not alone of bucket or
sling, but also of the daily motion of the earth round her own
axis, of her monthly motion round the common centre of gravity
of earth and moon, and of her annual motion round the sun.
And on that account each particle of the stone or the water
describes a line far removed from circular. Nor in fact does that
supposed axifugal conation exist, since it is not concerned with
some one axis in relation to absolute space, supposing that such a
space exists ; accordingly I do not see how that can be called a
single conation to which a truly circular motion corresponds as to
its proper and adequate effect.

63 No motion can be recognized or measured, unless through sensible things. Since then absolute space in no way affects the senses, it must necessarily be quite useless for the distinguishing of motions. Besides, determination or direction is essential to motion ; but that consists in relation. Therefore it is impossible that absolute motion should be conceived.

64 Further, since the motion of the same body may vary with the diversity of relative place, nay actually since a thing can be said in one respect to be in motion and in another respect to be at rest, to determine true motion and true rest, for the removal of ambiguity and for the furtherance of the mechanics of these philosophers who take the wider view of the system of things, it would be enough to bring in, instead of absolute space, relative space as confined to the heavens of the fixed stars, considered as at rest. But motion and rest marked out by such relative space can conveniently be substituted in place of the absolutes, which cannot be distinguished from them by any mark. For however forces may be impressed, whatever conations there are, let us grant that motion is distinguished by actions exerted on bodies ; never, however, will it follow that that space, absolute place, exists, and that change in it is true place.

65 The laws of motions and the effects, and theorems containing the proportions and calculations of the same for the different configurations of the paths, likewise for accelerations and different directions, and for mediums resisting in greater or less degree, all these hold without bringing absolute motion into account. As is plain from this that since according to the principles of those who introduce absolute motion we cannot know by any indication whether the whole frame of things is at rest, or is moved uniformly in a direction, clearly we cannot know the absolute motion of any body.

66 From the foregoing it is clear that the following rules will be of great service in determining the true nature of motion : (1) to distinguish mathematical hypotheses from the natures of things ; (2) to beware of abstractions ; (3) to consider motion as something sensible, or at least imaginable ; and to be content with relative measures. If we do so, all the famous theorems of the mechanical philosophy by which the secrets of nature are unlocked, and by which the system of the world is reduced to human calculation, will remain untouched ; and the study of motion will be freed from a thousand minutiæ, subtleties, and

abstract ideas. And let these words suffice about the nature of motion.

67 It remains to discuss the cause of the communication of motions. Most people think that the force impressed on the moveable body is the cause of motion in it. However that they do not assign a known cause of motion, and one distinct from the body and the motion is clear from the preceding argument. It is clear, moreover, that force is not a thing certain and determinate, from the fact that great men advance very different opinions, even contrary opinions, about it, and yet in their results attain the truth. For Newton says that impressed force consists in action alone, and is the action exerted on the body to change its state, and does not remain after the action. Torricelli contends that a certain heap or aggregate of forces impressed by percussion is received into the mobile body, and there remains and constitutes impetus. Borelli and others say much the same. But although Newton and Torricelli seem to be disagreeing with one another, they each advance consistent views, and the thing is sufficiently well explained by both. For all forces attributed to bodies are mathematical hypotheses just as are attractive forces in planets and sun. But mathematical entities have no stable essence in the nature of things ; and they depend on the notion of the definer. Whence the same thing can be explained in different ways.

68 Let us lay down that the new motion in the body struck is conserved either by the natural force by reason of which any body persists in its own uniform state of motion or of rest, or by the impressed force, received (while the percussion lasts) into the body struck, and there remaining ; it will be the same in fact, the difference existing only in name. Similarly when the striking moveable body loses motion, and the struck body acquires it, it is not worth disputing whether the acquired motion is numerically the same as the motion lost ; the discussion would lead into metaphysical and even verbal minutiæ about identity. And so it comes to the same thing whether we say that motion passes from the striker to the struck, or that motion is generated *de novo* in the struck, and is destroyed in the striker. In either case it is understood that one body loses motion, the other acquires it, and besides that, nothing.

69 That the Mind which moves and contains this universal, bodily mass, and is the true efficient cause of motion, is the same cause, properly and strictly speaking, of the communication thereof I would not deny. In physical philosophy, however, we

must seek the causes and solutions of phenomena among mechanical principles. Physically, therefore, a thing is explained not by assigning its truly active and incorporeal cause, but by showing its connection with mechanical principles, such as *action and reaction are always opposite and equal*. From such laws as from the source and primary principle, those rules for the communication of motions are drawn, which by the moderns for the great good of the sciences have been already found and demonstrated.

70 I, for my part, will content myself with hinting that that principle could have been set forth in another way. For if the true nature of things, rather than abstract mathematics, be regarded, it will seem more correct to say that in attraction or percussion, the passion of bodies, rather than their action, is equal on both sides. For example, the stone tied by a rope to a horse is dragged towards the horse just as much as the horse towards the stone ; for the body in motion impinging on a quiescent body suffers the same change as the quiescent body. And as regards real effect, the striker is just as the struck, and the struck as the striker. And that change on both sides, both in the body of the horse and in the stone, both in the moved and in the resting, is mere passivity. It is not established that there is force, virtue, or bodily action truly and properly causing such effects. The body in motion impinges on the quiescent body ; we speak, however, in terms of action and say that that impels this ; and it is correct to do so in mechanics where mathematical ideas, rather than the true natures of things, are regarded.

71 In physics sense and experience which reach only to apparent effects hold sway ; in mechanics the abstract notions of mathematicians are admitted. In first philosophy or metaphysics we are concerned with incorporeal things, with causes, truth, and the existence of things. The physicist studies the series or successions of sensible things, noting by what laws they are connected, and in what order, what precedes as cause, and what follows as effect. And on this method we say that the body in motion is the cause of motion in the other, and impresses motion on it, draws it also or impels it. In this sense second corporeal causes ought to be understood, no account being taken of the actual seat of the forces or of the active powers or of the real cause in which they are. Further, besides body, figure, and motion, even the primary axioms of mechanical science can be called causes or mechanical principles, being regarded as the causes of the consequences.

72 Only by meditation and reasoning can truly active causes be rescued from the surrounding darkness and be to some extent known. To deal with them is the business of first philosophy or metaphysics. Allot to each science its own province ; assign its bounds ; accurately distinguish the principles and objects belonging to each. Thus it will be possible to treat them with greater ease and clarity.

The Analyst

or

A Discourse Addressed to an Infidel Mathematician

Wherein it is examined whether the object, principles, and inferences of the modern Analysis are more distinctly conceived, or more evidently deduced, than religious Mysteries and points of Faith

First printed in 1734

EDITOR'S INTRODUCTION

AFTER his return from America late in 1731 Berkeley resided in London, in Green Street, waiting for the preferment which had been virtually promised him by the Court. In a letter to his friend Thomas Prior on 7 January 1734 he said that he had not been well and could not read, but rose early and passed ' my early hours in thinking of certain mathematical matters which may possibly produce something.' It produced the *Analyst*, the only philosophical work which Berkeley wrote in England. The *Analyst* was published in 1734 both in London and Dublin ; the two texts are not identical ; *e.g.* in S. 5 the London text writes ' plain,' the Dublin text ' plane.' According to Fraser (*LL*, p. 225) it appeared in March ; on 4 June it was advertised in the *Dublin Journal* as ' just published.'

In it Berkeley examines Newton's doctrine of the flowing quantity or fluxion. His interest in the doctrine was of long standing. Infinitesimals are often discussed in the *Philosophical Commentaries*. Fluxions are mentioned in No. 168 and, along with Leibniz's kindred doctrine of the differential calculus, in No. 333. In his essay ' Of Infinites ' Berkeley shows himself acquainted with the works of Wallis and Cheyne and the Marquis de l'Hospital and with the controversy between Leibniz and Nieuentiit on the *differentiæ differentiarum*. In his *Principles* (S. 130*ff*) he denies the infinitely small, and says ' Of late the speculations about Infinites have run so high and grown to such strange notions as have occasioned no small scruples and disputes among the geometers of the present age.'

Berkeley's primary concern with these mathematical doctrines was on the score of metaphysics. The infinitesimal gave colour to the belief in matter and its infinite divisibility, and Berkeley approached it as an immaterialist, anxious to see and answer the objections to his philosophical creed which could be urged from the mathematical angle. The religious interest was there as well. The title-page of the *Analyst* attributes it to ' The author of *The Minute Philosopher*,' and we must regard it as a sequel to that work as well as to the *Principles*. The *Analyst* has its place in Christian apologetic and in 'the design and connection' of Berkeley's philosophical works ; it was written in defence of the Christian religion—a proper task for a bishop-elect—and in defence of some out-works of immaterialism ; it develops suggestions made a quarter of a century previously in the *Principles* (SS. 123–34) and expressly refers (S. 50) to that passage. He had recently, he says, been called upon to make good those suggestions—presumably a reference to Andrew Baxter's challenging reflections on his mathematics in *An Enquiry into the nature of the human soul* (1733)—and the revival of public interest in his philosophy is evidenced by the edition of the Essay on Vision appended to the *Alciphron* and by the new editions of the *Principles* and the *Three Dialogues* of 1734.

The *Analyst* is addressed to 'an infidel mathematician,' and Section 1 gives such a pointed application of the address that we may be almost sure that Berkeley had some individual in mind. That individual was not Sir Isaac Newton, though Walton regarded Newton's interposition 'in prophecies and revelations' as a motive of the attack. Berkeley denies that charge (Appendix, S. 2), says that he had a high regard for Newton's writings on those subjects, and shows (*e.g.* Query 58) that he accepts Newton as a religious man. He clearly wished to lessen the authority of Newton, and if Dr. Jurin's servility to Newton ('*vestigia pronus adoro*') was typical, Berkeley was right to make the attempt, but he makes no personal attack on Newton, and certainly did not regard him as 'an infidel mathematician.'

The 'infidel' of the title can be no other than the person to whom Berkeley refers in his *Defence* (S. 7) when he says that Addison 'assured me that the infidelity of a certain noted mathematician, still living, was one principal reason assigned by a witty man of those times for his being an infidel.' Who was this mathematician ? Berkeley does not say, but Stock is in no doubt, and probably he had the authority of the bishop's brother for the statement which follows : 'The occasion [of the *Analyst*] was this : Mr. Addison had given the bishop an account of their common friend Dr. Garth's behaviour in his last illness, which was equally unpleasing to both those excellent advocates for revealed religion. For when Mr. Addison went to see the doctor, and began to discourse with him seriously about preparing for his approaching dissolution, the other made answer, " Surely, Addison, I have good reason not to believe those trifles, since my friend Dr. Halley who has dealt so much in demonstration has assured me that the doctrines of Christianity are incomprehensible, and the religion itself an imposture." The bishop therefore took arms against this redoubtable dealer in demonstration, and addressed the *Analyst* to him, with a view of shewing, that mysteries in faith were unjustly objected to by mathematicians, who admitted much greater mysteries, and even falsehoods, in science, of which he endeavoured to prove that the doctrine of fluxions furnished an eminent example.' Stock's statement fits in well with Berkeley's words quoted above, and I see no reason for doubting it. Fraser finds it a difficulty that Garth, the king's physician, died in January 1719, and Addison six months later, Berkeley being in Italy at the time. But Stock does not say that Addison told Berkeley by word of mouth, and Addison may well have written an account of Garth's last days to their mutual friend in Italy.

Edmund Halley (1656–1742), famous for his astronomical and meteorological discoveries, was Astronomer Royal from 1721. He had the name of being non-Christian, but in 1844 S. J. Rigaud took up the cudgels on his behalf in his *Defence of Halley against the charge of religious infidelity.* From his earliest days of authorship Berkeley had studied Halley's thought, and in his *Philosophical Commentaries* (No. 448) he notes that ' Halley's doctrine about the proportion between infinitely great quantities vanishes.'

To the ecclesiastics of the day the *Analyst* was a useful piece of tactics, a diversion, a counter-attack which helped to keep the mathematical theorists in their place. Gibson, the Bishop of London, refers to it in two letters to Berkeley (9 July 1735 and 7 February 1736) saying, ' the men of science (a conceited generation) are the greatest sticklers against revealed religion, and have been very open in their attacks upon it. And we are much obliged to your Lordship for retorting their arguments upon them, and finding them work in their own quarters. . . .' Its true religious interest lies deeper. As a work in defence of the faith, the *Analyst* has a precise, logical aim. It asks (Query 66), ' Whether the modern analytics do not furnish a strong *argumentum ad hominem* against the philomathematical infidels of these times ? ' It bids mathematicians examine their own principles before they exclaim against mystery ; it shows that mathematics has no monopoly of reason, or religion a monopoly of mystery, and it puts the whole case in the graphic epigram (S. 7) ' He who can digest a second or third fluxion . . . need not, methinks, be squeamish about any point in divinity.'

The *Analyst* is more than a Christian apologetic ; it is a work on mathematics for mathematicians ; and Bishop Gibson wrote better than he knew when he spoke of ' finding them work in their own quarters.' The *Analyst* started a controversy among mathematicians, which lasted for many years and is still remembered, which served to correct their principles, improve their methods, and advance the science.

Outline Analysis

Berkeley describes the *object* of the mathematical analysis (SS. 3–8). Lines are viewed as generated by the motion of points, planes by the motion of lines, and solids by the motion of planes. Quantities are determined from the velocities of their generating motions, and such velocities are called fluxions. Sometimes, instead of velocities the momentary increments or decrements of flowing quantities are considered, and are called moments. Moments are not finite particles, but the nascent principles of finite quantities. The fluxions are celerities proportional, not to the small finite increments, but to the moments or nascent increments. The fluxions of fluxions are called second fluxions ; the fluxions of second fluxions are called third fluxions, and so on with fourth and fifth fluxions *ad infinitum*. These are mysteries, which neither sense nor imagination can grasp. The incipient celerity of an incipient celerity, and the nascent augment of a nascent augment cannot be clearly conceived. Foreign mathematicians proceed somewhat differently, but the method of the differential calculus is, to all intents and purposes, the same as the method of fluxions. The consideration of differences of differences involves the consideration of quantities infinitely less than the least discernible quantity.

Berkeley then turns (SS. 9–16) to the principles of this analysis, and argues that they include error and false reasoning. The main point in the method of fluxions is to obtain the fluxion or momentum of the rectangle or product of two indeterminate quantities. The demonstration is taken from Newton's *Principia* (II. lem. 2), and it is so faulty, says Berkeley, that only an implicit deference to Newton's authority could have secured its acceptance. From this principle, so demonstrated, is derived the general rule for finding the fluxion of any power of a flowing quantity. Newton adopts a new method in establishing this rule, which looks as if he were conscious of defects in the former method. Berkeley examines this new method (SS. 13–16).

He then (S. 17) points out that Newton in his *Treatise of Quadratures* makes an important new departure, in effect adopting the method of the differential calculus, which involves first the supposition and then the rejection of quantities infinitely small. The latter process offends against the geometrical principle of exact accuracy. Berkeley then deals with the argument from results, *viz.* that there cannot be mistakes in the method ; for it yields valid conclusions. He takes an instance (S. 21) and shows how a twofold mistake by a compensation of errors can yield an apparently valid conclusion, and argues that the mathematicians commit this twofold mistake, and arrive at ' truth,' though not at science.

An alternative explanation considers velocities, increments, infinitesimals, etc. imprecisely ; on this showing mathematicians would compute and solve practical problems by aid of the method, just as a sailor can apply the rules and methods of astronomy and geometry without understanding them. Newton himself in this spirit used fluxions as the scaffolding of a building, to be laid aside as soon as their practical purpose was attained. ' And what are these fluxions ? The velocities of evanescent increments. And what are these same evanescent increments ? They are neither finite quantities, nor quantities infinitely small, nor yet nothing. May we not call them " the ghosts of departed quantities ? " ' (S. 35). Names and signs are easy to invent and to reckon by ; but if we lay aside the names and signs, it will not be found easy to conceive the velocities for which the names and signs are supposed to stand. In fact the exponents or notes representing fluxions are often confounded (S. 45 : Fraser mistakenly reads ' compounded ') with the fluxions themselves.

RECEPTION OF THE ANALYST

Opinions have differed among mathematicians as to what precisely Newton taught about fluxions at the varying stages of his thought, and in consequence it is not easy to determine the precise value or justice of Berkeley's particular criticisms ; but when the dust of controvery settled, notable tributes were paid by eminent mathematicians to his perspicuity and to the general truth of his contentions.[1]

G. A. Gibson wrote that Berkeley ' did a great service to sound reasoning in mathematics by the publication of the *Analyst*. . . .' F. Cajori in his *History of Mathematics* (p. 236) says, ' In England the principles of fluxions were boldly attacked by Bishop Berkeley, the eminent metaphysician, who argued with great acuteness, contending, among other things, that the fundamental idea of supposing a finite ratio to exist between terms absolutely evanescent—" the ghosts of departed quantities " as he called them— was absurd and unintelligible. The reply made by Jurin failed to remove all the objections. Berkeley was the first to point out what was again shown later by Lazare Carnot that correct answers were reached by a " compensation of errors." ' Cajori pays a further tribute to the *Analyst* in his *A History of the Conceptions of Limits and Fluxions in Great Britain from Newton to Woodhouse*, which has a portrait of Berkeley for frontispiece.

The immediate result of the *Analyst* was a battle of books. Dr. James Jurin, fellow of Trinity College, Cambridge, writing as Philalethes Cantabrigiensis, published in 1734 *Geometry no friend to infidelity, or a defence of Sir Isaac Newton and the British mathematicians in a Letter to the author of the Analyst*. . . . Jurin makes a counter-attack on the clergy and on the un-Christian spirit of the *Analyst*. He maintains that the doctrine of fluxions is the greatest proof of the extent of human abilities. He complains that Berkeley mistranslates Newton and puts phrases into his mouth that he never used. He denies the alleged twofold mistake and the compensation of errors, and argues that when dealing with vast spaces and celestial bodies, small increments are negligible and can be rejected without error. Finally he reverts to Berkeley's original attack on abstract general ideas, and tries to vindicate Locke's doctrine. J. Walton, apparently a Dublin school-master, published in 1735 *A Vindication of Sir Isaac Newton's principles of fluxions against the objections contained in the Analyst*. He goes somewhat fully into the mathematics of the case, tries to defend the detail of Newton's argument, and even maintains that Newton's method in the *Quadratures* is consistent with that of the second book of his *Principles*.

[1] See A. E. De Morgan, ' On the early history of Infinitesimals in England,' *London, Edinburgh, and Dublin Philosophical Magazine*, vol. 4, 4th series, London, 1852, p. 328, and J. O. Wisdom, ' The Analyst Controversy,' *Hermathena* LIX, 1942, G. A. Gibson, *Proc. Edin. Math. Soc.*, vol. 17, 1898–9, pp. 31–2.

Berkeley answered Jurin with *A Defence of Free-thinking in Mathematics* (see below p. 105), adding an Appendix concerning Mr. Walton's Vindication of Sir Isaac Newton's *Principles of Fluxions*. Jurin came back with *The minute mathematician, or the free-thinker no Just-thinker* (1735), an abusive tract to which Berkeley made no reply. Walton answered the Appendix in the same year with *The catechism of the author of the Minute Philosopher fully answer'd*. Berkeley replied with the short tract, *Reasons for not replying to Mr. Walton's Full Answer in a letter to P.T.P.*, which drew from Walton a further rejoinder in an Appendix to the second edition of his *Catechism*.

Berkeley made no further contribution to the issue, but the controversy was long continued among the mathematicians, and in 1744 Berkeley could say (*Siris*, S. 271*n*) about fluxions that 'within these ten years, I have seen published about twenty tracts and dissertations, whose authors being utterly at variance and inconsistent with each other, instruct bystanders what to think of their pretensions to evidence.' B. Robins, Jurin, H. Pemberton, T. Bayes, and J. Smith were amongst those who contributed to the debate, and the most important works which resulted were, *A discourse concerning the nature and certainty of Sir Isaac Newton's methods of fluxions* . . . (1735), by B. Robins and C. Maclaurin's *Treatise of fluxions* (1742).

The Analyst

The Text

THE ANALYST

1 Though I am a stranger to your person, yet I am not, Sir,
a stranger to the reputation you have acquired in that branch of
learning which hath been your peculiar study; nor to the authority
that you therefore assume in things foreign to your profession,
nor to the abuse that you, and too many more of the like character,
are known to make of such undue authority, to the misleading
of unwary persons in matters of the highest concernment, and
whereof your mathematical knowledge can by no means qualify
you to be a competent judge. Equity indeed and good sense would
incline one to disregard the judgment of men, in points which
they have not considered or examined. But several who make
the loudest claim to those qualities do nevertheless the very
thing they would seem to despise, clothing themselves in the
livery of other men's opinions, and putting on a general deference
for the judgment of you, Gentlemen, who are presumed to be
of all men the greatest masters of reason, to be most conversant
about distinct ideas, and never to take things upon trust, but
always clearly to see your way, as men whose constant employment is the deducing truth by the justest inference from the most
evident principles. With this bias on their minds, they submit
to your decisions where you have no right to decide. And that
this is one short way of making Infidels, I am credibly informed.

2 Whereas then it is supposed that you apprehend more
distinctly, consider more closely, infer more justly, conclude more
accurately than other men, and that you are therefore less religious
because more judicious, I shall claim the privilege of a Free-
thinker ; and take the liberty to inquire into the object, principles,
and method of demonstration admitted by the mathematicians of
the present age, with the same freedom that you presume to treat
the principles and mysteries of Religion ; to the end that all
men may see what right you have to lead, or what encourage-
ment others have to follow you. It hath been an old remark,
that Geometry is an excellent Logic. And it must be owned
that when the definitions are clear ; when the postulata cannot
be refused, nor the axioms denied ; when from the distinct

contemplation and comparison of figures, their properties are derived, by a perpetual well-connected chain of consequences, the objects being still kept in view, and the attention ever fixed upon them ; there is acquired an habit of reasoning, close and exact and methodical : which habit strengthens and sharpens the mind, and being transferred to other subjects is of general use in the inquiry after truth. But how far this is the case of our geometrical analysts, it may be worth while to consider.

3 The Method of Fluxions is the general key by help whereof the modern mathematicians unlock the secrets of Geometry, and consequently of Nature. And, as it is that which hath enabled them so remarkably to outgo the ancients in discovering theorems and solving problems, the exercise and application thereof is become the main if not sole employment of all those who in this age pass for profound geometers. But whether this method be clear or obscure, consistent or repugnant, demonstrative or precarious, as I shall inquire with the utmost impartiality, so I submit my inquiry to your own judgment, and that of every candid reader. Lines are supposed to be generated [1] by the motion of points, planes by the motion of lines, and solids by the motion of planes. And whereas quantities generated in equal times are greater or lesser according to the greater or lesser velocity wherewith they increase and are generated, a method hath been found to determine quantities from the velocities of their generating motions. And such velocities are called fluxions : and the quantities generated are called flowing quantities. These fluxions are said to be nearly as the increments of the flowing quantities, generated in the least equal particles of time ; and to be accurately in the first proportion of the nascent, or in the last of the evanescent increments. Sometimes, instead of velocities, the momentaneous increments or decrements of undetermined flowing quantities are considered, under the appellation of moments.

4 By moments we are not to understand finite particles. These are said not to be moments, but quantities generated from moments, which last are only the nascent principles of finite quantities. It is said that the minutest errors are not to be neglected in mathematics : that the fluxions are celerities, not proportional to the finite increments, though ever so small ; but only to the moments or nascent increments, whereof the proportion alone, and not the magnitude, is considered. And of

[1] *Introd. ad Quadraturam Curvarum.*

the aforesaid fluxions there be other fluxions, which fluxions of fluxions are called second fluxions. And the fluxions of these second fluxions are called third fluxions : and so on, fourth, fifth, sixth, &c. *ad infinitum*. Now, as our sense is strained and puzzled with the perception of objects extremely minute, even so the imagination, which faculty derives from sense, is very much strained and puzzled to frame clear ideas of the least particles of time, or the least increments generated therein : and much more so to comprehend the moments, or those increments of the flowing quantities in *statu nascenti*, in their very first origin or beginning to exist, before they become finite particles. And it seems still more difficult to conceive the abstracted velocities of such nascent imperfect entities. But the velocities of the velocities, the second, third, fourth, and fifth velocities, &c., exceed, if I mistake not, all human understanding. The further the mind analyseth and pursueth these fugitive ideas the more it is lost and bewildered ; the objects, at first fleeting and minute, soon vanishing out of sight. Certainly in any sense, a second or third fluxion seems an obscure mystery. The incipient celerity of an incipient celerity, the nascent augment of a nascent augment, *i.e.* of a thing which hath no magnitude : take it in what light you please, the clear conception of it will, if I mistake not, be found impossible ; whether it be so or no I appeal to the trial of every thinking reader. And if a second fluxion be inconceivable, what are we to think of third, fourth, fifth fluxions, and so on without end ?

5 The foreign mathematicians [1] are supposed by some, even of our own, to proceed in a manner less accurate, perhaps, and geometrical, yet more intelligible. Instead of flowing quantities and their fluxions, they consider the variable finite quantities as increasing or diminishing by the continual addition or sub-duction of infinitely small quantities. Instead of the velocities wherewith increments are generated, they consider the increments or decrements themselves, which they call differences, and which are supposed to be infinitely small. The difference of a line is an infinitely little line ; of a plain an infinitely little plain. They suppose finite quantities to consist of parts infinitely little, and curves to be polygons, whereof the sides are infinitely little, which by the angles they make one with another determine the curvity of the line. Now to conceive a quantity infinitely small,

[1] [Elsewhere Berkeley names Leibniz, Nieuentiit, and the Marquis de l'Hospital.—Ed.]

that is, infinitely less than any sensible or imaginable quantity, or than any the least finite magnitude is, I confess, above my capacity. But to conceive a part of such infinitely small quantity that shall be still infinitely less than it, and consequently though multiplied infinitely shall never equal the minutest finite quantity, is, I suspect, an infinite difficulty to any man whatsoever ; and will be allowed such by those who candidly say what they think ; provided they really think and reflect, and do not take things upon trust.

6 And yet in the *calculus differentialis*, which method serves to all the same intents and ends with that of fluxions, our modern analysts are not content to consider only the differences of finite quantities : they also consider the differences of those differences, and the differences of the differences of the first differences. And so on *ad infinitum*. That is, they consider quantities infinitely less than the least discernible quantity ; and others infinitely less than those infinitely small ones ; and still others infinitely less than the preceding infinitesimals, and so on without end or limit. Insomuch that we are to admit an infinite succession of infinitesimals, each infinitely less than the foregoing, and infinitely greater than the following. As there are first, second, third, fourth, fifth, &c. fluxions, so there are differences, first, second, third, fourth, &c., in an infinite progression towards nothing, which you still approach and never arrive at. And (which is most strange) although you should take a million of millions of these infinitesimals, each whereof is supposed infinitely greater than some other real magnitude, and add them to the least given quantity, it shall never be the bigger. For this is one of the modest *postulata* of our modern mathematicians, and is a corner-stone or ground-work of their speculations.

7 All these points, I say, are supposed and believed by certain rigorous exactors of evidence in religion, men who pretend to believe no further than they can see. That men who have been conversant only about clear points should with difficulty admit obscure ones might not seem altogether unaccountable. But he who can digest a second or third fluxion, a second or third difference, need not, methinks, be squeamish about any point in divinity. There is a natural presumption that men's faculties are made alike. It is on this supposition that they attempt to argue and convince one another. What therefore shall appear evidently impossible and repugnant to one may be presumed the same to another. But with what appearance of reason shall

any man presume to say that mysteries may not be objects of faith, at the same time that he himself admits such obscure mysteries to be the object of science ?

8 It must indeed be acknowledged the modern mathematicians do not consider these points as mysteries, but as clearly conceived and mastered by their comprehensive minds. They scruple not to say that by the help of these new analytics they can penetrate into infinity it self : that they can even extend their views beyond infinity : that their art comprehends not only infinite, but infinite of infinite (as they express it), or an infinity of infinites. But, notwithstanding all these assertions and pretensions, it may be justly questioned whether, as other men in other inquiries are often deceived by words or terms, so they likewise are not wonderfully deceived and deluded by their own peculiar signs, symbols, or species. Nothing is easier than to devise expressions or notations, for fluxions and infinitesimals of the first, second, third, fourth, and subsequent orders, proceeding in the same regular form without end or limit $\dot{x}$. $\ddot{x}$. $\dddot{x}$. $\ddddot{x}$. &c. or dx. ddx. $dddx$. $ddddx$. &c. These expressions indeed are clear and distinct, and the mind finds no difficulty in conceiving them to be continued beyond any assignable bounds. But if we remove the veil and look underneath, if, laying aside the expressions, we set ourselves attentively to consider the things themselves which are supposed to be expressed or marked thereby, we shall discover much emptiness, darkness, and confusion ; nay, if I mistake not, direct impossibilities and contradictions. Whether this be the case or no, every thinking reader is intreated to examine and judge for himself.

9 Having considered the object, I proceed to consider the principles of this new analysis by momentums, fluxions, or infinitesimals ; wherein if it shall appear that your capital points, upon which the rest are supposed to depend, include error and false reasoning ; it will then follow that you, who are at a loss to conduct your selves, cannot with any decency set up for guides to other men. The main point in the method of fluxions is to obtain the fluxion or momentum of the rectangle or product of two indeterminate quantities. Inasmuch as from thence are derived rules for obtaining the fluxions of all other products and powers ; be the coefficients or the indexes what they will, integers or fractions, rational or surd. Now, this fundamental point one would think should be very clearly made out, considering how much is built upon it, and that its influence extends throughout

the whole analysis. But let the reader judge. This is given for demonstration.[1] Suppose the product or rectangle AB increased by continual motion : and that the momentaneous increments of the sides A and B are a and b. When the sides A and B were deficient, or lesser by one half of their moments, the rectangle was $\overline{A - \frac{1}{2}a} \times \overline{B - \frac{1}{2}b}$ i.e. $AB - \frac{1}{2}aB - \frac{1}{2}bA + \frac{1}{4}ab$. And as soon as the sides A and B are increased by the other two halves of their moments, the rectangle becomes $\overline{A + \frac{1}{2}a} \times \overline{B + \frac{1}{2}b}$ or $AB + \frac{1}{2}aB + \frac{1}{2}bA + \frac{1}{4}ab$. From the latter rectangle subduct the former, and the remaining difference will be $aB + bA$. Therefore the increment of the rectangle generated by the intire increments a and b is $aB + bA$. Q.E.D. But it is plain that the direct and true method to obtain the moment or increment of the rectangle AB, is to take the sides as increased by their whole increments, and so multiply them together, $A + a$ by $B + b$, the product whereof $AB + aB + bA + ab$ is the augmented rectangle ; whence, if we subduct AB the remainder $aB + bA + ab$ will be the true increment of the rectangle, exceeding that which was obtained by the former illegitimate and indirect method by the quantity ab. And this holds universally be the quantities a and b what they will, big or little, finite or infinitesimal, increments, moments, or velocities. Nor will it avail to say that ab is a quantity exceeding small : since we are told that *in rebus mathematicis errores quam minimi non sunt contemnendi*.[2]

10 Such reasoning as this for demonstration, nothing but the obscurity of the subject could have encouraged or induced the great author of the fluxionary method to put upon his followers, and nothing but an implicit deference to authority could move them to admit. The case indeed is difficult. There can be nothing done till you have got rid of the quantity ab. In order to this the notion of fluxions is shifted : It is placed in various lights : Points which should be clear as first principles are puzzled ; and terms which should be steadily used are ambiguous. But notwithstanding all this address and skill the point of getting rid of ab cannot be obtained by legitimate reasoning. If a man, by methods not geometrical or demonstrative, shall have satisfied himself of the usefulness of certain rules ; which he afterwards shall propose to his disciples for undoubted truths ; which he undertakes to demonstrate in a subtile manner, and by the help of nice and

---

[1] *Naturalis Philosophiæ principia mathematica*, lib. 2. lem. 2.
[2] *Introd. ad Quadraturam Curvarum.*

intricate notions ; it is not hard to conceive that such his disciples may, to save themselves the trouble of thinking, be inclined to confound the usefulness of a rule with the certainty of a truth, and accept the one for the other ; especially if they are men accustomed rather to compute than to think ; earnest rather to go on fast and far, than solicitous to set out warily and see their way distinctly.

11 The points or mere limits of nascent lines are undoubtedly equal, as having no more magnitude one than another, a limit as such being no quantity. If by a momentum you mean more than the very initial limit, it must be either a finite quantity or an infinitesimal. But all finite quantities are expressly excluded from the notion of a momentum. Therefore the momentum must be an infinitesimal. And, indeed, though much artifice hath been employed to escape or avoid the admission of quantities infinitely small, yet it seems ineffectual. For ought I see, you can admit no quantity as a medium between a finite quantity and nothing, without admitting infinitesimals. An increment generated in a finite particle of time is it self a finite particle ; and cannot therefore be a momentum. You must therefore take an infinitesimal part of time wherein to generate your momentum. It is said, the magnitude of moments is not considered : And yet these same moments are supposed to be divided into parts. This is not easy to conceive, no more than it is why we should take quantities less than A and B in order to obtain the increment of AB, of which proceeding it must be owned the final cause or motive is very obvious ; but it is not so obvious or easy to explain a just and legitimate reason for it, or shew it to be geometrical.

12 From the foregoing principle, so demonstrated, the general rule for finding the fluxion of any power of a flowing quantity is derived.[1] But, as there seems to have been some inward scruple or consciousness of defect in the foregoing demonstration, and as this finding the fluxion of a given power is a point of primary importance, it hath therefore been judged proper to demonstrate the same in a different manner independent of the foregoing demonstration. But whether this other method be more legitimate and conclusive than the former, I proceed now to examine ; and in order thereto shall premise the following lemma. ' If with a view to demonstrate any proposition, a certain point is supposed, by virtue of which certain other points are attained ; and such supposed point be it self afterwards destroyed or rejected by a

---

[1] *Philosophiæ naturalis principia mathematica*, lib. 2. lem. 2.

contrary supposition ; in that case, all the other points attained thereby, and consequent thereupon, must also be destroyed and rejected, so as from thence forward to be no more supposed or applied in the demonstration.' This is so plain as to need no proof.

13 Now the other method of obtaining a rule to find the fluxion of any power is as follows. Let the quantity x flow uniformly, and be it proposed to find the fluxion of x^n. In the same time that x by flowing becomes $x + o$, the power x^n becomes $\overline{x + o}|^n$, i.e. by the method of infinite series

$$x^n + nox^{n-1} + \frac{nn - n}{2} oox^{n-2} + \&c.,$$

and the increments

$$o \text{ and } nox^{n-1} + \frac{nn - n}{2} oox^{n-2} + \&c.$$

are one to another as

$$1 \text{ to } nx^{n-1} + \frac{nn - n}{2} ox^{n-2} + \&c.$$

Let now the increments vanish, and their last proportion will be 1 to nx^{n-1}. But it should seem that this reasoning is not fair or conclusive. For when it is said, let the increments vanish, i.e. let the increments be nothing, or let there be no increments, the former supposition that the increments were something, or that there were increments, is destroyed, and yet a consequence of that supposition, i.e. an expression got by virtue thereof, is retained. Which, by the foregoing lemma, is a false way of reasoning. Certainly when we suppose the increments to vanish, we must suppose their proportions, their expressions, and every thing else derived from the supposition of their existence to vanish with them.

14 To make this point plainer, I shall unfold the reasoning, and propose it in a fuller light to your view. It amounts therefore to this, or may in other words be thus expressed. I suppose that the quantity x flows, and by flowing is increased, and its increment I call o, so that by flowing it becomes $x + o$. And as x increaseth, it follows that every power of x is likewise increased in a due proportion. Therefore as x becomes $x + o$, x^n will become $\overline{x + o}|^n$: that is, according to the method of infinite series,

$$x^n + nox^{n-1} + \frac{nn - n}{2} oox^{n-2} + \&c.$$

And if from the two augmented quantities we subduct the root and the power respectively, we shall have remaining the two increments, to wit,

$$o \text{ and } nox^{n-1} + \frac{nn - n}{2} oox^{n-2} + \&\text{c.}$$

which increments, being both divided by the common divisor o, yield the quotients

$$1 \text{ and } nx^{n-1} + \frac{nn - n}{2} ox^{n-2} + \&\text{c.}$$

which are therefore exponents of the ratio of the increments. Hitherto I have supposed that x flows, that x hath a real increment, that o is something. And I have proceeded all along on that supposition, without which I should not have been able to have made so much as one single step. From that supposition it is that I get at the increment of x^n, that I am able to compare it with the increment of x, and that I find the proportion between the two increments. I now beg leave to make a new supposition contrary to the first, *i.e.* I will suppose that there is no increment of x, or that o is nothing ; which second supposition destroys my first, and is inconsistent with it, and therefore with every thing that supposeth it. I do nevertheless beg leave to retain nx^{n-1}, which is an expression obtained in virtue of my first supposition, which necessarily presupposeth such supposition, and which could not be obtained without it : All which seems a most inconsistent way of arguing, and such as would not be allowed of in Divinity.

15 Nothing is plainer than that no just conclusion can be directly drawn from two inconsistent suppositions. You may indeed suppose any thing possible : But afterwards you may not suppose any thing that destroys what you first supposed : or, if you do, you must begin *de novo*. If therefore you suppose that the augments vanish, *i.e.* that there are no augments, you are to begin again and see what follows from such supposition. But nothing will follow to your purpose. You cannot by that means ever arrive at your conclusion, or succeed in what is called by the celebrated author, the investigation of the first or last proportions of nascent and evanescent quantities, by instituting the analysis in finite ones. I repeat it again : You are at liberty to make any possible supposition : And you may destroy one supposition by another : But then you may not retain the conse-

quences, or any part of the consequences, of your first supposition so destroyed. I admit that signs may be made to denote either any thing or nothing : and consequently that in the original notation $x + o$, o might have signified either an increment or nothing. But then which of these soever you make it signify, you must argue consistently with such its signification, and not proceed upon a double meaning : Which to do were a manifest sophism. Whether you argue in symbols or in words the rules of right reason are still the same. Nor can it be supposed you will plead a privilege in mathematics to be exempt from them.

16 If you assume at first a quantity increased by nothing, and in the expression $x + o$, o stands for nothing, upon this supposition as there is no increment of the root, so there will be no increment of the power ; and consequently there will be none except the first, of all those members of the series constituting the power of the binomial ; you will therefore never come at your expression of a fluxion legitimately by such method. Hence you are driven into the fallacious way of proceeding to a certain point on the supposition of an increment, and then at once shifting your supposition to that of no increment. There may seem great skill in doing this at a certain point or period. Since, if this second supposition had been made before the common division by o, all had vanished at once, and you must have got nothing by your supposition. Whereas, by this artifice of first dividing and then changing your supposition, you retain 1 and nx^{n-1}. But, notwithstanding all this address to cover it, the fallacy is still the same. For, whether it be done sooner or later, when once the second supposition or assumption is made, in the same instant the former assumption and all that you got by it is destroyed, and goes out together. And this is universally true, be the subject what it will, throughout all the branches of human knowledge ; in any other of which, I believe, men would hardly admit such a reasoning as this, which in mathematics is accepted for demonstration.

17 It may be not amiss to observe that the method for finding the fluxion of a rectangle of two flowing quantities, as it is set forth in the Treatise of Quadratures, differs from the above-mentioned taken from the second book of the Principles, and is in effect the same with that used in the *calculus differentialis*.[1] For the supposing a quantity infinitely diminished, and therefore rejecting it, is in effect the rejecting an infinitesimal ; and indeed it requires a marvellous sharpness of discernment to be able to

---

[1] *Analyse des infiniment petits*, part 1. prop. 2.

distinguish between evanescent increments and infinitesimal differences. It may perhaps be said that the quantity being infinitely diminished becomes nothing, and so nothing is rejected. But according to the received principles it is evident that no geometrical quantity can by any division or subdivision what-soever be exhausted, or reduced to nothing. Considering the various arts and devices used by the great author of the fluxionary method ; in how many lights he placeth his fluxions ; and in what different ways he attempts to demonstrate the same point ; one would be inclined to think, he was himself suspicious of the justness of his own demonstrations ; and that he was not enough pleased with any notion steadily to adhere to it. Thus much at least is plain, that he owned himself satisfied concerning certain points, which nevertheless he could not undertake to demon-strate to others.[1] Whether this satisfaction arose from tentative methods or inductions ; which have often been admitted by mathematicians (for instance, by Dr. Wallis in his Arithmetic of Infinites [2]), is what I shall not pretend to determine. But, whatever the case might have been with respect to the author, it appears that his followers have shewn themselves more eager in applying his method, than accurate in examining his principles.

18 It is curious to observe what subtilty and skill this great genius employs to struggle with an insuperable difficulty ; and through what labyrinths he endeavours to escape the doctrine of infinitesimals ; which as it intrudes upon him whether he will or no, so it is admitted and embraced by others without the least repugnance. Leibniz and his followers in their *calculus dif-ferentialis* making no manner of scruple, first to suppose, and secondly to reject, quantities infinitely small ; with what clear-ness in the apprehension and justness in the reasoning, any thinking man, who is not prejudiced in favour of those things, may easily discern. The notion or idea of an *infinitesimal quantity*, as it is an object simply apprehended by the mind, hath been already considered.[3] I shall now only observe as to the method of getting rid of such quantities, that it is done without the least ceremony. As in fluxions the point of first importance, and which paves the way to the rest, is to find the fluxion of a product of two indeterminate quantities, so in the *calculus differentialis* (which method is supposed to have been borrowed from the

[1] See letter to Collins, Nov. 8, 1676. [*Cf. Defence*, S. 37.—Ed.]
[2] [Mentioned in Berkeley's *Of Infinites* ; see also *PC* No. 482.—Ed.]
[3] Sect. 5 and 6.

former with some small alterations) the main point is to obtain the difference of such product. Now the rule for this is got by rejecting the product or rectangle of the differences. And in general it is supposed that no quantity is bigger or lesser for the addition or subduction of its infinitesimal : and that consequently no error can arise from such rejection of infinitesimals.

19 And yet it should seem that, whatever errors are admitted in the premises, proportional errors ought to be apprehended in the conclusion, be they finite or infinitesimal : and that therefore the ἀκρίβεια of geometry requires nothing should be neglected or rejected. In answer to this you will perhaps say, that the conclusions are accurately true, and that therefore the principles and methods from whence they are derived must be so too. But this inverted way of demonstrating your principles by your conclusions, as it would be peculiar to you gentlemen, so it is contrary to the rules of logic. The truth of the conclusion will not prove either the form or the matter of a syllogism to be true ; inasmuch as the illation might have been wrong or the premises false, and the conclusion nevertheless true, though not in virtue of such illation or of such premises. I say that in every other science men prove their conclusions by their principles, and not their principles by the conclusions. But if in yours you should allow your selves this unnatural way of proceeding, the consequence would be that you must take up with Induction, and bid adieu to Demonstration. And if you submit to this, your authority will no longer lead the way in points of Reason and Science.

20 I have no controversy about your conclusions, but only about your logic and method. How you demonstrate ? What objects you are conversant with, and whether you conceive them clearly ? What principles you proceed upon ; how sound they may be ; and how you apply them ? It must be remembered that I am not concerned about the truth of your theorems, but only about the way of coming at them ; whether it be legitimate or illegitimate, clear or obscure, scientific or tentative. To prevent all possibility of your mistaking me, I beg leave to repeat and insist, that I consider the geometrical analyst as a logician, *i.e.* so far forth as he reasons and argues ; and his mathematical conclusions, not in themselves, but in their premises ; not as true or false, useful or insignificant, but as derived from such principles, and by such inferences. And, forasmuch as it may perhaps seem an unaccountable paradox that mathematicians should deduce true propositions from false principles, be right

in the conclusion and yet err in the premises ; I shall endeavour particularly to explain why this may come to pass, and shew how error may bring forth truth, though it cannot bring forth science.

21 In order therefore to clear up this point, we will suppose for instance that a tangent is to be drawn to a parabola, and examine the progress of this affair as it is performed by infinitesimal differences. Let AB be a curve, the absciss $AP = x$, the ordinate $PB = y$, the difference of the absciss $PM = dx$, the difference of the ordinate $RN = dy$. Now, by supposing the curve to be a polygon, and consequently BN, the increment or difference of the curve, to be a straight line coincident with the tangent, and the differential triangle BRN to be similar to the triangle TPB, the subtangent PT is found a fourth proportional to $RN : RB : PB$: that is, to $dy : dx : y$. Hence the subtangent will be $\dfrac{y\,dx}{dy}$. But herein there is an error arising from the forementioned false supposition, whence the value of PT comes out

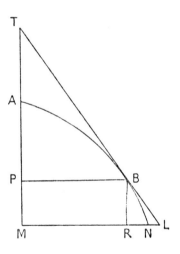

greater than the truth : for in reality it is not the triangle RNB but RLB, which is similar to PBT, and therefore (instead of RN) RL should have been the first term of the proportion, i.e. $RN+NL$, i.e. $dy + z$: whence the true expression for the subtangent should have been $\dfrac{y\,dx}{dy+z}$. There was therefore an error of defect in making dy the divisor : which error was equal to z, i.e. NL the line comprehended between the curve and the tangent. Now by the nature of the curve $yy = px$, supposing p to be the parameter, whence by the rule of differences $2y\,dy = p\,dx$ and $dy = \dfrac{pdx}{2y}$. But if you multiply $y + dy$ by it self, and retain the whole product without rejecting the square of the difference, it will then come out, by substituting the augmented quantities in the equation of the curve, that $dy = \dfrac{p\,dx}{2y} - \dfrac{dy\,dy}{2y}$ truly. There was therefore an error of excess in making $dy = \dfrac{p\,dx}{2y}$, which followed from the erroneous rule of differences. And the measure of this second error is $\dfrac{dy\,dy}{2y} = z$. Therefore the two errors being equal and contrary destroy each other ; the first error of defect being corrected by a second error of excess.

22 If you had committed only one error, you would not have come at a true solution of the problem. But by virtue of a twofold mistake you arrive, though not at science, yet at truth. For science it cannot be called, when you proceed blindfold, and arrive at the truth not knowing how or by what means. To demonstrate that z is equal to $\dfrac{dy\,dy}{2y}$, let BR or dx be m, and RN or dy be n. By the thirty third proposition of the first book of the Conics of Apollonius, and from similar triangles, as $2x$ to y so is m to $n + z = \dfrac{my}{2x}$. Likewise from the nature of the parabola $yy + 2yn + nn = xp + mp$, and $2yn + nn = mp$: wherefore $\dfrac{2yn + nn}{p} = m$: and because $yy = px$, $\dfrac{yy}{p}$ will be equal to x. Therefore substituting these values instead of m and x we shall have

$$n + z = \frac{my}{2x} = \frac{2\,yynp + ynnp}{2yyp} :$$

i.e.
$$n + z = \frac{2yn + nn}{2y} :$$

which being reduced gives

$$z = \frac{nn}{2y} = \frac{dy\,dy}{2y}\ Q.E.D.$$

23 Now, I observe in the first place, that the conclusion comes out right, not because the rejected square of dy was infinitely small ; but because this error was compensated by another contrary and equal error. I observe in the second place, that whatever is rejected, be it ever so small, if it be real and consequently makes a real error in the premises, it will produce a proportional real error in the conclusion. Your theorems there-

fore cannot be accurately true, nor your problems accurately solved, in virtue of premises which themselves are not accurate ; it being a rule in logic that *conclusio sequitur partem debiliorem*. Therefore I observe in the third place, that when the conclusion is evident and the premises obscure, or the conclusion accurate and the premises inaccurate, we may safely pronounce that such conclusion is neither evident nor accurate, in virtue of those obscure inaccurate premises or principles ; but in virtue of some other principles which perhaps the demonstrator himself never knew or thought of. I observe in the last place, that in case the differences are supposed finite quantities ever so great, the conclusion will nevertheless come out the same : inasmuch as the rejected quantities are legitimately thrown out, not for their smallness, but for another reason, to wit, because of contrary errors, which, destroying each other do upon the whole cause that nothing is really, though something is apparently, thrown out. And this reason holds equally with respect to quantities finite as well as infinitesimal, great as well as small, a foot or a yard long as well as the minutest increment.

24 For the fuller illustration of this point, I shall consider it in another light, and proceeding in finite quantities to the conclusion, I shall only then make use of one infinitesimal. Suppose the straight line MQ cuts the curve AT in the points R and S.

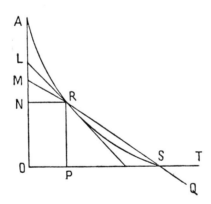

Suppose LR a tangent at the point R, AN the absciss, NR and OS ordinates. Let AN be produced to O, and RP be drawn parallel to NO. Suppose $AN = x$, $NR = y$, $NO = v$, $PS = z$, the subsecant $MN = s$. Let the equation $y = xx$ express the nature of the curve : and supposing y and x increased by their finite increments we get

$$y + z = xx + 2xv + vv :$$

whence the former equation being subducted there remains $z = 2xv + vv$. And by reason of similar triangles

$$PS : PR : : NR : NM, \text{ i.e. } z : v : : y : s = \frac{vy}{z},$$

wherein if for y and z we substitute their values, we get

$$\frac{vxx}{2\,xv + vv} = s = \frac{xx}{2\,x + v}.$$

And supposing NO to be infinitely diminished, the subsecant NM will in that case coincide with the subtangent NL, and v as an infinitesimal may be rejected, whence it follows that

$$S = NL = \frac{xx}{2x} = \frac{x}{2}$$

which is the true value of the subtangent. And since this was obtained by one only error, *i.e.* by once rejecting one only infinitesimal, it should seem, contrary to what hath been said, that an infinitesimal quantity or difference may be neglected or thrown away, and the conclusion nevertheless be accurately true, although there was no double mistake, or rectifying of one error by another, as in the first case. But, if this point be thoroughly considered, we shall find there is even here a double mistake, and that one compensates or rectifies the other. For, in the first place, it was supposed that when NO is infinitely diminished or becomes an infinitesimal then the subsecant NM becomes equal to the sub-tangent NL. But this is a plain mistake ; for it is evident that as a secant cannot be a tangent, so a subsecant cannot be a sub-tangent. Be the difference ever so small, yet still there is a difference. And if NO be infinitely small, there will even then be an infinitely small difference between NM and NL. Therefore NM or S was too little for your supposition (when you supposed it equal to NL) and this error was compensated by a second error in throwing out v, which last error made s bigger than its true value, and in lieu thereof gave the value of the subtangent. This is the true state of the case, however it may be disguised. And to this in reality it amounts, and is at bottom the same thing, if we should pretend to find the subtangent by having first found, from the equation of the curve and similar triangles, a general expression for all subsecants, and then reducing the subtangent under this general rule, by considering it as the subsecant when v vanishes or becomes nothing.

25 Upon the whole I observe, *First*, that v can never be nothing so long as there is a secant. *Secondly*, that the same line cannot be both tangent and secant. *Thirdly*, that when v or NO [1] vanisheth, PS and SR do also vanish, and with them the proportionality of the similar triangles. Consequently the whole expression, which was obtained by means thereof and grounded thereupon, vanisheth when v vanisheth. *Fourthly*, that the method for finding secants or the expression of secants, be it ever so general, cannot in common sense extend any further than to all secants whatsoever : and, as it necessarily supposeth similar triangles, it cannot be supposed to take place where there are not similar triangles. *Fifthly*, that the subsecant will always be less than the subtangent, and can never coincide with it ; which coincidence to suppose would be absurd ; for it would be supposing the same line at the same time to cut and not to cut another given line ; which is a manifest contradiction, such as subverts the hypothesis and gives a demonstration of its falsehood. *Sixthly*, if this be not admitted, I demand a reason why any other apagogical demonstration, or demonstration *ad absurdum* should be admitted in geometry rather than this : Or that some real difference be assigned between this and others as such. *Seventhly*, I observe that it is sophistical to suppose NO or RP, PS, and SR to be finite real lines in order to form the triangle, RPS, in order to obtain proportions by similar triangles ; and afterwards to suppose there are no such lines, nor consequently similar triangles, and nevertheless to retain the consequence of the first supposition, after such supposition hath been destroyed by a contrary one. *Eighthly*, that although, in the present case, by inconsistent suppositions truth may be obtained, yet that such truth is not demonstrated : That such method is not conformable to the rules of logic and right reason : That, however useful it may be, it must be considered only as a presumption, as a knack, an art, rather an artifice, but not a scientific demonstration.

26 The doctrine premised may be farther illustrated by the

[1] See the foregoing figure.

following simple and easy case, wherein I shall proceed by evanescent increments. Suppose $AB = x$, $BC = y$, $BD = o$, and that xx is equal to the area ABC : it is proposed to find the ordinate y or BC. When x by flowing becomes $x + o$, then xx becomes $xx + 2xo + oo$: And the area ABC becomes ADH, and the increment of xx will be equal to $BDHC$, the increment of the area, *i.e.* to $BCFD + CFH$. And if we suppose the curvilinear space CFH to be qoo, then

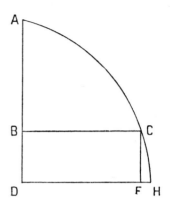

$$2xo + oo = yo + qoo$$

which divided by o gives $2x + o = y + qo$. And, supposing o to vanish, $2x = y$, in which case ACH will be a straight line, and the areas ABC, CFH, triangles. Now with regard to this reasoning, it hath been already remarked,[1] that it is not legitimate or logical to suppose o to vanish, *i.e.* to be nothing, *i.e.* that there is no increment, unless we reject at the same time with the increment it self every consequence of such increment, *i.e.* whatsoever could not be obtained but by supposing such increment. It must nevertheless be acknowledged that the problem is rightly solved, and the conclusion true, to which we are led by this method. It will therefore be asked, how comes it to pass that the throwing out o is attended with no error in the conclusion ? I answer, the true reason hereof is plainly this : because q being unit, qo is equal to o : and therefore

$$2x + o - qo = y = 2x,$$

the equal quantities qo and o being destroyed by contrary signs.

27 As on the one hand, it were absurd to get rid of o by saying, Let me contradict my self : Let me subvert my own hypothesis : Let me take it for granted that there is no increment, at the same time that I retain a quantity which I could never have got at but by assuming an increment : So on the other hand it would be equally wrong to imagine that in a geometrical demonstration we may be allowed to admit any error, though ever so small, or that it is possible, in the nature of things, an accurate

[1] Sect. 12 and 13 *supra*.

conclusion should be derived from inaccurate principles. There-fore o cannot be thrown out as an infinitesimal, or upon the principle that infinitesimals may be safely neglected. But only because it is destroyed by an equal quantity with a negative sign, whence $o - qo$ is equal to nothing. And as it is illegitimate to reduce an equation, by subducting from one side a quantity when it is not to be destroyed, or when an equal quantity is not subducted from the other side of the equation : So it must be allowed a very logical and just method of arguing to conclude that if from equals either nothing or equal quantities are subducted, they shall still remain equal. And this is a true reason why no error is at last produced by the rejecting of o. Which therefore must not be ascribed to the doctrine of differences, or infinitesimals, or evanescent quantities, or momentums, or fluxions.

28 Suppose the case to be general, and that x^n is equal to the area ABC, whence by the method of fluxions the ordinate is found nx^{n-1} which we admit for true, and shall inquire how it is arrived at. Now if we are content to come at the conclusion in a summary way, by supposing that the ratio of the fluxions of x and x^n are found [1] to be 1 and nx^{n-1}, and that the ordinate of the area is considered as its fluxion, we shall not so clearly see our way, or perceive how the truth comes out, that method as we have shewed before being obscure and illogical. But if we fairly delineate the area and its increment, and divide the latter into two parts $BCFD$ and CFH,[2] and proceed regularly by equations between the algebraical and geometrical quantities, the reason of the thing will plainly appear. For as x^n is equal to the area ABC, so is the increment of x^n equal to the increment of the area, *i.e.* to $BDHC$; that is to say

$$nox^{n-1} + \frac{nn - n}{2}oox^{n-2} + \&c. = BDFC + CFH.$$

And only the first members on each side of the equation being retained, $nox^{n-1} = BDFC$: And dividing both sides by o or BD, we shall get $nx^{n-1} = BC$. Admitting therefore that the curvilinear space CFH is equal to the rejectaneous quantity

$$\frac{nn - n}{2}oox^{n-2} + \&c.,$$

and that when this is rejected on one side, that is rejected on the other, the reasoning becomes just and the conclusion true. And

[1] Sect. 13. [2] See the figure in Sect. 26.

it is all one whatever magnitude you allow to *BD*, whether that of an infinitesimal difference or a finite increment ever so great. It is therefore plain that the supposing the rejectaneous algebraical quantity to be an infinitely small or evanescent quantity, and therefore to be neglected, must have produced an error, had it not been for the curvilinear spaces being equal thereto, and at the same time subducted from the other part or side of the equation, agreeably to the axiom, *If from equals you subduct equals, the remainders will be equal.* For those quantities which by the analysts are said to be neglected, or made to vanish, are in reality subducted. If therefore the conclusion be true, it is absolutely necessary that the finite space *CFH* be equal to the remainder of the increment expressed by

$$\frac{nn - n}{2}\,oox^{n-2} \ \&\text{c.}$$

equal, I say, to the finite remainder of a finite increment.

29 Therefore, be the power what you please, there will arise on one side an algebraical expression, on the other a geometrical quantity, each of which naturally divides itself into three members: The algebraical or fluxionary expression, into one which includes neither the expression of the increment of the absciss nor of any power thereof; another which includes the expression of the increment itself; and a third including the expression of the powers of the increment. The geometrical quantity also or whole increased area consists of three parts or members, the first of which is the given area; the second a rectangle under the ordinate and the increment of the absciss; and the third a curvilinear space. And, comparing the homologous or correspondent members on both sides, we find that as the first member of the expression is the expression of the given area, so the second member of the expression will express the rectangle or second member of the geometrical quantity, and the third, containing the powers of the increment, will express the curvilinear space, or third member of the geometrical quantity. This hint may perhaps be further extended, and applied to good purpose, by those who have leisure and curiosity for such matters. The use I make of it is to shew, that the analysis cannot obtain in augments or differences, but it must also obtain in finite quantities, be they ever so great, as was before observed.

30 It seems therefore upon the whole that we may safely pronounce the conclusion cannot be right, if in order thereto

any quantity be made to vanish, or be neglected, except that either one error is redressed by another ; or that secondly on the same side of an equation equal quantities are destroyed by contrary signs, so that the quantity we mean to reject is first annihilated ; or lastly, that from the opposite sides equal quantities are sub-ducted. And therefore to get rid of quantities by the received principles of fluxions or of differences is neither good geometry nor good logic. When the augments vanish, the velocities also vanish. The velocities or fluxions are said to be *primo* and *ultimo*, as the augments nascent and evanescent. Take therefore the *ratio* of the evanescent quantities, it is the same with that of the fluxions. It will therefore answer all intents as well. Why then are fluxions introduced ? Is it not to shun or rather to palliate the use of quantities infinitely small ? But we have no notion whereby to conceive and measure various degrees of velocity beside space and time ; or when the times are given beside space alone. We have even no notion of velocity prescinded from time and space. When therefore a point is supposed to move in given times, we have no notion of greater or lesser velocities, or of proportions between velocities, but only of longer or shorter lines, and of proportions between such lines generated in equal parts of time.

31 A point may be the limit of a line : A line may be the limit of a surface : A moment may terminate time. But how can we conceive a velocity by the help of such limits ? It neces-sarily implies both time and space, and cannot be conceived without them. And if the velocities of nascent and evanescent quantities, *i.e.* abstracted from time and space, may not be comprehended, how can we comprehend and demonstrate their proportions ? Or consider their *rationes primæ* and *ultimæ*. For, to consider the proportion or *ratio* of things implies that such things have magnitude : That such their magnitudes may be measured, and their relations to each other known. But, as there is no measure of velocity except time and space, the proportion of velocities being only compounded of the direct proportion of the spaces, and the reciprocal proportion of the times ; doth it not follow that to talk of investigating, obtaining, and considering the proportions of velocities, exclusively of time and space, is to talk unintelligibly ?

32 But you will say that, in the use and application of fluxions, men do not overstrain their faculties to a precise conception of the above-mentioned velocities, increments, infinitesimals, or any other such-like ideas of a nature so nice, subtile, and evanescent.

And therefore you will perhaps maintain that problems may be solved without those inconceivable suppositions ; and that, consequently, the doctrine of fluxions, as to the practical part, stands clear of all such difficulties. I answer that if in the use or application of this method those difficult and obscure points are not attended to, they are nevertheless supposed. They are the foundations on which the moderns build, the principles on which they proceed, in solving problems and discovering theorems. It is with the method of fluxions as with all other methods, which presuppose their respective principles and are grounded thereon ; although the rules may be practised by men who neither attend to, nor perhaps know the principles. In like manner, therefore, as a sailor may practically apply certain rules derived from astronomy and geometry, the principles whereof he doth not understand : And as any ordinary man may solve divers numerical questions, by the vulgar rules and operations of arithmetic, which he performs and applies without knowing the reasons of them : Even so it cannot be denied that you may apply the rules of the fluxionary method : You may compare and reduce particular cases to general forms : You may operate and compute and solve problems thereby, not only without an actual attention to, or an actual knowledge of, the grounds of that method, and the principles whereon it depends, and whence it is deduced, but even without having ever considered or comprehended them.

33 But then it must be remembered that in such case although you may pass for an artist, computist, or analyst, yet you may not be justly esteemed a man of science and demonstration. Nor should any man, in virtue of being conversant in such obscure analytics, imagine his rational faculties to be more improved than those of other men which have been exercised in a different manner and on different subjects ; much less erect himself into a judge and an oracle concerning matters that have no sort of connexion with or dependence on those species, symbols or signs, in the management whereof he is so conversant and expert. As you, who are a skilful computist or analyst, may not therefore be deemed skilful in anatomy : or *vice versa*, as a man who can dissect with art may, nevertheless, be ignorant in your art of computing : Even so you may both, notwithstanding your peculiar skill in your respective arts, be alike unqualified to decide upon logic, or metaphysics, or ethics, or religion. And this would be true, even admitting that you understood your own principles and could demonstrate them.

34 If it is said that fluxions may be expounded or expressed by finite lines proportional to them : Which finite lines, as they may be distinctly conceived and known and reasoned upon, so they may be substituted for the fluxions, and their mutual relations or proportions be considered as the proportions of fluxions : By which means the doctrine becomes clear and useful. I answer that, if in order to arrive at these finite lines proportional to the fluxions, there be certain steps made use of which are obscure and inconceivable, be those finite lines themselves ever so clearly conceived, it must nevertheless be acknowledged that your proceeding is not clear nor your method scientific. For instance, it is supposed that *AB* being the absciss, *BC* the ordinate, and *VCH* a

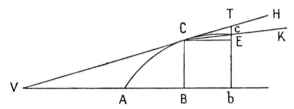

tangent of the curve *AC*, *Bb* or *CE* the increment of the absciss, *Ec* the increment of the ordinate, which produced meets *VH* in the point *T*, and *Cc* the increment of the curve. The right line *Cc* being produced to *K*, there are formed three small triangles, the rectilinear *CEc*, the mixtilinear *CEc*, and the rectilinear triangle *CET*. It is evident these three triangles are different from each other, the rectilinear *CEc* being less than the mixtilinear *CEc*, whose sides are the three increments above mentioned, and this still less than the triangle *CET*. It is supposed that the ordinate *bc* moves into the place *BC*, so that the point *c* is coincident with the point *C* ; and the right line *CK*, and consequently the curve *Cc*, is coincident with the tangent *CH*. In which case the mixtilinear evanescent triangle *CEc* will, in its last form, be similar to the triangle *CET* : and its evanescent sides *CE*, *Ec*, and *Cc*, will be proportional to *CE*, *ET*, and *CT*, the sides of the triangle *CET*. And therefore it is concluded that the fluxions of the lines *AB*, *BC*, and *AC*, being in the last ratio of their evanescent increments, are proportional to the sides of the triangle *CET*, or, which is all one, of the triangle *VBC* similar thereunto.[1] It is particularly remarked and insisted on by the great author, that the points *C* and *c* must not be distant one from another, by any

[1] *Introduct. ad Quad. Curv.*

the least interval whatsoever : but that, in order to find the ultimate proportions of the lines *CE*, *Ec*, and *Cc* (*i.e.* the proportions of the fluxions or velocities) expressed by the finite sides of the triangle *VBC*, the points *C* and *c* must be accurately coincident, *i.e.* one and the same. A point therefore is considered as a triangle, or a triangle is supposed to be formed in a point. Which to conceive seems quite impossible. Yet some there are who, though they shrink at all other mysteries, make no difficulty of their own, who strain at a gnat and swallow a camel.

35 I know not whether it be worth while to observe, that possibly some men may hope to operate by symbols and suppositions, in such sort as to avoid the use of fluxions, momentums, and infinitesimals, after the following manner. Suppose x to be an absciss of a curve, and z another absciss of the same curve. Suppose also that the respective areas are xxx and zzz : and that $z - x$ is the increment of the absciss, and $zzz - xxx$ the increment of the area, without considering how great or how small those increments may be. Divide now $zzz - xxx$ by $z - x$, and the quotient will be $zz + zx + xx$: and, supposing that z and x are equal, this same quotient will be $3xx$, which in that case is the ordinate, which therefore may be thus obtained independently of fluxions and infinitesimals. But herein is a direct fallacy : for, in the first place, it is supposed that the abscisses z and x are unequal, without which supposition no one step could have been made ; and in the second place, it is supposed they are equal ; which is a manifest inconsistency, and amounts to the same thing that hath been before considered.[1] And there is indeed reason to apprehend that all attempts for setting the abstruse and fine geometry on a right foundation, and avoiding the doctrine of velocities, momentums, &c. will be found impracticable, till such time as the object and end of geometry are better understood than hitherto they seem to have been. The great author of the method of fluxions felt this difficulty, and therefore he gave into those nice abstractions and geometrical metaphysics without which he saw nothing could be done on the received principles ; and what in the way of demonstration he hath done with them the reader will judge. It must, indeed, be acknowledged that he used fluxions, like the scaffold of a building, as things to be laid aside or got rid of as soon as finite lines were found proportional to them. But then these finite exponents are found by the help of fluxions. Whatever therefore is got by such exponents and

---

[1] *Sect.* 15.

proportions is to be ascribed to fluxions : which must therefore
be previously understood.   And what are these fluxions ?   The
velocities of evanescent increments ?   And what are these same
evanescent increments ?   They are neither finite quantities, nor
quantities infinitely small, nor yet nothing.   May we not call
them the ghosts of departed quantities ?

36 Men too often impose on themselves and others as if they
conceived and understood things expressed by signs, when in
truth they have no idea, save only of the very signs themselves.
And there are some grounds to apprehend that this may be the
present case.   The velocities of evanescent or nascent quantities
are supposed to be expressed, both by finite lines of a determinate
magnitude, and by algebraical notes or signs : but I suspect that
many who, perhaps never having examined the matter take it for
granted, would upon a narrow scrutiny find it impossible to frame
any idea or notion whatsoever of those velocities, exclusive of such
finite quantities and signs.

Suppose the line *KP* described by the motion of a point
continually accelerated, and that in equal particles of time the
unequal [1] parts *KL, LM, MN, NO,* &c. are generated.   Suppose
also that *a, b, c, d, e,* &c. denote the velocities of the generating
point, at the several periods of the parts or increments so generated.
It is easy to observe that these increments are each proportional
to the sum of the velocities with which it is described : That,
consequently, the several sums of the velocities, generated in equal
parts of time, may be set forth by the respective lines *KL, LM,
MN,* &c. generated in the same times :   It is likewise an easy
matter to say, that the last velocity generated in the first particle
of time may be expressed by the symbol *a*, the last in the second
by *b*, the last generated in the third by *c*, and so on : that *a* is the
velocity of *LM* in *statu nascenti*, and *b, c, d, e,* &c. are the velocities
of the increments *MN, NO, OP,* &c. in their respective nascent
estates.   You may proceed, and consider these velocities themselves as flowing or increasing quantities, taking the velocities of

---

[1] [I have reproduced Berkeley's diagram, which, however, does not correspond
quite accurately with his description in the text.—Ed.]

the velocities, and the velocities of the velocities of the velocities, *i.e.* the first, second, third, &c. velocities *ad infinitum* : which succeeding series of velocities may be thus expressed.

$$a.\ b - a.\ c - 2\,b + a.\ d - 3c + 3b - a\ \&c.$$

which you may call by the names of first, second, third, fourth fluxions. And for an apter expression you may denote the variable flowing line *KL, KM, KN,* &c. by the letter x ; and the first fluxions by $\dot{x}$, the second by $\ddot{x}$, the third by $\dddot{x}$, and so on *ad infinitum.*

37 Nothing is easier than to assign names, signs, or expressions to these fluxions, and it is not difficult to compute and operate by means of such signs. But it will be found much more difficult to omit the signs and yet retain in our minds the things which we suppose to be signified by them. To consider the exponents, whether geometrical, or algebraical, or fluxionary, is no difficult matter. But to form a precise idea of a third velocity for instance, in itself and by itself, *Hoc opus, hic labor.* Nor indeed is it an easy point to form a clear and distinct idea of any velocity at all, exclusive of and prescinding from all length of time and space ; as also from all notes, signs, or symbols whatsoever. This, if I may be allowed to judge of others by myself, is impossible. To me it seems evident that measures and signs are absolutely necessary in order to conceive or reason about velocities ; and that consequently, when we think to conceive the velocities simply and in themselves, we are deluded by vain abstractions.

38 It may perhaps be thought by some an easier method of conceiving fluxions to suppose them the velocities wherewith the infinitesimal differences are generated. So that the first fluxions shall be the velocities of the first differences, the second the velocities of the second differences, the third fluxions the velocities of the third differences, and so on *ad infinitum.* But not to mention the insurmountable difficulty of admitting or conceiving infinitesimals, and infinitesimals of infinitesimals, &c. it is evident that this notion of fluxions would not consist with the great author's view ; who held that the minutest quantity ought not to be neglected, that therefore the doctrine of infinitesimal differences was not to be admitted in geometry, and who plainly appears to have introduced the use of velocities or fluxions, on purpose to exclude or do without them.

39 To others it may possibly seem that we should form a

juster idea of fluxions by assuming the finite, unequal, isochronal increments *KL*, *LM*, *MN*, &c. and considering them in *statu nascenti*, also their increments in *statu nascenti*, and the nascent increments of those increments, and so on, supposing the first nascent increments to be proportional to the first fluxions or velocities, the nascent increments of those increments to be proportional to the second fluxions, the third nascent increments to be proportional to the third fluxions, and so onwards. And, as the first fluxions are the velocities of the first nascent increments, so the second fluxions may be conceived to be the velocities of the second nascent increments, rather than the velocities of velocities. By which means the analogy of fluxions may seem better preserved, and the notion rendered more intelligible.

40 And indeed it should seem that in the way of obtaining the second or third fluxion of an equation the given fluxions were considered rather as increments than velocities. But the considering them sometimes in one sense, sometimes in another, one while in themselves, another in their exponents, seems to have occasioned no small share of that confusion and obscurity which is found in the doctrine of fluxions. It may seem therefore that the notion might be still mended, and that instead of fluxions of fluxions, or fluxions of fluxions of fluxions, and instead of second, third, or fourth, &c. fluxions of a given quantity, it might be more consistent and less liable to exception to say, the fluxion of the first nascent increment, *i.e.* the second fluxion ; the fluxion of the second nascent increment, *i.e.* the third fluxion ; the fluxion of the third nascent increment, *i.e.* the fourth fluxion, which fluxions are conceived respectively proportional, each to the nascent principle of the increment succeeding that whereof it is the fluxion.

41 For the more distinct conception of all which it may be considered that if the finite increment *LM* [1] be divided into the isochronal parts *Lm*, *mn*, *no*, *oM* ; and the increment *MN* into the parts *Mp*, *pq*, *qr*, *rN* isochronal to the former ; as the whole increments *LM*, *MN* are proportional to the sums of their describing velocities, even so the homologous particles *Lm*, *Mp* are also proportional to the respective accelerated velocities with which they are described. And as the velocity with which *Mp* is generated, exceeds that with which *Lm* was generated, even so the particle *Mp* exceeds the particle *Lm*. And in general, as the isochronal velocities describing the particles of *MN* exceed the

---

[1] See the foregoing Scheme in Sect. 36.

isochronal velocities describing the particles of LM, even so the particles of the former exceed the correspondent particles of the latter. And this will hold, be the said particles ever so small. MN therefore will exceed LM if they are both taken in their nascent states : and that excess will be proportional to the excess of the velocity b above the velocity a. Hence we may see that this last account of fluxions comes, in the upshot, to the same thing with the first.[1]

42 But notwithstanding what hath been said it must still be acknowledged that the finite particles Lm or Mp, though taken ever so small, are not proportional to the velocities a and b ; but each to a series of velocities changing every moment, or which is the same thing, to an accelerated velocity, by which it is generated during a certain minute particle of time : That the nascent beginnings or evanescent endings of finite quantities, which are produced in moments or infinitely small parts of time, are alone proportional to given velocities : That therefore, in order to conceive the first fluxions, we must conceive time divided into moments, increments generated in those moments, and velocities proportional to those increments : That, in order to conceive second and third fluxions, we must suppose that the nascent principles or momentaneous increments have themselves also other momentaneous increments, which are proportional to their respective generating velocites : that the velocities of these second momentaneous increments are second fluxions : those of their nascent momentaneous increments third fluxions. And so on *ad infinitum*.

43 By subducting the increment generated in the first moment from that generated in the second, we get the increment of an increment. And by subducting the velocity generating in the first moment from that generating in the second, we get the fluxion of a fluxion. In like manner, by subducting the difference of the velocities generating in the two first moments from the excess of the velocity in the third above that in the second moment, we obtain the third fluxion. And after the same analogy we may proceed to fourth, fifth, sixth fluxions, &c. And if we call the velocities of the first, second, third, fourth moments, a, b, c, d, the series of fluxions will be as above, $a. b - a. c - 2b + a. d - 3c + 3b - a.$ *ad infinitum*, *i.e.* $\dot{x}. \ddot{x}. \dddot{x}. \ddddot{x}.$ *ad infinitum*.

44 Thus fluxions may be considered in sundry lights and shapes, which seem all equally difficult to conceive. And, indeed,

[1] Sect. 36.

as it is impossible to conceive velocity without time or space, without either finite length or finite duration,[1] it must seem above the powers of men to comprehend even the first fluxions. And if the first are incomprehensible what shall we say of the second and third fluxions, &c. ? He who can conceive the beginning of a beginning, or the end of an end, somewhat before the first or after the last, may be perhaps sharpsighted enough to conceive these things. But most men will, I believe, find it impossible to understand them in any sense whatever.

45 One would think that men could not speak too exactly on so nice a subject. And yet, as was before hinted, we may often observe that the exponents of fluxions or notes representing fluxions are confounded with the fluxions themselves. Is not this the case when, just after the fluxions of flowing quantities were said to be the celerities of their increasing, and the second fluxions to be the mutations of the first fluxions or celerities, we are told that $\overset{\shortparallel}{z}.\ \overset{\cdot}{z}.\ z.\ \dot{z}.\ \ddot{z}.\ \dot{z}.$[2] represents a series of quantities whereof each subsequent quantity is the fluxion of the preceding ; and each foregoing is a fluent quantity having the following one for its fluxion ?

46 Divers series of quantities and expressions, geometrical and algebraical, may be easily conceived, in lines, in surfaces, in species, to be continued without end or limit. But it will not be found so easy to conceive a series, either of mere velocities or of mere nascent increments, distinct therefrom and corresponding thereunto. Some perhaps may be led to think the author intended a series of ordinates, wherein each ordinate was the fluxion of the preceding and fluent of the following, i.e. that the fluxion of one ordinate was itself the ordinate of another curve ; and the fluxion of this last ordinate was the ordinate of yet another curve ; and so on ad infinitum. But who can conceive how the fluxion (whether velocity or nascent increment) of an ordinate should be itself an ordinate ? Or more than that each preceding quantity or fluent is related to its subsequent or fluxion, as the area of a curvilinear figure to its ordinate ; agreeably to what the author remarks, that each preceding quantity in such series is as the area of a curvilinear figure, whereof the absciss is z, and the ordinate is the following quantity ?

47 Upon the whole it appears that the celerities are dismissed, and instead thereof areas and ordinates are introduced. But, however expedient such analogies or such expressions may be found

[1] Sect. 31.   [2] De Quadratura Curvarum.

for facilitating the modern quadratures, yet we shall not find any light given us thereby into the original real nature of fluxions ; or that we are enabled to frame from thence just ideas of fluxions considered in themselves. In all this the general ultimate drift of the author is very clear, but his principles are obscure. But perhaps those theories of the great author are not minutely considered or canvassed by his disciples ; who seem eager, as was before hinted, rather to operate than to know, rather to apply his rules and his forms than to understand his principles and enter into his notions. It is nevertheless certain that, in order to follow him in his quadratures, they must find fluents from fluxions ; and in order to this, they must know to find fluxions from fluents ; and in order to find fluxions, they must first know what fluxions are. Otherwise they proceed without clearness and without science. Thus the direct method precedes the inverse, and the knowledge of the principles is supposed in both. But as for operating according to rules, and by the help of general forms, whereof the original principles and reasons are not understood, this is to be esteemed merely technical. Be the principles therefore ever so abstruse and metaphysical, they must be studied by whoever would comprehend the doctrine of fluxions. Nor can any geometrician have a right to apply the rules of the great author, without first considering his metaphysical notions whence they were derived. These how necessary soever in order to science, which can never be attained without a precise, clear, and accurate conception of the principles, are nevertheless by several carelessly passed over ; while the expressions alone are dwelt on and considered and treated with great skill and management, thence to obtain other expressions by methods suspicious and indirect (to say the least) if considered in themselves, however recommended by Induction and Authority ; two motives which are acknowledged sufficient to beget a rational faith and moral persuasion, but nothing higher.

48 You may possibly hope to evade the force of all that hath been said, and to screen false principles and inconsistent reasonings, by a general pretence that these objections and remarks are metaphysical. But this is a vain pretence. For the plain sense and truth of what is advanced in the foregoing remarks, I appeal to the understanding of every unprejudiced intelligent reader. To the same I appeal, whether the points remarked upon are not most incomprehensible metaphysics. And metaphysics not of mine, but your own. I would not be understood to infer that

your notions are false or vain because they are metaphysical. Nothing is either true or false for that reason. Whether a point be called metaphysical or no avails little. The question is, whether it be clear or obscure, right or wrong, well or ill deduced ?

49 Although momentaneous increments, nascent and evanescent quantities, fluxions and infinitesimals of all degrees, are in truth such shadowy entities, so difficult to imagine or conceive distinctly, that (to say the least) they cannot be admitted as principles or objects of clear and accurate science : and although this obscurity and incomprehensibility of your metaphysics had been alone sufficient to allay your pretensions to evidence ; yet it hath, if I mistake not, been further shewn, that your inferences are no more just than your conceptions are clear, and that your logics are as exceptionable as your metaphysics. It should seem therefore upon the whole, that your conclusions are not attained by just reasoning from clear principles ; consequently, that the employment of modern analysts, however useful in mathematical calculations and constructions, doth not habituate and qualify the mind to apprehend clearly and infer justly ; and, consequently, that you have no right, in virtue of such habits, to dictate out of your proper sphere, beyond which your judgment is to pass for no more than that of other men.

50 Of a long time I have suspected that these modern analytics were not scientifical, and gave some hints thereof to the public twenty-five years ago.[1] Since which time, I have been diverted by other occupations, and imagined I might employ myself better than in deducing and laying together my thoughts on so nice a subject. And though of late I have been called upon [2] to make good my suggestions ; yet, as the person who made this call doth not appear to think maturely enough to understand either those metaphysics which he would refute, or mathematics which he would patronize, I should have spared myself the trouble of writing for his conviction. Nor should I now have troubled you or myself with this address, after so long an intermission of these studies ; were it not to prevent, so far as I am able, your imposing on yourself and others in matters of much higher moment and concern. And, to the end that you may more clearly comprehend the force and design of the foregoing remarks,

[1] [See *Principles of Human Knowledge*, sects. 123–134.—ED.]
[2] [Apparently a reference to Andrew Baxter's attack on Berkeley's philosophy in *An Enquiry into the nature of the human soul*, 1733.—Ed.]

and pursue them still further in your own meditations, I shall subjoin the following Queries.

Qu. 1 Whether the object of geometry be not the proportions of assignable extensions? And whether there be any need of considering quantities either infinitely great or infinitely small?

Qu. 2 Whether the end of geometry be not to measure assignable finite extension? And whether this practical view did not first put men on the study of geometry?

Qu. 3 Whether the mistaking the object and end of geometry hath not created needless difficulties, and wrong pursuits in that science?

Qu. 4 Whether men may properly be said to proceed in a scientific method, without clearly conceiving the object they are conversant about, the end proposed, and the method by which it is pursued?

Qu. 5 Whether it doth not suffice, that every assignable number of parts may be contained in some assignable magnitude? And whether it be not unnecessary, as well as absurd, to suppose that finite extension is infinitely divisible?

Qu. 6 Whether the diagrams in a geometrical demonstration are not to be considered as signs, of all possible finite figures, of all sensible and imaginable extensions or magnitudes of the same kind?

Qu. 7 Whether it be possible to free geometry from insuperable difficulties and absurdities, so long as either the abstract general idea of extension, or absolute external extension be supposed its true object?

Qu. 8 Whether the notions of absolute time, absolute place, and absolute motion be not most abstractedly metaphysical? Whether it be possible for us to measure, compute, or know them?

Qu. 9 Whether mathematicians do not engage themselves in disputes and paradoxes concerning what they neither do nor can conceive? And whether the doctrine of forces be not a sufficient proof of this [1]?

Qu. 10 Whether in geometry it may not suffice to consider assignable finite magnitude, without concerning ourselves with infinity? And whether it would not be righter to measure large polygons having finite sides, instead of curves, than to suppose curves are polygons of infinitesimal sides, a supposition neither true nor conceivable?

[1] See a Latin treatise *De Motu*, published at London, in the year 1721.

Qu. 11 Whether many points which are not readily assented to are not nevertheless true? And whether those in the two following queries may not be of that number?

Qu. 12 Whether it be possible that we should have had an idea or notion of extension prior to motion? Or whether, if a man had never perceived motion, he would ever have known or conceived one thing to be distant from another?

Qu. 13 Whether geometrical quantity hath co-existent parts? And whether all quantity be not in a flux as well as time and motion?

Qu. 14 Whether extension can be supposed an attribute of a Being immutable and eternal?

Qu. 15 Whether to decline examining the principles, and unravelling the methods used in mathematics would not shew a bigotry in mathematicians?

Qu. 16 Whether certain maxims do not pass current among analysts which are shocking to good sense? And whether the common assumption that a finite quantity divided by nothing is infinite, be not of this number?

Qu. 17 Whether the considering geometrical diagrams absolutely or in themselves, rather than as representatives of all assignable magnitudes or figures of the same kind, be not a principal cause of the supposing finite extension infinitely divisible; and of all the difficulties and absurdities consequent thereupon?

Qu. 18 Whether from geometrical propositions being general, and the lines in diagrams being therefore general substitutes or representatives, it doth not follow that we may not limit or consider the number of parts into which such particular lines are divisible?

Qu. 19 When it is said or implied, that such a certain line delineated on paper contains more than any assignable number of parts, whether any more in truth ought to be understood, than that it is a sign indifferently representing all finite lines, be they ever so great. In which relative capacity it contains, *i.e.* stands for more than any assignable number of parts? And whether it be not altogether absurd to suppose a finite line, considered in itself or in its own positive nature, should contain an infinite number of parts?

Qu. 20 Whether all arguments for the infinite divisibility of finite extension do not suppose and imply, either general abstract ideas or absolute external extension to be the object of geometry?

And, therefore, whether, along with those suppositions, such arguments also do not cease and vanish?

Qu. 21 Whether the supposed infinite divisibility of finite extension hath not been a snare to mathematicians and a thorn in their sides? And whether a quantity infinitely diminished and a quantity infinitely small are not the same thing?

Qu. 22 Whether it be necessary to consider velocities of nascent or evanescent quantities, or moments, or infinitesimals? And whether the introducing of things so inconceivable be not a reproach to mathematics?

Qu. 23 Whether inconsistencies can be truths? Whether points repugnant and absurd are to be admitted upon any subject, or in any science? And whether the use of infinites ought to be allowed as a sufficient pretext and apology for the admitting of such points in geometry?

Qu. 24 Whether a quantity be not properly said to be known, when we know its proportion to given quantities? And whether this proportion can be known but by expressions or exponents, either geometrical, algebraical, or arithmetical? And whether expressions in lines or species can be useful but so far forth as they are reducible to numbers?

Qu. 25 Whether the finding out proper expressions or notations of quantity be not the most general character and tendency of the mathematics? And arithmetical operation that which limits and defines their use?

Qu. 26 Whether mathematicians have sufficiently considered the analogy and use of signs? And how far the specific limited nature of things corresponds thereto?

Qu. 27 Whether because, in stating a general case of pure algebra, we are at full liberty to make a character denote either a positive or a negative quantity, or nothing at all, we may therefore, in a geometrical case, limited by hypotheses and reasonings from particular properties and relations of figures, claim the same licence?

Qu. 28 Whether the shifting of the hypothesis, or (as we may call it) the *fallacia suppositionis* be not a sophism that far and wide infects the modern reasonings, both in the mechanical philosophy and in the abstruse and fine geometry?

Qu. 29 Whether we can form an idea or notion of velocity distinct from and exclusive of its measures, as we can of heat distinct from and exclusive of the degrees on the thermometer by which it is measured? And whether this be not supposed in the reasonings of modern analysts?

Qu. 30 Whether motion can be conceived in a point of space? And if motion cannot, whether velocity can? And if not, whether a first or last velocity can be conceived in a merc limit, either initial or final, of the described space?

Qu. 31 Where there are no increments, whether there can be any *ratio* of increments? Whether nothings can be considered as proportional to real quantities? Or whether to talk of their proportions be not to talk nonsense? Also in what sense we are to understand the proportion of a surface to a line, of an area to an ordinate? And whether species or numbers, though properly expressing quantities which are not homogeneous, may yet be said to express their proportion to each other?

Qu. 32 Whether if all assignable circles may be squared, the circle is not, to all intents and purposes, squared as well as the parabola? Or whether a parabolical area can in fact be measured more accurately than a circular?

Qu. 33 Whether it would not be righter to approximate fairly than to endeavour at accuracy by sophisms?

Qu. 34 Whether it would not be more decent to proceed by trials and inductions, than to pretend to demonstrate by false principles?

Qu. 35 Whether there be not a way of arriving at truth, although the principles are not scientific, nor the reasoning just? And whether such a way ought to be called a knack or a science?

Qu. 36 Whether there can be science of the conclusion where there is not science of the principles? And whether a man can have science of the principles without understanding them? And therefore whether the mathematicians of the present age act like men of science, in taking so much more pains to apply their principles than to understand them?

Qu. 37 Whether the greatest genius wrestling with false principles may not be foiled? And whether accurate quadratures can be obtained without new *postulata* or assumptions? And if not, whether those which are intelligible and consistent ought not to be preferred to the contrary? *See Sect*. 28 and 29.

Qu. 38 Whether tedious calculations in algebra and fluxions be the likeliest method to improve the mind? And whether men's being accustomed to reason altogether about mathematical signs and figures doth not make them at a loss how to reason without them?

Qu. 39 Whether, whatever readiness analysts acquire in stating a problem, or finding apt expressions for mathematical quantities, the same doth necessarily infer a proportionable ability in conceiving and expressing other matters?

Qu. 40 Whether it be not a general case or rule, that one and the same coefficient dividing equal products gives equal quotients? And yet whether such coefficient can be interpreted by *o* or nothing? Or whether any one will say that if the equation $2 \times o = 5 \times o$, be divided by *o*, the quotients on both sides are equal? Whether therefore a case may not be general with respect to all quantities and yet not extend to nothings, or include the case of nothing? And whether the bringing nothing under the notion of quantity may not have betrayed men into false reasoning?

Qu. 41 Whether in the most general reasonings about equalities and proportions men may not demonstrate as well as in geometry? Whether in such demonstrations they are not obliged to the same strict reasoning as in geometry? And whether such their reasonings are not deduced from the same axioms with those in geometry? Whether therefore algebra be not as truly a science as geometry?

Qu. 42 Whether men may not reason in species as well as in words? Whether the same rules of logic do not obtain in both cases? And whether we have not a right to expect and demand the same evidence in both?

Qu. 43 Whether an algebraist, fluxionist, geometrician, or demonstrator of any kind can expect indulgence for obscure principles or incorrect reasonings? And whether an algebraical note or species can at the end of a process be interpreted in a sense which could not have been substituted for it at the beginning? Or whether any particular supposition can come under a general case which doth not consist with the reasoning thereof?

Qu. 44 Whether the difference between a mere computer and a man of science be not, that the one computes on principles clearly conceived, and by rules evidently demonstrated, whereas the other doth not?

Qu. 45 Whether, although geometry be a science, and algebra allowed to be a science, and the analytical a most excellent method, in the application nevertheless of the analysis to geometry, men may not have admitted false principles and wrong methods of reasoning?

Qu. 46 Whether, although algebraical reasonings are admitted to be ever so just, when confined to signs or species as general representatives of quantity, you may not nevertheless fall into error, if, when you limit them to stand for particular things, you do not limit your self to reason consistently with the nature of such particular things? And whether such error ought to be imputed to pure algebra?

Qu. 47 Whether the view of modern mathematicians doth not rather seem to be the coming at an expression by artifice, than the coming at science by demonstration?

Qu. 48 Whether there may not be sound metaphysics as well as unsound? Sound as well as unsound logic? And whether the modern analytics may not be brought under one of these denominations, and which?

Qu. 49 Whether there be not really a *philosophia prima*, a certain transcendental science superior to and more extensive than mathematics, which it might behove our modern analysts rather to learn than despise?

Qu. 50 Whether, ever since the recovery of mathematical learning, there have not been perpetual disputes and controversies among the mathematicians? And whether this doth not disparage the evidence of their methods?

Qu. 51 Whether anything but metaphysics and logic can open the eyes of mathematicians and extricate them out of their difficulties?

Qu. 52 Whether, upon the received principles, a quantity can by any division or subdivision, though carried ever so far, be reduced to nothing?

Qu. 53 Whether, if the end of geometry be practice, and this practice be measuring, and we measure only assignable extensions, it will not follow that unlimited approximations compleatly answer the intention of geometry?

Qu. 54 Whether the same things which are now done by infinites may not be done by finite quantities? And whether this would not be a great relief to the imaginations and understandings of mathematical men?

Qu. 55 Whether those philomathematical physicians, anatomists, and dealers in the animal œconomy, who admit the doctrine of fluxions with an implicit faith, can with a good grace insult other men for believing what they do not comprehend?

Qu. 56 Whether the corpuscularian, experimental, and mathematical philosophy, so much cultivated in the last age, hath not too much engrossed men's attention ; some part whereof it might have usefully employed ?

Qu. 57 Whether from this and other concurring causes the minds of speculative men have not been borne downward, to the debasing and stupifying of the higher faculties ? And whether we may not hence account for that prevailing narrowness and bigotry among many who pass for men of science, their incapacity for things moral, intellectual, or theological, their proneness to measure all truths by sense and experience of animal life ?

Qu. 58 Whether it be really an effect of thinking, that the same men admire the great author for his fluxions, and deride him for his religion ?

Qu. 59 If certain philosophical virtuosi of the present age have no religion, whether it can be said to be for want of faith ?

Qu. 60 Whether it be not a juster way of reasoning, to recommend points of faith from their effects, than to demonstrate mathematical principles by their conclusions ?

Qu. 61 Whether it be not less exceptionable to admit points above reason than contrary to reason ?

Qu. 62 Whether mysteries may not with better right be allowed of in Divine Faith than in Human Science ?

Qu. 63 Whether such mathematicians as cry out against mysteries have ever examined their own principles ?

Qu. 64 Whether mathematicians, who are so delicate in religious points, are strictly scrupulous in their own science ? Whether they do not submit to authority, take things upon trust, and believe points inconceivable ? Whether they have not their mysteries, and what is more, their repugnancies and contradictions ?

Qu. 65 Whether it might not become men who are puzzled and perplexed about their own principles, to judge warily, candidly and modestly concerning other matters ?

Qu. 66 Whether the modern analytics do not furnish a strong *argumentum ad hominem* against the philomathematical infidels of these times ?

Qu. 67 Whether it follows from the above-mentioned remarks, that accurate and just reasoning is the peculiar character of the present age ? And whether the modern growth of infidelity can be ascribed to a distinction so truly valuable ?

FINIS

A Defence of Free-thinking in Mathematics

In answer to a pamphlet of Philalethes Cantabrigiensis, intituled *Geometry no friend to Infidelity, or a defence of Sir Isaac Newton and the British Mathematicians.* Also an Appendix concerning Mr. Walton's *Vindication of the principles of fluxions against the objections contained in* the Analyst ; wherein it is attempted to put this controversy in such a light as that every reader may be able to judge thereof

First printed in 1735

EDITOR'S INTRODUCTION

THE sting of the *Analyst* lay in the fact that its author was a bishop, and though Dr. Jurin did not, in so many words, tell the cobbler to stick to his last, it is easy to read his ' hands off mathematics ' between the lines of his tart reply. Hence the clever short title of Berkeley's rejoinder, *A Defence of Free-thinking in Mathematics*. He had attacked ' free-thinking ' in religion, where that term was a mask for infidelity ; but he believed in freedom of thought ; he claimed the right to analyse mathematical analysis, and he rightly stigmatized Jurin's exaggerated deference to the authority of Sir Isaac Newton, which is ' converting the republick of letters into an absolute monarchy . . . even introducing a kind of philosophic popery among a free people ' (S. 16).

The exact scope of the work is given in the full title : *A defence of free-thinking in mathematics in answer to a pamphlet of Philalethes Cantabrigiensis intituled Geometry no friend to infidelity or a defence of Sir Isaac Newton, and the British mathematicians also an Appendix concerning Mr. Walton's Vindication of the principles of fluxions against the objections contained in the Analyst—wherein it is attempted to put this controversy in such a light as that every reader may be able to judge thereof.* Quotations from Terence (*And. I.* i. 41) and Aristotle (*Metaph.* lib. xiii) ornament the title-page, which, like that of the *Analyst*, attributes the work to the author of the *Minute Philosopher* ; it was printed in Dublin by M. Rhames for R. Gunne in 1735.

The tract is an answer to Jurin point by point, and makes no positive contribution to the mathematical issue. Its chief interest to-day is its sparkling literary style and the hard-hitting, which show Berkeley a past-master in all the arts of controversial writing. Here is the sly humour of ' a page or two after, you very candidly represent your case to be that of an ass between two bottles of hay ; it is your own expression.' (S. 29). And note how the rolling period of the argument breaks at times into the short and sharp staccato—' My aim is truth. My reasons I have given. Confute them, if you can.'

To students of Berkeley's own philosophy the concluding sections (45–8) are of special interest ; for they help to refute the false opinion, invented in our day, that Berkeley in later life gave up the philosophy of his youth. His doctrine of abstract ideas has been a special target, as a result of Fraser's careless and indefensible remarks on the omission of three sections on abstract ideas from the third edition of the *Alciphron*. I have elsewhere [1] examined the question *in extenso* and have carried the argument to within a few months of Berkeley's death, showing that his doctrine of abstraction receives recognition, not alone in the early series, but also in *Siris* (1744), in the third edition of *Alciphron* (1752) and in the *De Motu* republished in the *Miscellany* (1752). Here I will only point out that Berkeley was fifty years old when he wrote this *Defence*, and that at that mature age he stood over every detail of his early doctrine of abstraction. Dr. Jurin had transcribed Section 125 of the Essay on Vision, had traversed Berkeley's statement that he could not form the general idea of a triangle, and had defended Locke from Berkeley's devastating criticism of the ' absurd triangle.' Did Berkeley withdraw or tone down, or plead youth and subsequent development ? Not at all. He re-states his old doctrine and his original criticism of Locke, distinguishing, as before, between abstract general ideas and general ideas, giving his reasons for rejecting the former, and adding, ' this doctrine of abstract general ideas seemed to me a capital errour, productive of numberless difficulties and disputes, that runs not only throughout Mr. Locke's book, but through most parts of learning.' (S. 48). It is clear from the following section, as also from Section 20, where he lists the *arcana* of the modern analysis that he regarded the key concepts of the doctrine of fluxions as instances of abstract general ideas.

The Appendix on Walton's *Vindication* is brief and patronizing, and one wonders why Berkeley troubled to notice ' this Dublin professor.' According to Fraser [2] it was ' added in a second issue of the *Defence*.' The edition of 1735 was issued in Dublin and London. The Dublin issue has the Appendix.

[1] *Berkeley and Malebranche*, cc. vii and viii, especially pp. 168–71.
[2] *Works* (1901), vol. iii, p. 97n.

A Defence of Free-thinking
in Mathematics

The Text

A DEFENCE OF FREE-THINKING
IN MATHEMATICS

1 When I read your Defence of the British Mathematicians, I could not, Sir, but admire your courage in asserting with such undoubting assurance things so easily disproved. This to me seemed unaccountable, till I reflected on what you say (p. 32) when, upon my having appealed to every thinking reader, whether it be possible to frame any clear conception of Fluxions, you express yourself in the following manner, ' Pray, Sir, who are those thinking readers you appeal to ? Are they geometricians or persons wholly ignorant of geometry ? If the former, I leave it to them : If the latter, I ask how well are they qualified to judge of the method of fluxions ? ' It must be acknowledged you seem by this dilemma secure in the favour of one part of your readers, and the ignorance of the other. I am nevertheless persuaded there are fair and candid men among the mathematicians. And for those who are not mathematicians, I shall endeavour so to unveil this mystery, and put the controversy between us in such a light as that every reader of ordinary sense and reflexion may be a competent judge thereof.

2 You express an extreme surprize and concern, ' that I should take so much pains to depreciate one of the noblest sciences, to disparage and traduce a set of learned men whose labours so greatly conduce to the honour of this island (p. 5) ; to lessen the reputation and authority of Sir Isaac Newton and his followers, by shewing that they are not such masters of reason as they are generally presumed to be ; and to depreciate the science they profess, by demonstrating to the world that it is not of that clearness and certainty as is commonly imagined.' All which, you insist, ' appears very strange to you and the rest of that famous University, who plainly see of how great use mathematical learning is to mankind.' Hence you take occasion to declaim on the usefulness of mathematics in the several branches, and then to redouble your surprize and amazement (p. 19 and 20). To all which declamation I reply that it is quite beside the purpose. For I allow, and always have allowed, its full claim of merit to

whatever is useful and true in the mathematics : But that which is not so, the less it employs men's time and thoughts the better. And after all you have said or can say, I believe the unprejudiced reader will think with me, that things obscure are not therefore sacred ; and that it is no more a crime to canvass and detect unsound principles or false reasonings in mathematics than in any other part of learning.

3 You are, it seems, much at a loss to understand the useful-ness, or tendency, or prudence of my attempt. I thought I had sufficiently explained this in the *Analyst*. But for your further satisfaction shall here tell you it is very well known that several persons who deride Faith and Mysteries in Religion admit the doctrine of Fluxions for true and certain. Now if it be shewn that fluxions are really most incomprehensible Mysteries, and that those who believe them to be clear and scientific do entertain an implicit faith in the author of that method ; will not this furnish a fair *argumentum ad hominem* against men who reject that very thing in religion which they admit in human learning ? And is it not a proper way to abate the pride, and discredit the pretensions of those who insist upon clear ideas in points of faith, if it be shewn that they do without them even in science ?

4 As to my timing this charge ; why now and not before, since I had published hints thereof many years ago [1] ? Surely I am obliged to give no account of this : If what hath been said in the *Analyst* be not sufficient ; suppose that I had not leisure, or that I did not think it expedient, or that I had no mind to it. When a man thinks fit to publish anything, either in mathematics or in any other part of learning, what avails it, or indeed what right hath any one to ask, Why at this or that time ; in this or that manner ; upon this or that motive ? Let the reader judge if it suffice not that what I publish is true, and that I have a right to publish such truths when and how I please, in a free country.

5 I do not say that mathematicians, as such, are infidels ; or that geometry is a friend to infidelity, which you untruly insinuate, as you do many other things ; whence you raise topics for invective : But I say there are certain mathematicians who are known to be so ; and that there are others who are not mathematicians who are influenced by a regard for their authority. Some perhaps who live in the University, may not be apprised of this ; but the intelligent and observing reader, who lives in the world,

[1] [See *Analyst*, S. 50, where Berkeley refers to his *Principles*, SS. 123-34.—Ed.]

and is acquainted with the humour of the times and the characters of men, is well aware there are too many that deride Mysteries, and yet admire Fluxions ; who yield that faith to a mere mortal which they deny to Jesus Christ, whose religion they make it their study and business to discredit. The owning this is not to own that men who reason well are enemies to religion, as you would represent it : On the contrary, I endeavour to shew that such men are defective in point of reason and judgment, and that they do the very thing they would seem to despise.

6 There are, I make no doubt, among the mathematicians many sincere believers in Jesus Christ ; I know several such myself ; but I addressed my *Analyst* to an infidel ; and on very good grounds, I supposed that, besides him, there were other deriders of faith who had nevertheless a profound veneration for fluxions ; and I was willing to set forth the inconsistence of such men. If there be no such thing as infidels who pretend to knowledge in the modern analysis, I own myself misinformed, and shall gladly be found in a mistake ; but even in that case, my remarks upon fluxions are not the less true ; nor will it follow that I have no right to examine them on the foot of human science, even though religion were quite unconcerned, and though I had no end to serve but truth. But you are very angry (p. 13 and 14) that I should enter the lists with reasoning infidels, and attack them upon their pretensions to science : And hence you take occasion to shew your spleen against the clergy. I will not take upon me to say that I know you to be a Minute Philosopher yourself ; but I know the Minute Philosophers make just such compliments as you do to our church, and are just as angry as you can be at any who undertake to defend religion by reason. If we resolve all into faith, they laugh at us and our faith : And if we attempt to reason, they are angry at us : They pretend we go out of our province, and they recommend to us a blind implicit faith. Such is the inconsistence of our adversaries. But it is to be hoped there will never be wanting men to deal with them at their own weapons ; and to shew they are by no means those masters of reason ; which they would fain pass for.

7 I do not say, as you would represent me, that we have no better reason for our religion than you have for fluxions : but I say that an infidel, who believes the doctrine of fluxions, acts a very inconsistent part in pretending to reject the Christian religion because he cannot believe what he doth not comprehend ; or because he cannot assent without evidence ; or because he

cannot submit his faith to authority. Whether there are such
infidels, I submit to the judgment of the reader. For my own
part I make no doubt of it, having seen some shrewd signs thereof
myself, and having been very credibly informed thereof by others.
Nor doth this charge seem the less credible, for your being so
sensibly touched, and denying it with so much passion. You,
indeed, do not stick to affirm, that the persons who informed me
are *a pack of base profligate and impudent liars* (p. 27). How far the
reader will think fit to adopt your passions, I cannot say ; but I
can truly say, the late celebrated Mr. Addison is one of the
persons whom you are pleased to characterize in these modest
and mannerly terms. He assured me that the infidelity of a certain
noted mathematician, still living, was one principal reason
assigned by a witty man of those times for his being an infidel.[1]
Not that I imagine geometry disposeth men to infidelity ; but
that, from other causes, such as presumption, ignorance, or
vanity, like other men geometricians also become infidels, and
that the supposed light and evidence of their science gains credit
to their infidelity.

8 You reproach me with 'calumny, detraction, and artifice'
(p. 15). You recommend such means as are 'innocent and just,
rather than the criminal method of lessening or detracting from
my opponents' (Ibid.). You accuse me of ' the *odium theologicum*,
the intemperate zeal of divines, that I do *stare super vias antiquas*'
(p. 13) ; with much more to the same effect. For all which
charge I depend on the reader's candour, that he will not take
your word, but read and judge for himself. In which case he will
be able to discern (though he should be no mathematician) how
passionate and unjust your reproaches are, and how possible it is
for a man to cry out against calumny and practise it in the same
breath. Considering how impatient all mankind are when their
prejudices are looked into, I do not wonder to see you rail and
rage at the rate you do. But if your own imagination be strongly
shocked and moved, you cannot therefore conclude that a sincere
endeavour to free a science, so useful and ornamental to human
life, from those subtilties, obscurities, and paradoxes which
render it inaccessible to most men, will be thought a criminal
undertaking by such as are in their right mind. Much less can
you hope that an illustrious Seminary of learned men, which hath
produced so many free-spirited inquirers after truth, will at once
enter into your passions, and degenerate into a nest of bigots.

[1] [See Stock's *Life of Berkeley* quoted above, p. 56.—Ed.]

9 I observe upon the inconsistency of certain infidel analysts. I remark some defects in the principles of the modern analysis. I take the liberty decently to dissent from Sir Isaac Newton. I propose some helps to abridge the trouble of mathematical studies, and render them more useful. What is there in all this that should make you declaim on the usefulness of practical mathematics? That should move you to cry out *Spain, inquisition, odium theologicum*? By what figure of speech do you extend what is said of the modern analysis to mathematics in general; or what is said of mathematical infidels to all mathematicians; or the confuting an errour in science to burning or hanging the authors? But it is nothing new or strange that men should choose to indulge their passions, rather than quit their opinions, how absurd soever. Hence the frightful visions and tragical uproars of bigoted men, be the subject of their bigotry what it will. A very remarkable instance of this you give (p. 27), where, upon my having said that a deference to certain mathematical infidels, as I was credibly informed, had been one motive to infidelity, you ask, with no small emotion, ' For God's sake are we in England or in Spain?' ' Is this the language of a familiar who is whispering an inquisitor, &c.?' And the page before you exclaim in the following words, ' Let us burn or hang up all the mathematicians in Great Britian, or halloo the mob upon them to tear them to pieces every mother's son of them, *Tros Rutulusve fuat*, laymen or clergymen, &c. Let us dig up the bodies of Dr. Barrow and Sir Isaac Newton, and burn them under the gallows,' &c.

10 The reader need not be a mathematician to see how vain all this tragedy of yours is. And if he be as thoroughly satisfied as I am that the cause of fluxions cannot be defended by reason, he will be as little surprised as I am to see you betake yourself to the arts of all bigoted men, raising terrour and calling in the passions to your assistance. Whether those rhetorical flourishes about the inquisition and the gallies are not quite ridiculous, I leave to be determined by the reader. Who will also judge (though he should not be skilled in geometry) whether I have given the least grounds for this and a world of such-like declamation? And whether I have not constantly treated those celebrated writers with all proper respect, though I take the liberty in certain points to differ from them?

11 As I heartily abhor an inquisition in faith, so I think you have no right to erect one in science. At the time of writing your *Defence* you seem to have been overcome with passion: But, now

you may be supposed cool, I desire you to reflect whether it be not wrote in the true spirit of an inquisitor. Whether this becomes a person so exceeding delicate himself upon that point? And whether your brethren the analysts will think themselves honoured or obliged by you, for having defended their doctrine in the same manner as any declaiming bigot would defend transubstantiation? The same false colours, the same intemperate sallies, and the same indignation against common sense!

12 In a matter of mere science, where authority hath nothing to do, you constantly endeavour to overbear me with authorities, and load me with envy. If I see a sophism in the writings of a great author, and, in complement to his understanding, suspect he could hardly be quite satisfyed with his own demonstration: This sets you on declaiming for several pages. It is pompously set forth, as a criminal method of detracting from great men, as a concerted project to lessen their reputation, as making them pass for impostors. If I publish my free thoughts, which I have as much right to publish as any other man, it is imputed to rashness, and vanity, and the love of opposition. Though perhaps my late publication,[1] of what had been hinted twenty-five years ago, may acquit me of this charge in the eyes of an impartial reader. But when I consider the perplexities that beset a man who undertakes to defend the doctrine of fluxions, I can easily forgive your anger.

13 Two sorts of learned men there are: one who candidly seek truth by rational means. These are never averse to have their principles looked into, and examined by the test of reason. Another sort there is who learn by *route* a set of principles and a way of thinking which happen to be in vogue. These betray themselves by their anger and surprise, whenever their principles are freely canvassed. But you must not expect that your reader will make himself a party to your passions or your prejudices. I freely own that Sir Isaac Newton hath shewed himself an extraordinary mathematician, a profound naturalist, a person of the greatest abilities and erudition. Thus far I can readily go, but I cannot go the lengths that you do. I shall never say of him as you do, *Vestigia pronus adoro* (p. 70). This same adoration that you pay to him, I will pay only to truth.

14 You may, indeed, yourself be an idolater of whom you please: But then you have no right to insult and exclaim at

---

[1] [The *Analyst*; in his *Principles* Sects. 123-34 he gave the hints about infinitesimals to which he here refers.—Ed.]

other men, because they do not adore your idol. Great as Sir Isaac Newton was, I think he hath, on more occasions than one, shewed himself not to be infallible. Particularly, his demonstration of the doctrine of fluxions I take to be defective, and I cannot help thinking that he was not quite pleased with it himself. And yet this doth not hinder but the method may be useful, considered as an art of invention. You, who are a mathematician, must acknowledge there have been divers such methods admitted in mathematics, which are not demonstrative. Such, for instance, are the inductions of Dr. Wallis, in his Arithmetic of Infinites ; and such what Harriot, and, after him, Descartes, have wrote concerning the roots of affected æquations. It will not, nevertheless, thence follow that those methods are useless ; but only that they are not to be allowed of as premises in a strict demonstration.

15 No great name upon earth shall ever make me accept things obscure for clear, or sophisms for demonstrations. Nor may you ever hope to deter me from freely speaking what I freely think, by those arguments *ab invidia* which at every turn you employ against me. You represent yourself (p. 52) as a man ' whose highest ambition is in the lowest degree to imitate Sir Isaac Newton.' It might, perhaps, have suited better with your appellation of *Philalethes*, and been altogether as laudable, if your highest ambition had been to discover truth. Very consistently with the character you give of yourself, you speak of it as a sort of crime (p. 70) to think it possible you should ever ' see further, or go beyond Sir Isaac Newton.' And I am persuaded you speak the sentiments of many more besides yourself. But there are others who are not afraid to sift the principles of human science, who think it no honour to imitate the greatest man in his defects, who even think it no crime to desire to know, not only beyond Sir Isaac Newton, but beyond all mankind. And whoever thinks otherwise, I appeal to the reader whether he can properly be called a philosopher.

16 Because I am not guilty of your mean idolatry, you inveigh against me as a person conceited of my own abilities ; not considering that a person of less abilities may know more on a certain point than one of greater ; not considering that a purblind eye, in a close and narrow view, may discern more of a thing than a much better eye in a more extensive prospect ; not considering that this is to fix a *ne plus ultra*, to put a stop to all future inquiries ; lastly, not considering that this is in fact, so much as in you lies,

converting the republick of letters into an absolute monarchy, that it is even introducing a kind of philosophic popery among a free people.

17 I have said (and I venture still to say) that a fluxion is incomprehensible : That second, third, and fourth fluxions are yet more incomprehensible : That it is not possible to conceive a simple infinitesimal : that it is yet less possible to conceive an infinitesimal of an infinitesimal, and so onward.[1] What have you to say in answer to this ? Do you attempt to clear up the notion of a fluxion or a difference ? Nothing like it. You only ' assure me (upon your bare word) from your own experience, and that of several others whom you could name, that the doctrine of fluxions may be clearly conceived and distinctly comprehended ; and that if I am puzzled about it and do not understand it, yet others do.' But can you think, Sir, I shall take your word, when I refuse to take your Master's ?

18 Upon this point every reader of common sense may judge as well as the most profound mathematician. The simple apprehension of a thing defined is not made more perfect by any subsequent progress in mathematics. What any man evidently knows, he knows as well as you or Sir Isaac Newton. And every one can know whether the object of this method be (as you would have us think) clearly conceivable. To judge of this no depth of science is requisite, but only a bare attention to what passes in his own mind. And the same is to be understood of all definitions in all sciences whatsoever. In none of which can it be supposed that a man of sense and spirit will take any definition or principle upon trust, without sifting it to the bottom, and trying how far he can or he cannot conceive it. This is the course I have taken, and shall take, however you and your brethren may declaim against it, and place it in the most invidious light.

19 It is usual with you to admonish me to look over a second time, to consult, examine, weigh the words of Sir Isaac. In answer to which I will venture to say that I have taken as much pains as (I sincerely believe) any man living to understand that great author, and to make sense of his principles. No industry, nor caution, nor attention, I assure you, have been wanting on my part. So that, if I do not understand him, it is not my fault but my misfortune. Upon other subjects you are pleased to compliment me with depth of thought and uncommon abilities (p. 5 and 84). But I freely own, I have no pretence to those

[1] *Analyst*, Sect. 4, 5, 6, &c.

things. The only advantage I pretend to is that I have always thought and judged for myself. And, as I never had a master in mathematics, so I fairly followed the dictates of my own mind in examining and censuring the authors I read upon that subject, with the same freedom that I used upon any other ; taking nothing upon trust, and believing that no writer was infallible. And a man of moderate parts, who takes this painful course in studying the principles of any science, may be supposed to walk more surely than those of greater abilities, who set out with more speed and less care.

20 What I insist on is, that the idea of a fluxion simply considered is not at all improved or amended by any progress, though ever so great, in the analysis : neither are the demonstrations of the general rules of that method at all cleared up by applying them. The reason of which is, because in operating or calculating men do not return to contemplate the original principles of the method, which they constantly presuppose, but are employed in working, by notes and symbols denoting the fluxions supposed to have been at first explained, and according to rules supposed to have been at first demonstrated. This I say to encourage those who are not far gone in these studies, to use intrepidly their own judgment, without a blind or a mean deference to the best of mathematicians, who are no more qualified than they are to judge of the simple apprehension, or the evidence of what is delivered in the first elements of the method ; men by further and frequent use or exercise becoming only more accustomed to the symbols and rules, which doth not make either the foregoing notions more clear, or the foregoing proofs more perfect. Every reader of common sense, that will but use his faculties, knows as well as the most profound analyst what idea he frames or can frame of velocity without motion, or of motion without extension, of magnitude which is neither finite nor infinite, or of a quantity having no magnitude which is yet divisible, of a figure where there is no space, of proportion between nothings, or of a real product from nothing multiplied by something. He need not be far gone in geometry to know that obscure principles are not to be admitted in demonstration : That if a man destroys his own hypothesis, he at the same time destroys what was built upon it : That errour in the premises, not rectified, must produce errour in the conclusion.

21 In my opinion the greatest men have their prejudices. Men learn the elements of science from others : and every learner

hath a deference more or less to authority, especially the young learners, few of that kind caring to dwell long upon principles, but inclining rather to take them upon trust : And things early admitted by repetition become familiar : And this familiarity at length passeth for evidence. Now to me it seems there are certain points tacitly admitted by mathematicians which are neither evident nor true. And such points or principles ever mixing with their reasonings do lead them into paradoxes and perplexities. If the great author of the fluxionary method was early imbued with such notions, it would only shew he was a man. And if by virtue of some latent errour in his principles a man be drawn into fallacious reasonings, it is nothing strange that he should take them for true : And, nevertheless, if, when urged by perplexities and uncouth consequences, and driven to arts and shifts, he should entertain some doubt thereof, it is no more than one may naturally suppose might befall a great genius grappling with an insuperable difficulty : Which is the light in which I have placed Sir Isaac Newton.[1] Hereupon you are pleased to remark that I represent the great author not only as a weak but an ill man, as a deceiver and an impostor. The reader will judge how justly.

22 As to the rest of your colourings and glosses, your reproaches and insults and outcries, I shall pass them over, only desiring the reader not to take your word, but read what I have written, and he will want no other answer. It hath been often observed that the worst cause produceth the greatest clamour ; and indeed you are so clamorous throughout your defence that the reader, although he should be no mathematician, provided he understands common sense and hath observed the ways of men, will be apt to suspect that you are in the wrong. It should seem, therefore, that your brethren the analysts are but little obliged to you for this new method of declaiming in mathematics. Whether they are more obliged by your reasoning I shall now examine.

23 You ask me (p. 32) where I find Sir Isaac Newton using such expressions as the velocities of velocities, the second, third, and fourth velocities &c. This you set forth as a pious fraud and unfair representation. I answer, that if according to Sir Isaac Newton a fluxion be the velocity of an increment, then according to him I may call the fluxion of a fluxion the velocity of a velocity. But for the truth of the antecedent see his Introduction to the Quadrature of Curves, where his own words are,

[1] *Analyst*, Sect. 18.

Motuum vel incrementorum velocitates nominando fluxiones. See also the second lemma of the second book of his Mathematical Principles of Natural Philosophy, where he expresseth himself in the following manner, *Velocitates incrementorum ac decrementorum quas etiam, motus, mutationes, & fluxiones quantitatum nominare licet.* And that he admits fluxions of fluxions, or second, third, fourth fluxions, &c. see his Treatise of the Quadrature of Curves. I ask now, is it not plain that if a fluxion be a velocity, then the fluxion of a fluxion may agreeably thereunto be called the velocity of a velocity? In like manner if by a fluxion is meant a nascent augment, will it not then follow that the fluxion of a fluxion or second fluxion is the nascent augment of a nascent augment? Can anything be plainer? Let the reader now judge who is unfair.

24 I had observed that the great author had proceeded illegitimately, in obtaining the fluxion or moment of the rectangle of two flowing quantities; and that he did not fairly get rid of the rectangle of the moments. In answer to this you alledge that the errour arising from the omission of such rectangle (allowing it to be an errour) is so small that it is insignificant. This you dwell upon and exemplify to no other purpose but to amuse your reader and mislead him from the question; which in truth is not concerning the accuracy of computing or measuring in practice, but concerning the accuracy of the reasoning in science. That this was really the case, and that the smallness of the practical errour no wise concerns it, must be so plain to any one who reads the *Analyst* that I wonder how you could be ignorant of it.

25 You would fain persuade your reader that I make an absurd quarrel against errours of no significancy in practice, and represent mathematicians as proceeding blindfold in their approximations, in all which I cannot help thinking there is on your part either great ignorance or great disingenuity. If you mean to defend the reasonableness and use of approximations or of the method of indivisibles, I have nothing to say. But then you must remember this is not the doctrine of fluxions: it is none of that analysis with which I am concerned. That I am far from quarelling at approximations in geometry is manifest from the thirty-third and fifty-third queries in the *Analyst*. And that the method of fluxions pretends to somewhat more than the method of indivisibles is plain; because Sir Isaac disclaims this method as not geometrical.[1] And that the method of fluxions is supposed

See the Scholium at the end of the first Section. **Lib. 1. *Phil. Nat. Prin. Math.***

accurate in geometrical rigour is manifest to whoever considers what the great author writes about it ; especially in his Introduction to the Quadrature of Curves, where he saith, *In rebus mathematicis errores quam minimi non sunt contemnendi*. Which expression you have seen quoted in the *Analyst*, and yet you seem ignorant thereof, and indeed of the very end and design of the great author in this his invention of fluxions.

26 As oft as you talk of finite quantities inconsiderable in practice Sir Isaac disowns your apology. *Cave*, saith he, *intellexeris finitas*. And, although quantities less than sensible may be of no account in practice, yet none of your masters, nor will even you yourself venture to say they are of no account in theory and in reasoning. The application in gross practice is not the point questioned, but the rigour and justness of the reasoning. And it is evident that, be the subject ever so little, or ever so inconsiderable, this doth not hinder but that a person treating thereof may commit very great errours in logic, which logical errours are in no wise to be measured by the sensible or practical inconveniences thence arising, which, perchance, may be none at all. It must be owned that, after you have mislead and amused your less qualified reader (as you call him), you return to the real point in controversy, and set yourself to justify Sir Isaac's method of getting rid of the above-mentioned rectangle. And here I must entreat the reader to observe how fairly you proceed.

27 First then you affirm (p. 44), ' that neither in the demonstration of the rule for finding the fluxion of the rectangle of two flowing quantities, nor in anything preceding or following it, is any mention so much as once made of the increment of the rectangle of such flowing quantities.' Now I affirm the direct contrary. For in the very passage by you quoted in this same page, from the first case of the second lemma of the second book of Sir Isaac's Principles, beginning with *Rectangulum quodvis motu perpetuo auctum*, and ending with *igitur laterum incrementis totis a et b generatur rectanguli incrementum aB + bA* Q.E.D., in this very passage, I say, is express mention made of the increment of such rectangle. As this is matter of fact, I refer it to the reader's own eyes. Of what rectangle have we here the increment ? Is it not plainly of that whose sides have *a* and *b* for their *incrementa tota*, that is, of *AB* ? Let any reader judge whether it be not plain from the words, the sense, and the context, that the great author in the end of his demonstration understands his *incrementum* as belonging to the *rectangulum quodvis* at the beginning. Is not

the same also evident from the very lemma it self prefixed to the demonstration? The sense whereof is (as the author there explains it), that if the moments of the flowing quantities *A* and *B* are called *a* and *b*, then the *momentum vel mutatio geniti rectanguli AB* will be *aB* × *bA*. Either therefore the conclusion of the demonstration is not the thing which was to be demonstrated, or the *rectanguli incrementum aB* × *bA* belongs to the rectangle *AB*.

28 All this is so plain that nothing can be more so; and yet you would fain perplex this plain case by distinguishing between an increment and a moment. But it is evident to every one who has any notion of demonstration that the *incrementum* in the conclusion must be the *momentum* in the lemma; and to suppose it otherwise is no credit to the author. It is in effect supposing him to be one who did not know what he would demonstrate. But let us hear Sir Isaac's own words: *Earum (quantitatum scilicet fluentium) incrementa vel decrementa momentanea sub nomine momentorum intelligo.* And you observe yourself that he useth the word *moment* to signify either an increment or decrement. Hence with an intention to puzzle me you propose the increment and decrement of *AB*, and ask which of these I would call the moment? The case you say is difficult. My answer is very plain and easy, to wit, Either of them. You, indeed, make a different answer, and from the author's saying that by a moment he understands either the momentaneous increment or decrement of the flowing quantities, you would have us conclude, by a very wonderful inference, that his moment is neither the increment nor decrement thereof. Would it not be as good an inference, because a number is either odd or even, to conclude it is neither? Can any one make sense of this? Or can even your self hope that this will go down with the reader, how little soever qualified? It must be owned, you endeavour to intrude this inference on him, rather by mirth and humour than by reasoning. You are merry, I say, and (p. 46) represent the two mathematical quantities as pleading their rights, as tossing up cross and pile,[1] as disputing amicably. You talk of their claiming preference, their agreeing, their boyishness, and their gravity. And after this ingenious digression you address me in the following words—Believe me, there is no remedy, you must acquiesce. But my answer is that I will neither believe you nor acquiesce; there is a plain remedy

[1] ['cross and pile,' *i.e.* heads and tails; the cross was often stamped on the obverse of a coin; the pile was the reverse, and took its name from the impress of a machine used in minting.—Ed.]

in common sense ; and that to prevent surprise I desire the reader always to keep the controverted point in view, to examine your reasons, and be cautious how he takes your word, but most of all when you are positive or eloquent or merry.

29 A page or two after, you very candidly represent your case to be that of an ass between two bottles of hay : it is your own expression. The cause of your perplexity is that you know not whether the velocity of *AB* increasing, or of *AB* decreasing is to be esteemed the fluxion, or proportional to the moment of the rectangle. My opinion, agreeably to what hath been premised, is that either may be deemed the fluxion. But you tell us (p. 49) ' that you think, the venerable ghost of Sir Isaac Newton whispers you, the velocity you seek for is neither the one nor the other of these, but is the velocity which the flowing rectangle hath, not while it is greater or less than *AB*, but at that very instant of time that it is *AB*.' For my part, in the rectangle *AB* considered simply in itself, without either increasing or diminishing, I can conceive no velocity at all. And if the reader is of my mind, he will not take either your word, or even the word of a ghost how venerable soever, for velocity without motion. You proceed and tell us that, in like manner, the moment of the rectangle is neither its increment or decrement. This you would have us believe on the authority of his ghost, in direct opposition to what Sir Isaac himself asserted when alive. *Incrementa* (saith he) *vel decrementa momentanea sub nomine momentorum intelligo : ita ut incrementa pro momentis addititiis seu affirmativis, ac decrementa pro subductitiis seu negativis habeantur.*[1] I will not in your style bid the reader believe me, but believe his eyes.

30 To me it verily seems that you have undertaken the defence of what you do not understand. To mend the matter, you say, ' you do not consider *AB* as lying at either extremity of the moment, but as extended to the middle of it ; as having acquired the one half of the moment, and as being about to acquire the other ; or, as having lost one half of it, and being about to lose the other.' Now, in the name of truth, I intreat you to tell what this moment is, to the middle whereof the rectangle is extended ? This moment, I say, which is acquired, which is lost, which is cut in two, or distinguished into halfs ? Is it a finite quantity, or an infinitesimal, or a mere limit, or nothing at all ? Take it in what sense you will, I cannot make your defence either consistent or intelligible. For if you take it in either of the two

[1] *Princip. Phil. Nat.* Lib. II. Lem. II.

former senses, you contradict Sir Isaac Newton. And if you take it in either of the latter, you contradict common sense ; it being plain, that what hath no magnitude, or is no quantity, cannot be divided. And here I must intreat the reader to preserve his full freedom of mind intire, and not weakly suffer his judgment to be overborne by your imagination and your prejudices, by great names and authorities, by ghosts and visions, and above all by that extreme satisfaction and complacency with which you utter your strange conceits ; if words without a meaning may be called so. After having given this unintelligible account, you ask with your accustomed air, ' What say you, Sir ? Is this a just and legitimate reason for Sir Isaac's proceeding as he did ? I think you must acknowledge it to be so.' But, alas ! I acknowledge no such thing. I find no sense or reason in what you say. Let the reader find it if he can.

31 In the next place (p. 50) you charge me with want of caution. ' Inasmuch (say you) as that quantity which Sir Isaac Newton through his whole lemma, and all the several cases of it, constantly calls a *moment*, without confining it to be either an increment or decrement, is by you inconsiderately and arbitrarily, and without any shadow of reason given, supposed and determined to be an increment.' To which charge I reply that it is as untrue as it is peremptory. For that, in the foregoing citation from the first case of Sir Isaac's lemma, he expressly determines it to be an increment. And, as this particular instance or passage was that which I objected to, it was reasonable and proper for me to consider the moment in that same light. But, take it increment or decrement as you will, the objections still lie and the difficulties are equally insuperable. You then proceed to extoll the great author of the fluxionary method, and to bestow some *brusqueries* upon those who unadvisedly dare to differ from him. To all which I shall give no answer.

32 Afterwards to remove (as you say) all scruple and difficulty about this affair, you observe that the moment of the rectangle determined by Sir Isaac Newton, and the increment of the rectangle determined by me are perfectly and exactly equal, supposing a and b to be diminished *ad infinitum* : and for proof of this, you refer to the first lemma of the first section of the first book of Sir Isaac's Principles. I answer that if a and b are real quantities, then $a\,b$ is something, and consequently makes a real difference : but if they are nothing, then the rectangles whereof they are coefficients become nothing likewise : and

consequently the *momentum* or *incrementum*, whether Sir Isaac's or mine, are in that case nothing at all. As for the above-mentioned lemma, which you refer to, and which you wish I had consulted sooner, both for my own sake and for yours ; I tell you I had long since consulted and considered it. But I very much doubt whether you have sufficiently considered that lemma, its demonstration, and its consequences. For, however, that way of reasoning may do in the method of *exhaustions*, where quantities less than assignable are regarded as nothing ; yet, for a fluxionist writing about momentums to argue that quantities must be equal because they have no assignable difference seems the most injudicious step that could be taken : it is directly demolishing the very doctrine you would defend. For, it will thence follow that all homogeneous momentums are equal, and consequently the velocities, mutations, or fluxions, proportional thereto, are all likewise equal. There is, therefore, only one proportion of equality throughout, which at once overthrows the whole system you undertake to defend. Your moments (I say) not being themselves assignable quantities, their differences cannot be assignable : and, if this be true, by that way of reasoning it will follow, they are all equal, upon which supposition you cannot make one step in the method of fluxions. It appears from hence, how unjustly you blame me (p. 32) for omitting to give any account of that first section of the first book of the *Principia*, wherein (you say) the foundation of the method of fluxions is geometrically demonstrated and largely explained, and difficulties and objections against it are clearly solved. All which is so far from being true that the very first and fundamental lemma of that section is incompatible with and subversive of the doctrine of fluxions. And, indeed, who sees not that a demonstration *ad absurdum more veterum*, proceeding on a supposition that every difference must be some given quantity, cannot be admitted in, or consist with, a method wherein quantities less than any given, are supposed really to exist, and be capable of division ?

33 The next point you undertake to defend is that method for obtaining a rule to find the fluxion of any power of a flowing quantity, which is delivered in the Introduction to the Quadratures, and considered in the *Analyst*.[1] And here the question between us is, whether I have rightly represented the sense of those words, *evanescant jam augmenta illa*, in rendering them, let the increments vanish, *i.e.* let the increments be nothing, or

[1] Sect. 13, 14, &c.

let there be no increments ? This you deny, but, as your manner is, instead of giving a reason you declaim. I, on the contrary, affirm, the increments must be understood to be quite gone, and absolutely nothing at all. My reason is, because without that supposition you can never bring the quantity or expression

$$nx^{n-1} + \frac{nn - n}{2}ox^{n-2} + \&c. \text{ down to } nx^{n-1},$$

the very thing aimed at by supposing the evanescence. Say whether this be not the truth of the case ? Whether the former expression is not to be reduced to the latter ? And whether this can possibly be done so long as o is supposed a real quantity ? I cannot indeed say you are scrupulous about your affirmations, and yet I believe that even you will not affirm this ; it being most evident, that the product of two real quantities is something real ; and that nothing real can be rejected either according to the ἀκρίβεια of geometry,[1] or according to Sir Isaac's own Principles ; for the truth of which I appeal to all who know anything of these matters. Further by *evanescant* must either be meant, let them (the increments) vanish and become nothing, in the obvious sense, or else let them become infinitely small. But that this latter is not Sir Isaac's sense is evident from his own words in the very same page, that is, in the last of the Introduction to his Quadratures, where he expressly saith, *volui ostendere quod in methodo fluxionum non opus sit figuras infinite parvas in geometriam introducere.* Upon the whole, you seem to have considered this affair so very superficially as greatly to confirm me in the opinion, you are so angry with, to wit, that Sir Isaac's followers are much more eager in applying his method than accurate in examining his principles. You raise a dust about evanescent augments, which may perhaps amuse and amaze your reader, but I am much mistaken if it ever instructs or enlightens him. For, to come to the point, those evanescent augments either are real quantities, or they are not. If you say they are ; I desire to know how you get rid of the rejectaneous quantity ? If you say they are not ; you indeed get rid of those quantities in the composition whereof they are coefficients ; but then you are of the same opinion with me, which opinion you are pleased to call (p. 58) ' a most palpable, inexcusable, and unpardonable blunder,' although it be a truth most palpably evident.

[1] [*Cf. PC* No. 313.—Ed.]

34 Nothing, I say, can be plainer to any impartial reader than that by the evanescence of augments in the above-cited passage, Sir Isaac means their being actually reduced to nothing. But, to put it out of all doubt that this is the truth, and to convince even you, who shew so little disposition to be convinced, I desire you to look into his *Analysis per Æquationes Infinitas* (p. 20), where, in his preparation for demonstrating the first rule for the squaring of simple curves, you will find that on a parallel occasion, speaking of an augment which is supposed to vanish, he interprets the word *evanescere* by *esse nihil*. Nothing can be plainer than this, which at once destroys your defence. And yet, plain as it is, I despair of making you acknowledge it ; though I am sure you feel it, and the reader if he useth his eyes must see it. The words *evanescere sive esse nihil* do (to use your own expression) stare us in the face. Lo ! This is what you call (p. 56) ' so great, so unaccountable, so horrid, so truly Bœotian a blunder,' that, according to you, it was not possible Sir Isaac Newton could be guilty of it. For the future, I advise you to be more sparing of hard words : Since, as you incautiously deal them about, they may chance to light on your friends as well as your adversaries. As for my part, I shall not retaliate. It is sufficient to say you are mistaken. But I can easily pardon your mistakes. Though, indeed, you tell me on this very occasion, that I must expect no quarter from Sir Isaac's followers. And I tell you that I neither expect nor desire any. My aim is truth. My reasons I have given. Confute them, if you can. But think not to overbear me either with authorities or harsh words. The latter will recoil upon your selves : The former, in a matter of science, are of no weight with indifferent readers ; and as for bigots, I am not concerned about what they say or think.

35 In the next place you proceed to declaim upon the following passage taken from the seventeenth section of the *Analyst*. ' Considering the various arts and devices used by the great author of the fluxionary method : In how many lights he placeth his fluxions ; and in what different ways he attempts to demonstrate the same point : One would be inclined to think he was himself suspicious of the justness of his own demonstrations.' This passage you complain of as very hard usage of Sir Isaac Newton. You declaim copiously, and endeavour to shew that placing the same point in various lights is of great use to explain it ; which you illustrate with much rhetoric. But the fault of that passage is not the hard usage it contains : But on the contrary,

that it is too modest, and not so full and expressive of my sense as perhaps it should have been. Would you like it better if I should say, the various *inconsistent* accounts which this great author gives of his momentums and his fluxions may convince every intelligent reader that he had no clear and steady notions of them, without which there can be no demonstration? I own frankly that I see no clearness or consistence in them. You tell me indeed, in Miltonic verse, that the fault is in my own eyes,

> So thick a drop serene has quench'd their orbs
> Or dim suffusion veil'd.

At the same time you acknowledge your self obliged for those various lights which have enabled you to understand his doctrine. But as for me who do not understand it, you insult me, saying: 'For God's sake what is it you are offended at, who do not still understand him?' May not I answer, that I am offended for this very reason; because I cannot understand him or make sense of what he says? You say to me that I am all in the dark. I acknowledge it, and entreat you who see so clearly to help me out.

36 You, Sir, with the bright eyes, be pleased to tell me, whether Sir Isaac's momentum be a finite quantity, or an infinitesimal, or a mere limit? If you say a finite quantity: Be pleased to reconcile this with what he saith in the scholium of the second lemma of the first section of the first book of his Principles: *Cave intelligas quantitates magnitudine determinatas, sed cogita semper diminuendas sine limite.* If you say, an infinitesimal: reconcile this with what is said in the Introduction to his Quadratures: *Volui ostendere quod in methodo fluxionum non opus sit figuras infinite parvas in geometriam introducere.* If you should say, it is a mere limit; be pleased to reconcile this with what we find in the first case of the second lemma in the second book of his *Principles*: *Ubi de lateribus A et B deerant momentorum dimidia, &c.* where the moments are supposed to be divided. I should be very glad a person of such a luminous intellect would be so good as to explain whether by fluxions we are to understand the nascent or evanescent quantities themselves, or their motions, or their velocities, or simply their proportions: and having interpreted them in what sense you will, that you would then condescend to explain the doctrine of second, third, and fourth fluxions, and shew it to be consistent with common sense if you can. You seem to be very sanguine when you express yourself in the following terms.

' I do assure you, Sir, from my own experience, and that of many others whom I could name that the doctrine may be clearly conceived and distinctly comprehended.' (p. 31.) And it may be uncivil not to believe what you so solemnly affirm, from your own experience. But I must needs own I should be better satisfied of this, if, instead of entertaining us with your rhetoric, you would vouchsafe to reconcile those difficulties, and explain those obscure points above mentioned. If either you, or any one of those many whom you could name will but explain to others what you so clearly conceive yourselves, I give you my word that several will be obliged to you who, I may venture to say, understand those matters no more than myself. But, if I am not much mistaken, you and your friends will modestly decline this task.

37 I have long ago done what you so often exhort me to do, diligently read and considered the several accounts of this doctrine given by the great author in different parts of his writings : and upon the whole I could never make it out to be consistent and intelligible. I was even led to say that ' one would be inclined to think he was himself suspicious of the justness of his own demonstrations : and that he was not enough pleased with any one notion steadily to adhere to it.' After which I added, ' Thus much is plain, that he owned himself satisfied concerning certain points, which nevertheless he could not undertake to demonstrate to others.' See the seventeenth section of the *Analyst*. It is one thing when a doctrine is placed in various lights : and another when the principles and notions are shifted. When new devices are introduced and substituted for others, a doctrine instead of being illustrated may be explained away. Whether there be not something of this in the present case, I appeal to the writings of the great author. His *Methodus rationum primarum et ultimarum*, His second lemma in the second book of his *Principles*, his Introduction and Treatise of the Quadrature of Curves. In all which it appears to me, there is not one uniform doctrine explained and carried throughout the whole, but rather sundry inconsistent accounts of this new method, which still grows more dark and confused the more it is handled : I could not help thinking, the greatest genius might lye under the influence of false principles ; and where the object and notions were exceeding obscure, he might possibly distrust even his own demonstrations. ' At least thus much seemed plain, that Sir Isaac had sometime owned himself satisfied, where he could not demonstrate to others. In proof whereof I mentioned his letter to Mr. Collins ; hereupon

you tell me : there is a great deal of difference between saying, I cannot undertake to prove a thing, and I will not undertake it.' But in answer to this, I desire you will be pleased to consider that I was not making a precise extract out of that letter, in which the very words of Sir Isaac should alone be inserted. But I made my own remark and inference from what I remembered to have read in that letter ; where, speaking of a certain mathematical matter, Sir Isaac expresseth himself in the following terms. ' It is plain to me by the fountain I draw it from ; though I will not undertake to prove it to others.' Now, whether my inference may not be fairly drawn from those words of Sir Isaac Newton ; and whether the difference as to the sense be so great between *will* and *can* in that particular case, I leave to be determined by the reader.

38 In the next paragraph you talk big but prove nothing. You speak of driving out of intrenchments, of sallying, and attacking, and carrying by assault ; of slight and untenable works, of a new-raised and undisciplined militia, and of veteran regular troops. Need the reader be a mathematician to see the vanity of this paragraph ? After this you employ (p. 65) your usual colouring, and represent the great author of the Method of Fluxions ' as a good old gentleman fast asleep, and snoring in his easy chair ; while dame Fortune is bringing him her apron full of beautiful theorems and problems, which he never knows or thinks of.' This you would have pass for a consequence of my notions. But I appeal to all those who are ever so little knowing in such matters, whether there are not divers fountains of experiment, induction, and analogy, whence a man may derive and satisfy himself concerning the truth of many points in mathematics and mechanical philosophy, although the proofs thereof afforded by the modern analysis should not amount to demonstration ? I further appeal to the conscience of all the most profound mathematicians, whether they can, with perfect acquiescence of mind, free from all scruple, apply any proposition merely upon the strength of a demonstration involving second or third fluxions, without the aid of any such experiment, or analogy, or collateral proof whatsoever ? Lastly, I appeal to the reader's own heart, whether he cannot clearly conceive a medium between being fast asleep and demonstrating ? But, you will have it that I represent Sir Isaac's conclusions as coming out right, because one errour is compensated by another contrary and equal errour, which perhaps he never knew himself nor thought of : that by a

twofold mistake he arrives though not at science yet at truth : that he proceeds blindfold, &c. All which is untruly said by you, who have misapplied to Sir Isaac what was intended for the Marquis de l'Hospital [1] and his followers ; for no other end (as I can see) but that you may have an opportunity to draw that ingenious pourtraiture of Sir Isaac Newton and dame Fortune, as will be manifest to whoever reads the *Analyst*.

39 You tell me (p. 70) if I think fit to persist in asserting ' that this affair of a double errour is entirely a new discovery of my own, which Sir Isaac and his followers never knew or thought of, that you have unquestionable evidence to convince me of the contrary, and that all his followers are already apprised that this very objection of mine was long since foreseen, and clearly and fully removed by Sir Isaac Newton, in the first section of the first book of his *Principia*.' All which I do as strongly deny as you affirm. And I do aver that this is an unquestionable proof of the matchless contempt which you, *Philalethes*, have for truth. And I do here publickly call upon you to produce that evidence which you pretend to have, and to make good that fact which you so confidently affirm. And, at the same time, I do assure the reader that you never will, nor can.

40 If you defend Sir Isaac's notions, as delivered in his *Principia*, it must be on the rigorous foot of rejecting nothing, neither admitting nor casting away infinitely small quantities. If you defend the Marquis, whom you also style your Master, it must be on the foot of admitting that there are infinitesimals, that they may be rejected, that they are nevertheless real quantities, and themselves infinitely subdivisible. But you seem to have grown giddy with passion, and in the heat of controversy to have mistaken and forgot your part. I beseech you, Sir, to consider that the Marquis (whom alone, and not Sir Isaac, this double errour in finding the subtangent doth concern) rejects indeed infinitesimals, but not on the foot that you do, to wit, their being inconsiderable in practical geometry or mixed mathematics. But he rejects them in the accuracy of speculative knowledge : in which respect there may be great logical errours, although there should be no sensible mistake in practice : which, it seems, is what you cannot comprehend. He rejects them likewise in vertue of a

[1] [A French mathematician (1661–1704) whose *Analyse des infiniment petits* is mentioned in Berkeley's ' Of Infinites.'—Ed.]

postulatum, which I venture to call rejecting them without
ceremony. And, though he inferreth a conclusion accurately true,
yet he doth it, contrary to the rules of logic, from inaccurate and
false premises. And how this comes about, I have at large
explained in the *Analyst*, and shewed in that particular case of
tangents, that the rejectaneous quantity might have been a finite
quantity of any given magnitude, and yet the conclusion have
come out exactly the same way ; and, consequently, that the
truth of this method doth not depend on the reason assigned by
the Marquis, to wit, the postulatum for throwing away infinitesimals and therefore that he and his followers acted blindfold, as
not knowing the true reason for the conclusions coming out
accurately right, which I shew to have been the effect of a double
errour.

41 This is the truth of the matter, which you shamefully
misrepresent and declaim upon, to no sort of purpose but to
amuse and mislead your reader. For which conduct of yours
throughout your remarks, you will pardon me if I cannot otherwise account, than from a secret hope that the reader of your
Defence would never read the *Analyst*. If he doth, he cannot but
see what an admirable method you take to defend your cause :
How, instead of justifying the reasoning, the logic, or the theory
of the case specified, which is the real point, you discourse of
sensible and practical errours : And how all this is a manifest
imposition upon the reader. He must needs see that I have
expressly said, ' I have no controversy except only about your
logic and method : that I consider how you demonstrate ; what
objects you are conversant about ; and whether you conceive
them clearly.' That I have often expressed myself to the same
effect, desiring the reader to remember, ' that I am only concerned about the way of coming at your theorems, whether it be
legitimate or illegitimate, clear or obscure, scientific or tentative :
that I have, on this very occasion, to prevent all possibility of
mistake, repeated and insisted that I consider the geometrical
analyst as a logician, *i.e.* so far forth as he reasons and argues ;
and his mathematical conclusions not in themselves but in their
premises ; not as true or false, useful or insignificant, but as
derived from such principles, and by such inferences.' [1] You
affirm (and indeed what can you not affirm ?) that the difference
between the true subtangent and that found without any compensation is absolutely nothing at all. I profess myself of a contrary

[1] *Analyst*, Sect. 20.

opinion. My reason is, because nothing cannot be divided into parts. But this difference is capable of being divided into any, or into more than any given number of parts ; for the truth of which consult the Marquis de l'Hospital. And, be the errour in fact or in practice ever so small, it will not thence follow that the errour in reasoning, which is what I am alone concerned about, is one whit the less, it being evident that a man may reason most absurdly about the minutest things.

42 Pray answer me fairly, once for all, whether it be your opinion that whatsoever is little and inconsiderable enough to be rejected without inconvenience in practice, the same may in like manner be safely rejected and overlooked in theory and demonstration. If you say *No*, it will then follow that all you have been saying here and elsewhere, about yards, and inches, and decimal fractions, setting forth and insisting on the extreme smallness of the rejectaneous quantity, is quite foreign to the argument, and only a piece of skill to impose upon your reader. If you say *Yes*, it follows that you then give up at once all the orders of fluxions and infinitesimal differences ; and so most imprudently turn all your sallies and attacks and veterans to your own overthrow. If the reader is of my mind, he will despair of ever seeing you get clear of this dilemma. The points in controversy have been so often and so distinctly noted in the *Analyst* that I very much wonder how you could mistake, if you had no mind to mistake. It is very plain, if you are in earnest, that you neither understand me nor your Masters. And what shall we think of other ordinary analysts, when it shall be found that even you, who like a champion step forth to defend their principles, have not considered them ?

43 The impartial reader is intreated to remark throughout your whole performance how confident you are in asserting, and withall how modest in proving or explaining : How frequent it is with you to employ figures and tropes instead of reasons : How many difficulties proposed in the *Analyst* are discreetly overlooked by you, and what strange work you make with the rest : How grossly you mistake and misrepresent, and how little you practise the advice which you so liberally bestow. Believe me, Sir, I had long and maturely considered the principles of the modern analysis, before I ventured to publish my thoughts thereupon in the *Analyst*. And, since the publication thereof, I have myself

freely conversed with mathematicians of all ranks, and some of
the ablest professors, as well as made it my business to be informed
of the opinions of others, being very desirous to hear what could
be said towards clearing my difficulties or answering my objections. But, though you are not afraid or ashamed to represent
the analysts as very clear and uniform in their conception of these
matters, yet I do solemnly affirm (and several of themselves know
it to be true) that I found no harmony or agreement among them,
but the reverse thereof, the greatest dissonance, and even con-
trariety of opinions, employed to explain what after all seemed
inexplicable.

44 Some fly to proportions between nothings. Some reject
quantities because infinitesimal. Others allow only finite quantities and reject them because inconsiderable. Others place the
method of fluxions on a foot with that of *exhaustions*, and admit
nothing new therein. Some maintain the clear conception of
fluxions. Others hold they can demonstrate about things incomprehensible. Some would prove the algorism of fluxions by *re-
ductio ad absurdum* ; others *a priori*. Some hold the evanescent
increments to be real quantities, some to be nothings, some to be
limits. As many men, so many minds : Each differing one from
another, and all from Sir Isaac Newton. Some plead inaccurate
expressions in the great author, whereby they would draw him
to speak their sense ; not considering that if he meant as they do,
he could not want words to express his meaning. Others are
magisterial and positive, say they are satisfied, and that is all,
not considering that we, who deny Sir Isaac Newton's authority,
shall not submit to that of his disciples. Some insist that the
conclusions are true, and therefore the principles, not considering
what hath been largely said in the *Analyst* [1] on that head. Lastly
several (and those none of the meanest) frankly owned the objections to be unanswerable. All which I mention by way of antidote
to your false colours : and that the unprejudiced inquirer after
truth may see it is not without foundation that I call on the
celebrated mathematicians of the present age to clear up these
obscure analytics, and concur in giving to the publick some
consistent and intelligible account of the principles of their great
Master : which if they do not, I believe the world will take it
for granted that they cannot.

45 Having gone through your defence of the British mathematicians, I find in the next place, that you attack me on a

[1] Sect. 19, 20, &c.

point of metaphysics [1] with what success the reader will determine.
I had upon another occasion many years ago wrote against
abstract general ideas.[2]   In opposition to which, you declare
yourself to adhere to the vulgar opinion, that neither geometry
nor any other general science can subsist without general ideas
(p. 74).   This implies that I hold there are no general ideas.
But I hold the direct contrary, that there are indeed general
ideas, but not formed by abstraction in the manner set forth
by Mr. Locke.   To me it is plain there is no consistent idea the
likeness whereof may not really exist : whatsoever therefore is
said to be somewhat which cannot exist, the idea thereof must
be inconsistent.   Mr. Locke acknowledgeth it doth require pains
and skill to form his general idea of a triangle.   He further
expressly saith it must be neither oblique nor rectangular, neither
equilateral nor scalenum ; but all and none of these at once.
He also saith it is an idea wherein some parts of several different
and inconsistent ideas are put together.[3]   All this looks very like
a contradiction.   But to put the matter past dispute, it must be
noted that he affirms it to be somewhat imperfect that cannot exist ;
consequently the idea thereof is impossible or inconsistent.

46 I desire to know whether it is not possible for anything
to exist which doth not include a contradiction : And if it is,
whether we may not infer that what cannot possibly exist, the
same doth include a contradiction :   I further desire to know,
whether the reader can frame a distinct idea of anything that
includes a contradiction ?   For my part, I cannot, nor consequently of the above-mentioned triangle ; though you (who it
seems know better than myself what I can do) are pleased to
assure me of the contrary.   Again, I ask whether that which
it is above the power of man to form a compleat idea of, may

---

[1] [Dr. Jurin's attack, at first sight irrelevant, is a tribute to Berkeley's
clear vision of the epistemological consequences of Locke's doctrine of abstract
ideas. Berkeley rejected that doctrine because it helped to bolster up belief
in matter, and because by taking attention from concrete reality it is ' productive of numberless difficulties and disputes ' such as those about infinitesimals. Fraser in his note on this passage speaks of Berkeley's ' withdrawal
in the third edition (of the *Alciphron*) against abstract general ideas.' This
was a bad blunder on Fraser's part which has seriously misled scholars for the
past half-century. Berkeley never withdrew or weakened on abstract ideas,
and in the third edition of the *Alciphron* he is just as strong on the point, as he
is here or in the *Principles*.—Ed.]
[2] Introduction to a *Treatise concerning the Principles of Human Knowledge* printed
in the year MDCCX.
[3] *Essay on Human Understanding*, bk. IV. c. vii. § 9.

not be called incomprehensible ? And whether the reader can frame a complete idea of this imperfect impossible triangle ? And if not, whether it doth not follow that it is incomprehensible ? It should seem that a distinct aggregate of a few consistent parts was nothing so difficult to conceive or impossible to exist ; and that, therefore, your comment must be wide of the author's meaning. You give me to understand (p. 82) that this account of a general triangle was a trap which Mr. Locke set to catch fools. Who is caught therein let the reader judge.

47 It is Mr. Locke's opinion that every general name stands for a general *abstract* idea, which prescinds from the species or individuals comprehended under it. Thus, for example, according to him, the general name *colour* stands for an idea which is neither blue, red, green, nor any other particular colour, but somewhat distinct and abstracted from them all. To me it seems the word *colour* is only a more general name applicable to all and each of the particular colours ; while the other specific names, as blue, red, green, and the like, are each restrained to a more limited signification. The same may be said of the word triangle. Let the reader judge whether this be not the case ; and whether he can distinctly frame such an idea of colour as shall prescind from all the species thereof, or of a triangle which shall answer Mr. Locke's account, prescinding and abstracting from all the particular sorts of triangles, in the manner aforesaid.

48 I intreat my reader to think. For if he doth not, he may be under some influence from your confident and positive way of talking. But any one who thinks may, if I mistake not, plainly perceive that you are deluded, as it often happens, by mistaking the terms for ideas. Nothing is easier than to define in terms or words that which is incomprehensible in idea ; forasmuch as any words can be either separated or joined as you please, but ideas always cannot. It is as easy to say a round square as an oblong square, though the former be inconceivable. If the reader will but take a little care to distinguish between the definition and the idea, between words or expressions and the conceptions of the mind, he will judge of the truth of what I now advance, and clearly perceive how far you are mistaken in attempting to illustrate Mr. Locke's doctrine, and where your mistake lies. Or, if the reader is minded to make a short work, he needs only at once to try whether, laying aside the words, he can frame in his mind the idea of an impossible triangle ; upon which trial the issue of this dispute may be fairly put. This doctrine of

abstract general ideas seemed to me a capital errour, productive of numberless difficulties and disputes, that runs not only throughout Mr. Locke's book, but through most parts of learning. Consequently, my animadversions thereupon were not an effect of being inclined to carp or cavil at a single passage, as you would wrongfully insinuate, but proceeded from a love of truth, and a desire to banish, so far as in me lay, false principles and wrong ways of thinking, without respect of persons. And indeed, though you and other party-men are violently attached to your respective Masters, yet I, who profess myself only attached to truth, see no reason why I may not as freely animadvert on Mr. Locke or Sir Isaac Newton, as they would on Aristotle or Descartes. Certainly the more extensive the influence of any errour, and the greater the authority which supports it, the more it deserves to be considered and detected by sincere inquirers after knowledge.

49 In the close of your performance, you let me understand that your zeal for truth and the reputation of your Masters hath occasioned your reprehending me with the utmost freedom. And it must be owned you have shewn a singular talent therein. But I am comforted under the severity of your reprehensions, when I consider the weakness of your arguments, which, were they as strong as your reproofs, could leave no doubt in the mind of the reader concerning the matters in dispute between us. As it is, I leave him to reflect and examine by your light how clearly he is enabled to conceive a fluxion, or the fluxion of a fluxion, a part infinitely small subdivided into an infinity of parts, a nascent or evanescent increment, that which is neither something nor nothing, a triangle formed in a point, velocity without motion, and the rest of those *arcana* of the modern analysis. To conclude, I had some thoughts of advising you how to conduct yourself for the future, in return for the advice you have so freely imparted to me : but, as you think it becomes me rather to inform myself than instruct others, I shall, for my further information, take leave to propose a few Queries to those learned gentlemen of Cambridge, whom you associate with yourself and represent as being equally surprised at the tendency of my *Analyst*.

50 I desire to know whether those who can neither demonstrate nor conceive the principles of the modern analysis, and yet give in to it, may not be justly said to have faith, and be styled believers of mysteries? Whether it is impossible to find among the physicians, mechanical philosophers, mathematicians and philomathematicians of the present age, some such believers

who yet deride Christians for their belief of mysteries ? Whether with such men it is not a fair, reasonable, and legitimate method to use the *argumentum ad hominem* ? And being so, whether it ought to surprise either Christians or scholars ? Whether in an age wherein so many pretenders to science attack the Christian religion, we may not be allowed to make reprisals, in order to shew that the irreligion of those men is not to be presumed an effect of deep and just thinking ? Whether an attempt to detect false reasonings, and remedy defects in mathematics, ought to be ill received by mathematicians ? Whether the introducing more easy methods and more intelligible principles in any science should be discountenanced ? Whether there may not be fair objections as well as cavils ? And whether to inquire diligently into the meaning of terms and the proof of propositions, not excepting against anything without assigning a reason, nor affecting to mistake the signification of words, or stick at an expression where the sense was clear, but considering the subject in all lights, sincerely endeavouring to find out any sense or meaning whatsoever, candidly setting forth what seems obscure and what fallacious, and calling upon those who profess the know-ledge of such matters to explain them, whether I say such a proceeding can be justly called cavilling ? Whether there be an *ipse dixit* erected ? And, if so, when, where, by whom, and upon what authority ? Whether even where authority was to take place, one might not hope the mathematics, at least, would be excepted ? Whether the chief end, in making mathematics so considerable a part of academical education, be not to form in the minds of young students habits of just and exact reasoning ? And whether the study of abstruse and subtile matters can con-duce to this end, unless they are well understood, examined, and sifted to the bottom ? Whether, therefore, the bringing geo-metrical demonstrations to the severest test of reason should be reckoned a discouragement to the studies of any learned society ? Whether to separate the clear parts of things from the obscure, to distinguish the real principles whereon truths rest and whence they are derived, and to proportion the just measures of assent according to the various degrees of evidence, be an useless or unworthy undertaking ? Whether the making more of an argu-ment than it will bear, and placing it in an undue rank of evidence, be not the likely way to disparage it ? Whether it may not be of some use, to provoke and stir up the learned professors to explain a part of mathematical learning which is acknowledged to be most profound, difficult, and obscure, and at the same time set forth by *Philalethes* and many others as the greatest instance that has ever been given of the extent of human abilities ? Whether for the sake of a great man's discoveries, we must adopt his errours ? Lastly, whether in an age wherein all other principles are canvassed with the utmost freedom, the principles of Fluxions are to be alone excepted ?

AN APPENDIX

CONCERNING

MR WALTON'S VINDICATION OF SIR ISAAC NEWTON'S
PRINCIPLES OF FLUXIONS

1 I HAD no sooner considered the performance of *Philalethes*, but Mr. Walton's *Vindication of Fluxions* was put into my hands. As this Dublin professor gleans after the *Cantabrigian*, only endeavouring to translate a few passages from Sir Isaac Newton's *Principia*, and enlarge on a hint or two of *Philalethes*, he deserves no particular notice. It may suffice to advertise the reader that the foregoing defence contains a full and explicit answer to Mr. Walton, as he will find, if he thinks it worth his pains to read what this gentleman hath written, and compare it therewith : Particularly with Sect. 18, 20, 30, 32, 33, 34, 35, 36, 43. It is not, I am sure, worth mine to repeat the same things, or confute the same notions twice over, in mere regard to a writer who hath copied even the manners of *Philalethes*, and whom in answering the other I have, if I am not much mistaken, sufficiently answered.

2 Mr. Walton touches on the same points that the other had touched upon before him. He pursues a hint which the other had given [1] about Sir Isaac's first Section concerning the *rationes primæ et ultimæ*. He discreetly avoids, like the other, to say one syllable of second, third, or fourth fluxions, and of divers other points mentioned in the *Analyst*, about all which I observe in him a most prudent and profound silence. And yet he very modestly gives his reader to understand that he is able to clear up all difficulties and objections that have ever been made (p. 5). Mr. Walton, in the beginning, like *Philalethes*, from a particular case makes a general inference, supposing that Infidelity to be imputed to mathematicians in general which I suppose only in the person to whom the *Analyst* was addressed, and certain other persons of the same mind with him. Whether this extraordinary way of reasoning be the cause or effect of his passion, I know not : But before I had got to the end of his *Vindication*, I ceased to be surprized at his

---

[1] *Philalethes*, p. 32.

logic and his temper in the beginning. The double errour, which in the *Analyst* was plainly meant to belong to others, he with *Philalethes* (whose very oversights he adopts) supposeth to have been ascribed to Sir Isaac Newton (p. 36). And this writer also, as well as the *Cantabrigian*, must needs take upon him to explain the motive of my writing against fluxions : which he gives out, with great assurance, to have been because Sir Isaac Newton had presumed to interpose in prophecies and revelations, and to decide in religious affairs (p. 4) ; which is so far from being true that, on the contrary, I have a high value for those learned remains of that great man, whose original and free genius is an eternal reproach to that tribe of followers who are always imitating but never resemble him. This specimen of Mr. Walton's truth will be a warning to the reader to use his own eyes, and in obscure points never to trust the gentleman's candour, who dares to misrepresent the plainest.

3 I was thinking to have said no more concerning this author's performance, but, lest he should imagine himself too much neglected, I intreat the reader to have the patience to peruse it ; and if he finds any one point of the doctrine of fluxions cleared up, or any one objection in the *Analyst* answered, or so much as fairly stated, let him then make his compliments to the author. But, if he can no more make sense of what this gentleman has written than I can, he will need no answer to it. Nothing is easier than for a man to translate, or copy, or compose a plausible discourse of some pages in technical terms, whereby he shall make a shew of saying somewhat, although neither the reader nor himself understand one tittle of it. Whether this be the case of Mr. Walton, and whether he understands either Sir Isaac Newton, or me, or himself (whatever I may think), I shall not take upon me to say. But one thing I know, that many an unmeaning speech passeth for significant by the mere assurance of the speaker, till he cometh to be catechised upon it ; and then the truth sheweth itself. This vindicator, indeed, by his dissembling nine parts in ten of the difficulties proposed in the *Analyst*, sheweth no inclination to be catechised by me. But his scholars have a right to be informed. I therefore recommend it to them not to be imposed on by hard words and magisterial assertions, but carefully to pry into his sense, and sift his meaning, and particularly to insist on a distinct answer to the following Questions.

4 Let them ask him, whether he can conceive velocity without motion, or motion without extension, or extension without magnitude ? If he answers that he can, let him teach them to do

the same.   If he cannot, let him be asked, how he reconciles the idea of a fluxion which he gives (p. 13) with common sense ?— Again, let him be asked, whether nothing be not the product of nothing multiplied by something ?   And, if so, when the difference between the gnomon and the sum of the rectangles [1] vanisheth, whether the rectangles themselves do not also vanish ? *i.e.* when *ab* is nothing, whether $Ab + Ba$ be not also nothing ? *i.e.* whether the momentum of *AB* be not nothing ?   Let him then be asked, what his momentums are good for, when they are thus brought to nothing ?   Again, I wish he were asked to explain the difference between a magnitude infinitely small and a magnitude infinitely diminished.   If he saith, there is no difference :   Then let him be further asked, how he dares to explain the method of fluxions, by the *ratio* of magnitudes infinitely diminished (p. 9), when Sir Isaac Newton hath expressly excluded all consideration of quantities infinitely small ? [2]   If this able vindicator should say that quantities infinitely diminished are nothing at all, and consequently that, according to him, the first and last *ratios* are proportions between nothings, let him be desired to make sense of this, or explain what he means by *proportion between nothings*.   If he should say, the ultimate proportions are the *ratios* of mere limits, then let him be asked how the limits of lines can be proportioned or divided ?   After all, who knows but this gentleman, who hath already complained of me for an uncommon way of treating mathematics and mathematicians (p. 5), may (as well as the *Cantabrigian*) cry out *Spain* and the *Inquisition !* when he finds himself thus closely pursued and beset with interrogatories ?   That we may not, therefore, seem too hard on an innocent man, who probably meant nothing, but was betrayed by following another into difficulties and straits that he was not aware of, I shall propose one single expedient, by which his disciples (whom it most concerns) may soon satisfy themselves whether this Vindicator really understands what he takes upon him to vindicate.   It is, in short, that they would ask him to explain the second, third, or fourth fluxions upon his principles.   Be this the touchstone of his Vindication.   If he can do it, I shall own myself much mistaken :   If he cannot, it will be evident that he was much mistaken in himself, when he presumed to defend fluxions without so much as knowing what they are.   So having put the merits of the cause on this issue, I leave him to be tried by his scholars.

---

[1] See *Vindication*, p. 17.   [2] See *the Introduction to his Quadratures.*

Reasons for not replying to Mr. Walton's *Full Answer*

in a letter to P. T. P.

First printed in 1735

EDITOR'S INTRODUCTION

WALTON dealt with the questions propounded in Berkeley's appendix to his *Defence* in *The Catechism of the author of The Minute Philosopher fully answered.* Berkeley replied with his *Reasons for not replying to Mr. Walton's full answer in a letter to P. T. P.*, both tracts appearing in 1735. Berkeley undertakes (S. 3) to examine Walton's work ' throughout every article of his full answer,' and the title of the tract therefore contains a touch of humour, probably intentional. Berkeley replies with reasons for not replying, which consist in his rather laboured pretence, not consistently sustained, that Walton was attacking Newton under guise of defending him. Let the fluxionists answer Walton ; it is not for Berkeley to fall out with his secret friend and ally !

The dispute made some noise, and Walton was evidently more regarded than Berkeley would have us think ; for his *Catechism* went to two editions in the one year, and to the second edition Walton appended a serious and detailed reply to Berkeley's *Reasons for not replying* . . .

This pamphlet was Berkeley's last utterance [1] on the questions raised by the *Analyst*, and from this on the debate was confined to the mathematicians themselves.

Berkeley addresses his ' Letter ' to ' P.T.P.', and I have found no suggestion as to the identity of the addressee. In the tar-water correspondence Berkeley addressed several public letters to his friend and Dublin agent, Thomas Prior, and possibly we have the same name here, slightly disguised. In the Berkeley Papers in the British Museum (MS. 39306, pp. 1–5) there is a manuscript copy of the tract in Berkeley's hand, corrected fair and corresponding closely with the printed text.

The tract was published in Dublin, ' Printed by M. Rhames, for R. Gunne, Bookseller in Capel Street.' The title-page bears the inscription, ' By the author of *The Minute Philosopher* ' with the motto, *Ex fumo lucem.*

[1] Professor Furlong points out that *Siris*, though not treating the mathematical problems directly, shows by implication that Berkeley's views had remained unchanged ; see Sects. 208–9, and, especially, Sect. 271, where Berkeley's footnote makes a slighting reference to the mathematicians and ' their doctrine of fluxions.'

REASONS FOR NOT REPLYING
TO MR. WALTON'S FULL ANSWER, &c.

1 THERE are some men that can neither give nor take an answer, but writing merely for the sake of writing multiply words to no purpose. There are also certain careless writers that in defiance of common sense publish such things as, though they are not ashamed to utter, yet, other men may well be ashamed to answer. Whether there be anything in Mr. Walton's method of vindicating Fluxions, that might justify my taking no further notice of him on the above-mentioned considerations, I leave you and every other reader to judge. But those, Sir, are not the reasons I shall assign for not replying to Mr. Walton's full answer. The true reason is, that he seems at bottom a facetious man, who under the colour of an opponent writes on my side of the question, and really believes no more than I do of Sir Isaac Newton's doctrine about fluxions, which he exposes, contradicts, and confutes with great skill and humour, under the masque of a grave vindication.

2 At first I considered him in another light, as one who had good reason for keeping to the beaten track, who had been used to dictate, who had terms of art at will, but was indeed at small trouble about putting them together, and perfectly easy about his reader's understanding them. It must be owned, in an age of so much ludicrous humour, it is not every one can at first sight discern a writer's real design. But, be a man's assertions ever so strong in favour of a doctrine, yet if his reasonings are directly levelled against it, whatever question there may be about the matter in dispute, there can be none about the intention of the writer. Should a person, so knowing and discreet as Mr. Walton, thwart and contradict Sir Isaac Newton under pretence of defending his fluxions, and should he at every turn say such uncouth things of these same fluxions, and place them in such odd lights as must set all men in their wits against them, could I hope for a better second in this cause? Or could there remain any doubt of his being a disguised Freethinker in mathematics, who defended fluxions just as a certain Freethinker in religion did the rights of the Christian church?

3 Mr. Walton indeed after his free manner calls my *Analyst* a libel.[1] But this ingenious gentleman well knows a bad vindication is the bitterest libel. Had you a mind, Sir, to betray and ridicule any cause under the notion of vindicating it, would you not think it the right way to be very strong and dogmatical in the affirmative, and very weak and puzzled in the argumentative parts of your performance? To utter contradictions and paradoxes without remorse, and to be at no pains about reconciling or explaining them? And with great good humour, to be at perpetual variance with yourself and the author you pretend to vindicate? How successfully Mr. Walton hath practised these arts, and how much to the honour of the great client he would seem to take under his protection, I shall particularly examine throughout every article of his full answer.

4 First then, saith Mr. Walton, ' I am to be asked, whether I can conceive velocity without motion, or motion without extension, or extension without magnitude? ' To which he answereth in positive terms, that he can conceive velocity and motion in a point (p. 7). And to make out this he undertakes to demonstrate, ' that if a thing be moved by an agent operating continually with the same force, the velocity will not be the same in any two different points of the described space. But that it must vary upon the least change of space.' Now admitting thus much to be demonstrated, yet I am still at a loss to conceive how Mr. Walton's conclusion will follow, to wit, ' that I am greatly mistaken in imagining there can be no motion, no velocity, in a point of space (p. 10). Pray, Sir, consider his reasoning. The same velocity cannot be in two points of space ; therefore velocity can be in a point of space. Would it not be just as good reasoning to say, the same man cannot be in two nutshels ; therefore a man can be in a nutshel? Again, velocity must vary upon the least change of space ; therefore there may be velocity without space. Make sense of this if you can. What have these consequences to do with their premises? Who but Mr. Walton could have inferred them? Or how could even he have inferred them had it not been in jest?

5 Suppose the center of a falling body to describe a line, divide the time of its fall into equal parts, for instance, into minutes. The spaces described in those equal parts of time will be unequal. That is, from whatsoever points of the described line you measure a minute's descent, you will still find it a different

[1] *Vindication*, p. 1.

space. This is true. But how or why from this plain truth a man should infer, that motion can be conceived in a point, is to me as obscure as any the most obscure mysteries that occur in this profound author. Let the reader make the best of it. For my part, I can as easily conceive Mr. Walton should walk without stirring, as I can his idea of motion without space. After all, the question was not whether motion could be proved to exist in a point, but only whether it could be conceived in a point. For, as to the proof of things impossible, some men have a way of proving that may equally prove anything. But I much question whether any reader of common sense will undertake to conceive what this pleasant man at inference undertakes to prove.

6 If Mr. Walton really meant to defend the author of the fluxionary method, would he not have done it in a way consistent with this illustrious author's own principles? Let us now see what may be Sir Isaac's notion about this matter. He distinguisheth two sorts of motion, absolute and relative. The former he defineth to be a translation from absolute place to absolute place, the latter from one relative place to another.[1] Mr. Walton's is plainly neither of these sorts of motion, but some third kind, which what it is, I am at a loss to comprehend. But I can clearly comprehend that, if we admit motion without space, then Sir Isaac Newton's account of it must be wrong : For place by which he defines motion is, according to him, a part of space. And if so, then this notable defender hath cut out new work for himself to defend and explain. But about this, if I mistake not, he will be very easy. For, as I said before, he seems at bottom a back friend [2] to that great man ; which opinion you will see further confirmed in the sequel.

7 I shall no more ask Mr. Walton to explain anything. For I can honestly say, the more he explains, the more I am puzzled. But I will ask his readers to explain, by what art a man may conceive motion without space. And, supposing this to be done, in the second place to explain, how it consists with Sir Isaac Newton's account of motion. Is it not evident that Mr. Walton hath deserted from his old master, and been at some pains to expose him, while he defends one part of his principles by overturning another? Let any reader tell me, what Mr. Walton means by motion, or if he can guess, what this third kind is,

---

[1] See Schol. def. VIII. *Philos. Nat. Princip. Math.*
[2] [' Backfriend, a friend who *kept back*, and did not come forward to assist. . . .' O.E. Dict.—Ed.]

which is neither absolute nor relative, which exists in a point, which may be conceived without space. This learned professor saith, ' I have no clear conception of the principles of motion ' (p. 24). And in another place (p. 7) he saith, ' I might have conceived velocity in a point, if I had understood and considered the nature of motion.' I believe I am not alone in not understanding his principles. For myself, I freely confess the case to be desperate. I neither understand them, nor have any hopes of ever being able to understand them.

8 Being now satisfied that Mr. Walton's aim is not to clear up or defend Sir Isaac's principles, but rather to contradict and expose them, you will not, I suppose, think it strange, if instead of putting questions to this intrepid answerer, who is never at a loss, how often soever his readers may, I entreat you, or any other man of plain sense, to read the following passage, cited from the thirty-first section of the *Analyst*, and then try to apply Mr. Walton's answer to it : Whereby you will clearly perceive what a vein of raillery that gentleman is master of. ' Velocity necessarily implies both time and space, and cannot be conceived without them. And if the velocities of nascent or evanescent quantities, *i.e.* abstracted from time and space, may not be comprehended, how can we comprehend and demonstrate their proportions ? Or consider their *rationes primæ & ultimæ*. For to consider the proportion or ratio of things implieth that such things have magnitude : That such their magnitudes may be measured, and their relations to each other known. But, as there is no measure of velocity except time and space, the proportion of velocities being only compounded of the direct proportion of the spaces and the reciprocal proportion of the times ; doth it not follow, that to talk of investigating, obtaining, and considering the proportions of velocities, exclusively of time and space, is to talk unintelligibly ? ' Apply now, as I said, Mr. Walton's full answer, and you will soon find how fully you are enlightened about the nature of fluxions.

9 In the following article of Mr. Walton's full answer, he saith divers curious things, which being derived from this same principle, that motion may be conceived in a point, are altogether as incomprehensible as the origine from whence they flow. It is obvious and natural to suppose *Ab* and *Ba* [1] to be rectangles produced from finite lines multiplied by increments. Mr. Walton indeed supposeth that when the increments vanish or

[1] See *Nat. Phil. Princip. Math.* l. 2. lem. 2.

become nothing the velocities remain, which being multiplied by finite lines produce those rectangles (p. 13). But admitting the velocities to remain, yet how can any one conceive a rectangular surface to be produced from a line multiplied by velocity, otherwise than by supposing such line multiplied by a line or increment which shall be exponent of or proportional to such velocity? You may try to conceive it otherwise. I must own I cannot. Is not the increment of a rectangle itself a rectangle? must not then *Ab* and *Ba* be rectangles? and must not the coefficients or sides of rectangles be lines? Consequently are not *b* and *a* lines, or (which is the same thing) increments of lines? These increments may indeed be considered as proportional to and exponents of velocity. But exclusive of such exponents to talk of rectangles under lines and velocities is, I conceive, to talk unintelligibly. And yet this is what Mr. Walton doth, when he maketh *b* and *a* in the rectangles *Ab* and *Ba* to denote mere velocities.

10 As to the question, whether nothing be not the product of nothing multiplied by something, Mr. Walton is pleased to answer in the affirmative. And nevertheless, when *ab* is nothing, that is, when *a* and *b* are nothing, he denies that *Ab* + *Ba* is nothing. This is one of those many inconsistencies which I leave the reader to reconcile. But, saith Mr. Walton, the sides of the given rectangle still remain, which two sides according to him must form the increment of the flowing rectangle. But in this he directly contradicts Sir Isaac Newton, who asserts that *Ab* +*Ba* and not *A* +*B* is the increment of the rectangle *AB*. And, indeed, how is it possible a line should be the increment of a surface? *Laterum incrementis totis a et b generatur rectanguli incrementum Ab +Ba,* are the words of Sir Isaac,[1] which words seem utterly inconsistent with Mr. Walton's doctrine. But no wonder that gentleman should not agree with Sir Isaac, since he cannot agree even with himself; but contradicts what he saith elsewhere as the reader may see, even before he gets to the end of that same section, wherein he hath told us, that ' the gnomon and the sum of the two rectangles are turned into those two sides by a retroverted motion ' (p. 11 and 12). Which proposition if you or any other person shall try to make sense of, you may possibly be convinced that this profound author is as much at variance with common sense as he is with himself and Sir Isaac Newton.

11 Mr. Walton in the ninth page of his Vindication, in order to explain the nature of fluxions, saith that ' to obtain

---

[1] See *Nat. Phil. Princip. Math.* l. 2. lem. 2.

the last ratio of synchronal increments, the magnitude of those increments must be infinitely diminished.' Notwithstanding which, in the twenty-third page of his full answer he chargeth me as greatly mistaken, in supposing that he explained the doctrine of fluxions by the ratio of magnitudes infinitely diminished. It is an easy matter for any author to write so as to betray his readers into mistakes about his meaning. But then it is not easy to conceive what right he hath to upbraid them with such their mistakes. If I have mistaken his sense, let any one judge if he did not fairly lead me into the mistake. When a man puzzleth his reader, saith and unsaith, useth ambiguous terms and obscure terms, and putteth them together in so perverse a manner that it is odds you can make out no sense at all, or, if any, wrong sense, pray who is in fault but the writer himself? Let any one consider Mr. Walton's own words, and then say whether I am not justified in making this remark.

12 In the twentieth page of his full answer, Mr. Walton tells us that ' fluxions are measured by the first or last proportions of isochronal increments generated or destroyed by motion.' A little after he saith, these ratios subsist when the isochronal increments have no magnitude. Now, I would fain know whether the isochronal increments themselves subsist when they have no magnitude? Whether by isochronal increments we are not to understand increments generated in equal times? Whether there can be an increment where there is no increase, or increase where there is no magnitude? Whether if magnitudes are not generated in those equal times, what else is generated therein, or what else is it that Mr. Walton calls isochronal? I ask the reader these questions. I dare not ask Mr. Walton. For, as I hinted before, the subject grows still more obscure in proportion as this able writer attempts to illustrate it.

13 We are told (p. 22) ' that the first or last ratio of the isochronal spaces hath a real existence, forasmuch as it is equal to the ratio of the two motions of two points ; which motions, subsisting when the isochronal spaces are nothing, preserve the existence of the first or last ratio of these spaces, or keep it from being a ratio of nothings.' In order to assist your understanding, it must not be omitted that the said two points are supposed to exist at the same time in one point, and to be moved different ways without stirring from that point. Mr. Walton hath the conscience to call this riddle a full and clear answer : to make sense of which you must suppose it one of his ironies. In the

next and last article of his performance, you still find him proceed in the same vein of raillery upon fluxions.

14 It will be allowed that who ever seriously undertook to explain the second, third, and fourth fluxions of Sir Isaac Newton would have done it in a way agreeable to that great man's own doctrine. What Sir Isaac's precise notion is I will not pretend to say. And yet I will venture to say, it is something that cannot be explained by the three dimensions of a cube. I frankly own, I do not understand Sir Isaac's doctrine so far as to frame a positive idea of his fluxions. I have, nevertheless, a negative conception thereof, so far as to see that Mr. Walton is in jest, or (if in earnest) that he understands it no more than I do.

15 Sir Isaac tells us that he considers indeterminate quantities as flowing, or in other words, as increasing or decreasing by a perpetual motion. Which quantities he denotes by the latter letters of the alphabet, and their fluxions or celerities of increasing by the same letters pointed over head, and the fluxions of fluxions or second fluxions, *i.e.* the mutations more or less swift of the first celerities, by the same letters pointed with double points; and the mutations of those mutations of the first mutations or fluxions or celerities of increasing, which he calls fluxions of fluxions of fluxions, or third fluxions, by three points; the fourth fluxions by four points; the fifth by five; and so on.[1] Sir Isaac, you see, speaks of quantity in general. And in the *Analyst* the doctrine is exemplified and the case is put in lines. Now in lines, where there is only one dimension, how are we enabled to conceive second, third, or fourth fluxions, by conceiving the generation of three dimensions in a cube? Let any one but read what Sir Isaac Newton or what I have said, and then apply what Mr. Walton hath written about the three dimensions of a cube, and see whether the difficulties are solved or the doctrine made one whit the clearer by this explication.

16 That you may the better judge of the merit of this part of Mr. Walton's performance, I shall beg leave to set down a passage or two from the *Analyst*. ' As it is impossible to conceive velocity without time or space, without either finite length or finite duration, it must seem above the power of man to comprehend even the first fluxions. And if the first are incomprehensible, what shall we say of the second and third fluxions, &c.? He who can conceive the beginning of a beginning, or the end of an end, somewhat before the first or after the last, may perhaps

[1] See his Treatise *De Quadratura Curvarum.*

be sharpsighted enough to conceive these things. But most men, I believe, will find it impossible to understand them in any sense whatsoever. One would think that men could not speak too exactly on so nice a subject. And yet we may often observe that the exponents of fluxions, or notes representing fluxions are confounded with the fluxions themselves. Is not this the case when, just after the fluxions of flowing quantities were said to be the celerities of their increasing, and the second fluxions to be the mutations of the first fluxions or celerities, we are told that $\overset{"}{z}.\ \overset{\cdot}{z}.\ z.\ \dot{z}.\ \ddot{z}.\ \dot{z}.$ represents a series of quantities whereof each subsequent quantity is the fluxion of the preceding ; and each foregoing is a fluent quantity having the following one for its fluxion ? Divers series of quantities and expressions, geometrical and algebraical, may be easily conceived in lines, in surfaces, in species, to be continued without end or limit. But it will not be found so easy to conceive a series, either of mere velocities or of mere nascent increments, distinct therefrom and corresponding thereunto.' [1] Compare what is here said with Mr. Walton's genesis of a cube, and you will then clearly see how far this answerer is from explaining the nature of second, third, and fourth fluxions : And how justly I might repay that gentleman in kind, and tell him in his own language, that *all his skill is vain and impertinent.* (*Vind.* p. 36.)

17 But it doth not become me to find fault with this learned professor, who at bottom militates on my side, and in this very section makes it his business directly to overthrow Sir Isaac Newton's doctrine. For he saith in plain terms that there can be no fourth fluxion of a cube (p. 25), that is, there can be no second fluxion of a line, and *à fortiori*, no third, fourth, fifth, &c. Insomuch that, with one single dash of his pen, Mr. Walton destroys, to the great relief of the learned world, an indefinite rank of fluxions of different orders that might have reached from pole to pole. I had distinctly pointed out the difficulties, in several parts both of my *Analyst* and *Defence*, and I leave you to judge whether he explains or even attempts to explain one of them. Instead thereof he tell us of the trine dimension of a cube generated by motion : Whence he takes occasion, as hath been observed, to explode Sir Isaac's own doctrine, which is utterly inconsistent with Mr. Walton's. And can you now doubt the real design of this egregious vindicator ?

18 Before ever Sir Isaac Newton thought of his fluxions,

[1] *Analyst,* Sect. 44, 45, 46.

everybody knew there were three dimensions in a cube, and that a solid might be generated by the motion of a surface, a surface by the motion of a line, and a line by the motion of a point. And this in effect is all we know from Mr. Walton's explication. As for his dwelling so minutely on the genesis of the solid parts of a cube, a thing so foreign from the purpose, the only rational account I can give of it is that Mr. Walton, by puzzling the imagination of his vulgar readers, hoped the better to disguise his betraying the doctrine of his great client, which to a discerning eye he manifestly gives up ; and instead thereof humourously substitutes what all the world knew before Sir Isaac was born, to wit, the three dimensions of a cube and the genesis thereof by motion.

19 Upon the whole, I appeal to you and every intelligent reader, whether this thing, which Mr. Walton is pleased ironically to call a full answer, doth not carry throughout a sly insinuation that the profound science of fluxions cannot be maintained but by the help of most unintelligible paradoxes and inconsistencies. So far, indeed, as affirmations go, he sheweth himself an able support of Sir Isaac Newton. But then in his reasonings he drops that great man upon the most important points, to wit, his doctrine of motion and his doctrine of fluxions ; not regarding how far the demonstration of his famous *Principia* is interested therein. To convince you still more and more of the truth hereof, do but reflect a little on Mr. Walton's conduct. Can you think it probable that so learned and clear-headed a writer would have laid down such a direct repugnancy to common sense, as his idea of motion in a point, for the groundwork of his explanation, had it been his real intention to explain ? Or can you suppose he would have been absolutely silent on so many points urged home both in the *Analyst* and *Defence*, which it concerned a vindicator of Sir Isaac not to have overlooked ? Can you imagine that if he meant seriously to defend the doctrine of fluxions, he would have contented himself with barely asserting that ' Sir Isaac Newton in the Introduction to his Quadrature of Curves, in the second lemma of the second book and in the scholium to the first section of the first book of his Principles of Philosophy, hath delivered his doctrine of fluxions in so clear and distinct a manner, without the least inconsistency in terms or arguments, that one would have thought it impossible for any person not to have understood him ? ' (p. 30.)

20 Is it possible, I say, that Mr. Walton could in earnest

hope we should take his bare word, as so much more credible than Sir Isaac's, and not rather have endeavoured to answer the questions, and reconcile the difficulties set forth in my *Defence of Free-thinking*, for instance, in Sect. 36 ?   Wherein I intreat my antagonist to explain ' whether Sir Isaac's momentum be a finite quantity, or an infinitesimal, or a mere limit,' adding, ' If you say a finite quantity, be pleased to reconcile this with what he saith in the scholium of the second lemma of the first section of the first book of his Principles : *Cave intelligas quantitates magnitudine determinatas, sed cogita semper diminuendas sine limite.*   If you say, an infinitesimal : Reconcile this with what is said in the Introduction to his Quadratures : *Volui ostendere quod in methodo fluxionum non opus sit figuras infinite parvas in geometriam introducere.* If you should say it is a mere limit, be pleased to reconcile this with what we find in the first case of the second lemma in the second book of his Principles : *Ubi de lateribus A & B deerant momentorum dimidia, &c.* where the moments are supposed to be divided.' I shall scarce think it worth my while to bestow a serious thought on any writer who shall pretend to maintain Sir Isaac's doctrine, and yet leave this passage without a reply. And the reader, I believe, will think with me that, in answer to difficulties distinctly proposed and insisted on, to offer nothing but a magisterial assertion is a mere grimace of one who made merry with fluxions, under the notion of defending them. And he will be further confirmed in this way of thinking, when he observes that Mr. Walton hath not said one syllable in reply to those several sections of my *Defence* which I had particularly referred to, as containing a full answer to his *Vindication*. But it is no wonder, if with Sir Isaac's doctrine, he should drop also his own arguments in favour thereof.

21 I have been at the pains once for all to write this short comment on Mr. Walton, as the only way I could think of for making him intelligible, which will also serve as a key to his future writings on this subject. And I was the rather inclined to take this trouble, because it seemeth to me there is no part of learning that wants to be cleared up more than this same doctrine of fluxions, which hath hitherto walked about in a mist to the stupefaction of the literati of the present age. To conclude, I accept this professor's recantation ; nor am at all displeased at the ingenious method he takes to disguise it. Some zealous fluxionists may perhaps answer him.

FINIS

Arithmetica
and
Miscellanea Mathematica

First printed in 1707

EDITOR'S INTRODUCTION

THIS little work is curiously constructed. It is one book, and yet two. It is paged continuously throughout, but its two divisions are sharply separated, each having its own dedication and title-page. There is only one Preface which explains the aim of the *Arithmetica*, and the two title-pages partially overlap. We may fairly infer that the original nucleus of the work was the *Arithmetica* or (as it appears on the first part of the first title-page) *Arithmetica absque Algebra aut Euclide demonstrata,* and that the material covered by the second part of that title, *cui accesserunt cogitata nonnulla de radicibus surdis, de æstu aeris, de ludo algebraico, etc.* was later expanded by Berkeley and received the full length description on the second title-page, *Miscellanea Mathematica sive cogitata nonnulla de radicibus surdis, de æstu aeris, de cono æquilatero & cylindro eidem sphæræ circumscriptis, de ludo algebraico ; & parænetica quædam ad studium matheseos, præsertim algebræ.*

It was Berkeley's first publication, and he did not set his name on the title-page, which gives ' Autore . . . Art. Bac. Trin. Coll. Dub.' The authorship, however, has never been in doubt. Stock mentions the book in his *Life* of Berkeley and includes it in his edition of the works. The internal evidence, too, is conclusive. The imprint gives ' Londini ' with the date 1707. The mention of the author as a B.A. is sufficient to date the work in the earlier portion of that year ; for Berkeley took out his M.A. in July.

Most of these pieces, Berkeley says in his Preface, had been in his desk for nearly three years. They belong therefore to the earlier portion of the interval between his graduation as B.A. (1704) and his election to a fellowship which took place on 7 June 1707. Their publication early in that year may well have been made with an eye to that election and the statutory examination which preceded it. The work has the look of a fellowship thesis, specially designed to remove the impression that he disliked mathematics. We know from the *Philosophical Commentaries* that Berkeley about this time held very scornful views about some mathematics and some mathematicians, and if he did not keep those views to himself, College gossip would soon make him out ignorant of mathematics or prejudiced against them, and such gossip might weaken his chances of election.   Without some such background it would be hard to explain the repeated praise of ' suavissimum matheseos studium,' and the marked thanks to his tutor, Dr. Hall, the Vice-Provost, for encouraging him to study mathematics.

We must remember that after graduating B.A. Berkeley stayed on in College waiting for a vacancy on the staff, occupying his time with private tuitions (young Molyneux and Palliser were his pupils), with reading for fellowship, with miscellaneous writing, and with deep thinking about immaterialism.   A vacancy in the body of fellows occurred in the autumn of 1706, when Mr. Mullart resigned his fellowship, and ' went out on a College living.'   An election on the following Trinity Monday would be announced at once, and the candidates would at once begin to prepare for the open competitive examination, and of course a candidate with a book to his credit would improve his chances. In these pages Berkeley more than once refers to his other reading ' *aliis studiis occupato* ' ;   he admits the slight character of the publication (' *tenues istas studiorum meorum primitias* '), and promises a more important yield in days to come (' *potiora forsan posthac daturus* ').

A. C. Fraser in his notes repeatedly speaks as if there were two editions of the work ;   but no solid grounds for that supposition appear, and it is most unlikely that there would be any general demand for such a trifle.   There are three copies in the Trinity College Library, one of which has coloured end-papers and lacks the list of *Errata* and *Addenda* and the note ' *Ne quis forte putet . . .*' on the last page.   Fraser probably took his text from this imperfect copy (which may have been a presentation copy rushed through the press before the corrected issue was ready), and subsequently noticed the points of difference.

The biographical interest of the piece is considerable, and from his Game of Algebra, one can piece together vivid little pictures of College life in Berkeley's days, the gamblers, and chess-players, and the sad seclusion of the ' swots.'   The work further provides some striking evidence of the breadth and quality of Berkeley's education.   Here is a young student, barely twenty years of age, able to treat objectively and systematically of the principles and rules of Arithmetic, and able to express himself about them in good, idiomatic, and racy Latin.

An English translation of the work is contained in G. N. Wright's edition (1843) and is reproduced in G. Sampson's edition (1897).

The *Arithmetica* is dedicated to D. W. Palliser, son of the Archbishop of Cashel ; *the Miscellanea Mathematica* is dedicated to Samuel Molyneux. Both title-pages designate the author as ' Art. Bac. Trin. Col. Dub.', and along with the date, 1707, have the imprint, ' Londini : Typis J. Matthews, Impensis A. & J. Churchill, ad insigne Nigri Cygni in vico dicto Pater Noster Row : & Jer. Pepyat Dubl. Bibliop.'

Summary of Contents

Arithmetica Absque Algebra Aut Euclide Demonstrata

Preface. The rules of arithmetic may be demonstrated from the principles of arithmetic, without recourse to algebra (like Tacquet) or geometry. Part I. The notation and use of the numerical signs are set forth ; addition, subtraction, multiplication, and division, squares and square root, cube and cube root are explained. Part II. Fractions are explained, their addition, subtraction, multiplication, division, and reduction to lowest terms. Part III deals with proportion, alligation, arithmetical and geometrical progression, and logarithms.

De Radicibus Surdis

Advocates the use of a corresponding letter of the Greek alphabet in place of the radical sign. The radical sign covers a number of heterogeneous operations, and if it be discarded, the theory of surds can be more easily explained.

De Æstu Aeris

Criticizes the theory of the atmospheric tide in relation to the shape of the earth, put forth by Dr. Richard Mead, F.R.S. in his *De imperio solis et lunæ*, London, 1704, translated into English, 1708.

De Cono Æquilatero et Cylindro Eidem Sphæræ Circumscriptis

Between an equilateral cone and a cylinder circumscribed about the same sphere, there is the same sesquialterate ratio as to the whole surfaces, the solids, altitudes, and bases. Tacquet prided himself on the discovery, and puts it forth as rivalling those of Archimedes. ' It cannot be such a wonderful discovery,' says Berkeley, ' for I, a mere beginner in mathematics, discovered it myself two years ago.'

De Ludo Algebraico

Berkeley invented this ' game of algebra ' to furnish students with a mental exercise at once interesting and useful. On a small board, like that used for chess or draughts, mark a circle inscribed in a square. Set the figures, letters, angles, symbols, etc. as in the given diagram. The eye as it follows round the lines, angles, and symbols, forms algebraic equations with unknown quantities which provide the *question*. On the advantages of mathematics in general and of algebra in particular Berkeley quotes the *Philosophical Transactions*, Bacon, Descartes, Malebranche, and Locke's *On the conduct of the understanding*.

Arithmetica absque Algebra
aut Euclide demonstrata

The Text

MAXIMÆ SPEI PUERO,
D. GULIELMO PALLISER [1]

REVERENDISSIMI ARCHIEPISCOPI CASSELENSIS
FILIO UNICO, INGENIO, SOLERTIA, ERUDITIONE,
ANNOS LONGE PRÆEUNTI
NUMERISQUE ADEO OMNIBUS AD PRÆSTANDUM,
INGENS ALIQUOD SCIENTIIS LUMEN AC INCREMENTUM NATO,
HUNC ARITHMETICÆ TRACTATUM,
IN EXIGUUM SUMMI AMORIS PIGNUS,
OFFERT & DICAT
AUTHOR

---

[1] [Palliser entered Trinity College 1 July 1709 at the age of 14. He took his B.A. in 1712 and M.A. in 1716. His father (see *Dict. Nat. Biog.*) was elected Fellow, 1668, Professor of Divinity, 1678, and was appointed Archbishop of Cashel, 1694 ; he died in 1727, leaving a large collection of books to the College Library, where his name is commemorated in the Bibliotheca Palliseriana.—Ed.]

PRÆFATIO

PLEROSQUE scientiarum mathematicarum procos in ipso earundem limine cæcutientes, sentio simul et doleo. Nimirum cum ea sit, apud nos saltem, mathemata discendi ratio, ut primo arithmetica, deinde geometria, postremo algebra addiscatur, Tacqueti [1] vero *Arithmeticam* legamus, eam autem nemo probe intelligat, qui algebram non prælibarit ; hinc fit ut plerique mathesi operam navantes, dum bene multorum minoris usus theorematum demonstrationes studiose evolvunt, interea operationum arithmeticarum, quarum ea est vis et præstantia, ut non modo cæteris disciplinis mathematicis, verum etiam hominum cujuscunque demum sortis usibus commodissime famulentur, principia ac rationes intactas prætereant. Quod si quis tandem aliquando, post emensum matheseos cursum, oculos in prædictum Tacqueti librum retorqueat, multa ibi methodo obscura et quæ intellectum non tam illuminet quam convincat, demonstrata ; multa horrido porismatum et theorematum satellitio stipata inveniet.

Sed nec alius quisquam, quod sciam, arithmeticam seorsim ab algebra demonstravit. Proinde e re tyronum futurum ratus, si hæc mea qualiacunque in lucem emitterem, ea postquam, si minus omnia, pleraque certe per integrum fere triennium in scriniis delituerint, publici juris facio. Quæ cum præter ipsos operandi modos, eorundem etiam demonstrationes ex propriis et genuinis arithmeticæ principiis petitas complectantur, mirabitur fortasse quispiam, quod noster hic tractatus mole vulgares arithmeticorum libros, in quibus praxis tantum tradatur, haud exæquet. Hoc autem exinde provenit, quod cum operationum τὸ διότι explicarem in præceptis et exemplis, quæ vulgus arithmeticorum ad nauseam usque prosequitur, contractior fui ; nec eo forsan obscurior. Quippe tametsi cæco ad singulos fere gressus regendos opus sit manuductore, in clara tamen demonstrationum luce versanti sufficit, si quis tenendum tramitem vel strictim exponat. Quamobrem omnes matheseos candidati ad regularum arith-

---

[1] [Andrea Tacquet, 1612–60, of Antwerp, a Jesuit mathematician, author of *Arithmeticæ theoria et praxis*, 1665 and other treatises. His *Catoptrics* is mentioned by Barrow in the passage quoted by Berkeley, *Theory of Vision*, S. 29.—Ed.]

meticæ rationes ac fundamenta percipiendum animos adjungant, summopere velim et exoptem.

Neque id tanti moliminis est, ut plerique fortasse imaginentur. Quas attulimus demonstrationes faciles (ni fallor) sunt et concisæ ; nec principia aliunde mutuantur ; ex algebra nihil, nihil ex Euclide tanquam notum supponitur. Ubique malui obvia et familiari aliqua ratione a priori veritatem praxeos comprobare, quam per prolixam demonstrationum apagogicarum seriem ad absurdum deducere. Radicum quadratarum et cubicarum doctrinam ex ipsa involutionis arithmeticæ natura eruere tentavi. Atque ea, meo quidem judicio, ad numerosam radicum extractionem illustrandum magis accommoda videtur, quam quæ ex Elemento secundo Euclidis, aut ex analysi potestatum algebraicarum vulgo adferri solent. Regula vulgaris pro alligatione plurium rerum non nisi difficulter admodum et per species demonstratur : ejus igitur loco novam, quæ vix ulla demonstratione indigeat, e proprio penu substitui. Regulam falsi, utpote mancam et fere inutilem, consulto prætermisi. Ac, si nihil aliud, novitas fortassis aliqua placebit.

Neminem transcripsi ; nullius scrinia expilavi. Nempe id mihi imprimis propositum fuerat, ut numeros tractandi leges ex ipsis principiis, proprii exercitii et recreationis causa, deducerem. Quod et deinceps horis subsecivis prosecutus sum. Nec mihi hoc in loco, absque ingrati animi labe, præterire liceat Reverendum Virum Johannem Hall, S.T.D. Academiæ nostræ Vice-præpositum ibidemque linguæ Hebraicæ Professorem dignissimum,[1] cui viro optimo quum me multis nominibus obstringi lubens agnoscam, tum non id minimum duco, quod illius hortatu ad suavissimum Matheseos studium incitatus fuerim.

Monstravi porro ad quem collimaverim scopum,[2] quousque ipsum assecutus sim, penes æquos rerum æstimatores esto judicium. Candido quippe horum examini istas studiorum meorum primitias libenter submitto ; quicquid interim scioli sentiant et malevoli parum solicitus.

---

[1] [John Hall, entered Trinity College 1677 aged 18 ; elected Fellow, 1685 ; Vice-Provost, 1697–1713 ; Rector of Ardstraw and Rahy, 1713 ; died 1735. He was Berkeley's tutor.—Ed.]

[2] [Scopum, no doubt an echo of Malebranche's Rules of Method, *Recherche*, Book VI, Part 2, where Taylor translates, ' Still having before your eyes the scope you aim at.'—Ed.]

ARITHMETICÆ

PARS PRIMA

CAP. I

DE NOTATIONE ET ENUNCIATIONE NUMERORUM

NOVEM sunt notæ numerales, *viz.* 1, 2, 3, 4, 5, 6, 7, 8, 9, quibus una cum cyfra (o) utuntur arithmetici, ut tantum non infinitos numerorum ordines exprimant. Omne illius rei artificium in eo positum est, quod notarum numeralium loci ratione decupla progrediantur. Series autem numerorum, ea lege quoad locorum valores procedentium, in membra sive periodos enunciationis causa secatur. Rem totam oculis conspiciendam subjecta exhibet Tabella :

Notarum Numeralium Series

Centuriæ . .			Unesimæ . .		
Decades . .	349	Quintilionum	Decimæ . .	568	Millesimarum
Unitates . .			Centesimæ . .		
Centuriæ . .			Unesimæ . .		
Decades . .	758	Quatrilionum	Decimæ . .	918	Millionesimarum
Unitates . .			Centesimæ . .		
Centuriæ . .			Unesimæ . .		
Decades . .	192	Trilionum	Decimæ . .	300	Bilionesimarum
Unitates . .			Centesimæ . .		
Centuriæ . .			Unesimæ . .		
Decades . .	003	Bilionum	Decimæ . .	052	Trilionesimarum
Unitates . .			Centesimæ . .		
Centuriæ . .			Unesimæ . .		
Decades . .	505	Millionum	Decimæ . .	704	Quatrilionesimarum
Unitates . .			Centesimæ . .		
Centuriæ . .					
Decades . .	739	Millium			
Unitates . .					
Centuriæ . .					
Decades . .	047	Integrorum			
Unitates } . .					
Unesimæ∫ . .					
Decimæ . .	32	Partes			
Centesimæ . .					

qua exponitur notarum numeralium series, in terniones distribuTa : membra autem seu periodi millecupla, loci decupla ratione progrediuntur. *E.g.* Numerus positus in loco unitatum (is per subjectum punctum dignoscitur) denotat septem res integras quascunque, vel saltem ut integras spectatas ; numerus ei a dextris proximus, tres partes decimas ejusdem integri ; qui vero locum immediate præcedentem occupat, indigitat quatuor decadas eorundem integrorum. Eadem proportione decupla locus quilibet sequentem superat, a præcedente superatur.

Porro cum infinita unitatum multiplicatione et divisione, notarum series infinite ultra citraque unitatum locum producatur, adeoque innumeri oriantur loci, ut distincti eorum valores exprimantur ; opus est solummodo trium vocum continua repetitione ; modo ternio quivis sive periodus suo insigniatur nomine, uti factum in Tabella. Nam progrediendo a loco unitatum versus sinistram, prima periodus numerat simpliciter unitates, sive integra ; secunda, millia ; tertia, milliones ; quarta, biliones; atque ita porro. Similiter, servata analogia, in periodis infra unitatem descendentibus, occurrunt primo partes simpliciter, dein millesimæ, millionesimæ, bilionesimæ, &c. atque hæ quidem partiendæ in unesimas, decimas, centesimas ; illi vero colligendi in unitates, decades, centurias.

Ut itaque enunciemus numerum quavis e tota serie figura designatum, 1°, respiciendum est ad valorem notæ simplicem ; 2°, ad valorem loci ; postremo, periodi. *E.g.* enuncianda sit 9, in quinta sinistrorsum periodo, nota simpliciter sumpta valet novem : ratione loci, novem decadas ; ratione demum periodi, novem decadas trilionum. Proponatur 5, in tertia periodo, simpliciter sumpta dicit quinque ; ratione loci, quinque unitates ; ratione periodi, quinque unitates millionum, seu quinque milliones. In secunda infra unitatem periodo, detur 8, simplex notæ valor est octo, ratione loci, octo centesimæ ; ratione periodi, octo centesimæ millesimarum.

Quod si numerus enunciandus non habeat adscripta vocabula valores periodorum locorumque indigitantia, is punctatione a loco unitatum dextrorsum sinistrorsumque instituta in terniones distinguatur ; deinde, cuique loco et periodo assignato nomine, proferatur. Sit, *e.g.* numerus propositus 73·480·195. Notis in periodos distinctis, primum quæro quinam sint valores figuræ ad sinistram primæ ; quæ, quoniam collocatur in secundo loco tertiæ periodi, valet septem decadas millionum, quia vero numeri ratione decupla progrediuntur, intellecto notæ primæ valore, cæterarum valores ordine sequuntur. Sic ergo enunciabimus numerum propositum, septem decades et tres unitates millionum, quatuor centuriæ et octo decades millium, una centuria, novem decades et quinque unitates ; vel contractius, septuaginta tres milliones, quadringenta octuaginta [1] millia, centum nonaginta quinque ; hinc cernimus quod cyfra, licet per se nil valeat, necessario tamen scribatur, ut unicuique notæ debitum assignemus locum.

Facillimum erit numeros quantumvis magnos scribere et enunciare, modo quæ dicta sunt perpendantur, quorum etiam scientia in sequentibus maximi erit momenti, siquidem qua ratione operationes arithmeticæ in digitis perficiantur ipsa docet natura ; arte vero opus est ad easdem in numeris grandioribus accurate exercendas, quæ sane omnis in eo versatur, ut quod opus simul et uno quasi ictu peragi non sinit humanæ mentis angustia, id in plures partiamur opellas, sigillatim inquirentes digitorum aggregata, differentias, producta, &c. dein hæc ita componamus ut exhibeant summam, residuum, aut productum &c. totale ; cujus rei ratio omnis et artificium petitur ex simplici locorum progressione, et in ea ultimo fundatur.

N.B. Non me latet arithmeticos nonnullos numerorum seriem aliter ac a nobis factum est partiri ; sc. in senarios (composita denominatione) loco ternionum. Cum vero methodum quam tradimus sequantur etiam alii,[2] visum est et nobis eam (utpote simpliciorem) retinere.

---

[1] [octuaginta, usually octoginta.—Ed.]

[2] v.g. Cl. Wallisius in *Mathes. Univers.*, et le Père Lamy dans ses *Elémens des Mathématiques.*

[John Wallis, 1616–1703, Savilian Professor of Geometry, Oxford, wrote *Arithmetica infinitorum*, 1655, which Berkeley mentions in his ' Of Infinites ' ; *cf. PC* No. 482 ; for his *Mathesis Universalis* to which Berkeley refers here, see his collected mathematical works, published 1693–99. Bernard Lamy, 1640–1715, a priest of the Oratory, wrote on mathematics and theology. In 1680 he published a treatise on arithmetic, algebra, and analysis, the second edition of which came out in 1691 with the title *Elémens des mathématiques.*—Ed.]

CAP. II

DE ADDITIONE

ADDITIONE quæritur duorum pluriumve numerorum aggregatum, quod ut obtineatur, numeri aggregandi sub invicem scribantur ea lege, ut unitates unitatibus, decades decadibus, partes decimæ decimis, &c. respondeant.   Quamobrem ubi adnexæ fuerint partes decimales, oportet unitatis locum adjecto commate insignire, deinde sumpto a dextris initio notæ in primo loco occurrentes una addantur ;   decades autem siquæ proveniant, adjectis punctulis notatæ sequenti loco annumerandæ sunt, cujus itidem numeris (reservatis interim decadibus, quæ ad locum sequentem pertinent) in unam summam aggregati infra scribantur.   Atque ita porro.

E.g. In primo, infra-scriptorum exemplo, 9 et 5 faciunt 14 ; decadem punctatam servo, cum 4 progredior ;   4 et 8 sunt 12, punctata igitur decade, 2 subscribo ;   ad secundum locum accedens, reperio 6, quibus addo 2, *scil.*, decadas in primo punctatas, 8 et 2 faciunt decadem, quam notatam servans, quæ sola superest 1 subscribo.   Et sic deinceps.

			£	s.	d.
Addend.	2 0 1 8·	523,9702	7	8	9
	8·2 2·5·	81,35	3	12·	5
	4 3 6 9	60,2005	0	7	2
Sum.	1 4 6 1 2	665,5207	11	8	4

Quod si proponantur colligendæ res diversarum specierum, simili prorsus methodo operandum, dummodo habeatur ratio proportionis, juxta quam progrediuntur diversa rerum genera. *E.g.* Quoniam *Lib. Sol.* et *Den.* non ratione decupla ut numeri progrediuntur ;   adeoque non 10 denarii sed 12 constituant solidum ;   non 10 solidi sed 20, libram.   Propterea in hisce speciebus addendis, loco decadis, numerus quilibet in denariis, duodenarius, in solidis, vicenarius, sequenti loco adscribendus est.

CAP. III

DE SUBDUCTIONE

SUBDUCTIONE quæritur duorum numerorum differentia, sive quodnam superfuerit residuum sublato uno ex altero, cujus obtinendi causa, numeri minoris nota quælibet notæ majoris ejusdem loci subscribatur ; deinde subducendi prima dextrorsum nota ex nota suprascripta auferatur, residuumque infra notetur ; atque ita porro, usque dum perficiatur subductio totius.

Si vero accidat numerum aliquem minorem esse quam ut ex eo nota subscripta auferri possit, is decade augeatur, mutuata scil. unitate a loco sequente.

Detur 1189 subtrahendus ex 32034. Numeris ut in exemplo subjecto scriptis, aggredior subductionem notæ primæ 9 ex supraposita 4 ; verum cum 4 ne semel quidem contineat 9, adjecta decade, fiat 14 ; ex 14 subductis 9, restant 5. Dein versus sinistram pergens, reperio 8, a 2 (loco 3, habita nimirum ratione mutuatæ decadis) subducenda, quod quoniam fieri nequit, aufero 8 a 12, et restant 4 ; proxima subducendi nota est 1, quæ quia a nihilo, sive 0, non potest subtrahi, loco cyfræ 0, substituo 9, (9 inquam, quoniam, mutuata decas unitate numero præcedenti jam ante adjecta truncatur) ablata demum 1 ab 1, restat nihil. Porro peracta subductione restant 3, quæ itidem subscribo.

Haud dissimili ratione subductio specierum diversarum perficitur : modo advertamus non semper decadem, sed numerum qui dicit quotuplus locus quilibet sit præcedentis, in supplementum defectus notæ alicujus mutuandum esse.

			£	s.	d.
Subduc.	32034	7329,645	4	8	3
	1189	3042,100	2	6	5
Resid.	30845	4287,545	2	1[1]	10

N.B. Ex dictis liquet arithmeticæ (quam hactenus tradidimus) artificium consistere in perficiendo per partes id quod una vice fieri nequeat ; rationem vero in additione, reservandi, in subductione, mutuandi decadas, a decupla locorum progressione omnino petendam esse.

[1] [Text mistakenly has 2.—Ed.]

CAP. IV

DE MULTIPLICATIONE

MULTIPLICATIONE toties ponitur multiplicandus quoties jubet multiplicans, seu quæritur numerus qui eandem habeat rationem ad multiplicandum, quam multiplicans ad unitatem. Numerus autem iste appellatur productum sive rectangulum ; cujus latera seu factores dicuntur uterque tum multiplicandus, tum numerus per quem multiplicatur.

Ut productum duorum numerorum inveniamus, scripto numero multiplicante sub multiplicando, hic multiplicetur per quamlibet notam illius, incipiendo a dextris ; cujusque autem producti nota prima directe subscribatur notæ multiplicanti, reliquæ versus lævam ordine sequantur.

Peracta multiplicatione, producta particularia in unam colligantur summam, ut habeatur, productum totale, in quo tot loci partibus sunt assignandi, quot sunt in utroque factore.

Proponatur 30,94 ducendus in (sive multiplicandus per) 26,5. Quinquies 4 dant 20, cujus primam figuram 0 subscribo notæ multiplicanti (5), reliquam 2 servo ; porro 5 in 9 dant 45 ; 5 cum 2 servatis faciunt 7, quæ subscribo 4 sequenti loco ponenda servans ; et sic deinceps.

	30,94 26,5	52896 24	6000 56
	15470 18564 6188	211584 105792	36 30
Prod. tot.	819,910	1269504	336000

Quoniam numeri cujusque duplex est valor, ut multiplicatio recte instituatur, oportet utriusque rationem haberi ; adeo ut nota quævis multiplicetur juxta valorem cum simplicem tum localem figuræ multiplicantis. Hinc nota prima cujusque particularis producti scribitur sub nota multiplicante. *E.g.* in secundi exempli multiplicatore, nota 2 valet duas (non unitates sed) decadas ; ergo in 6 (primam multiplicandi notam) ducta producet duodecim (non quidem unitates, verum) decadas.   Proinde primam producti notam in loco decadum *h. e.* directe sub nota multiplicante 2, poni oportet.

Ob eandem rationem, ubi in factoribus occurrunt partes, numerus ex prima multiplicandi nota in primam multiplicantis ducta genitus, tot locis detrudendus est infra notam multiplicatam, quot multiplicans dextrorsum ab unitate distat ; adeoque tot loci in producto totali partibus seponendi sunt, quot fuerant in utroque factore.

N.B. Si factori utrique aut alterutri a dextris accedant cyfræ non interruptæ, multiplicatione in reliquis notis instituta omittantur istæ mox producto totali adjiciendæ, quippe cum loci proportione decupla progrediantur, liquet numerum decuplum, centuplum, millecuplum, &c. suiipsius evadere, si modo uno, duobus aut tribus locis promoveatur.

CAP. V

DE DIVISIONE

Divisio opponitur multiplicationi, nempe productum quod hæc conficit, illa sibi dissolvendum sive dividendum proponit. Numerus in divisione inventus, dicitur *Quotiens*, siquidem dicit quoties dividendus continet divisorem vel (quod idem est) rationem dividendi ad divisorem ; seu denique, partem dividendi a divisore denominatam.

In divisione, scriptis dividendo et divisore sicut in exemplorum subjectorum primo, captoque initio a sinistris, pars dividendi divisori æqualis, vel eum proxime superans (intelligo valorem tantum simplicem) interposito puncto seponatur : Quærendum dein quoties divisor in membro isto contineatur, numerusque proveniens erit prima quotientis nota ; porro divisor ducatur in notam inventam, productoque a membro dividendo ablato, residuum infra notetur, cui adscripta sequente dividendi nota, confit novum membrum dividendum, unde eruatur nota secunda quotientis, mox in divisorem ducenda, ut producto ex membro proxime diviso ablato, residuum una cum sequente dividendi nota, præbeat novum membrum ; atque ita porro, usque dum absoluta fuerit operatio. Subductis demum locis decimalibus divisoris ab iis qui sunt in dividendo, residuum indicabit quot loci partibus assignandi sunt in quotiente ; quod si nequeat fieri subductio, adjiciantur dividendo tot cyfræ decimales quot opus est.

Peracta divisione, si quid superfuerit, adjectis cyfris decimalibus continuari poterit divisio, donec vel nihil restet, vel id tam exiguum sit, ut tuto negligi possit ; aut etiam quotienti apponantur notæ residuæ, subscripto iisdem divisore.

Si uterque, dividendus nempe et divisor, desinat in cyfras, hæ æquali numero utrinque rescindantur ; si vero divisor solus cyfris terminetur, eæ omnes inter operandum negligantur, totidemque postremæ dividendi notæ abscissæ, sub finem operationis restituantur, scripto infra lineolam divisore.

Proponatur 45832, dividendus per 67. Quoniam divisor major est quam 45, adjecta nota sequente fiat 458, membrum primo dividendum ; hoc interposito puncto a reliquis dividendi notis secerno. 6 in 45 continetur septies, et superest 3 ; veruntamen quoniam 7 non itidem septies in 28 reperitur, ideo minuendus est quotiens. Sumatur 6 ; 6 in 45 invenitur sexies, atque

insuper 9, quin et 98 continet 7 sexies, est igitur 6 nota prima
quotientis ; hæc in divisorem ducta procreat subducendum 402,
quo sublato a 458, restant 56 ; his adscribo 3, proximam dividendi
notam, unde confit novum membrum, nimirum 563, quod sicuti
prius dividens, invenio 8 pro nota secunda quotientis : 8 in 67
dat 536, hunc subduco a membro 563, residuoque 27 adjiciens
reliquam dividendi notam, viz, 2, habeo 272 pro novo dividendo,
quod divisum dat 4, qua primo in quotiente scripta, dein in
divisorem ducta, productoque ex 272 ablato, restant 4 quotienti,
scripto infra lineolam divisore, adjicienda.

Expeditior est operatio, ubi subductio cujusque notæ multiplicationem immediate sequitur ; ipsa autem multiplicatio a
sinistra dextrorsum instituitur. *E.g.* Sit 12199980 dividendus per
156 (*vide* exempl. 3) sub 1219 primo dividendi membro scripto
divisore, constat hunc in illo septies contineri, quamobrem 7
scribo in quotiente. Septies 1 est 7, quibus subductis ex 12,
deleo tum notam multiplicatam 1, tum 12 partem membri unde
auferebatur productum, residuum 5 supra notans ; dein accedo
ad proximam divisoris notam 5 ; 7 in 5 dat 35 ; 35 ex 51 ablatis,
restant 16, quæ supra scribo deletis 51 et 5. Deinde autem 7
in 6 duco, productoque 42 ex 69 subtracto, supersunt 27, quæ
proinde noto, deletis interim tum 69 tum 6, ultima dividendi
figura. Porro divisorem jam integre deletum, denuo versus
dextram uno loco promotum scribo, perque illum membrum
suprascriptum (quod quidem fit ex residuo membri proxime divisi
sequente nota aucto) quemadmodum præcedens divido. Eodem
modo divisor usque promoveatur quoad dividendum totum
percurrerit.

$67)458\cdot32(684\frac{4}{67}$	$200)8200$	$4\!\!\!/1$
402		$1\!\!\!/2\!\!\!/3$ $\not{2}$
———	$2)$ 82 $(41$	$\not{5}\not{6}\not{7}1\not{7}\not{3}$
563	8	$1\!\!\!/2\!\!\!/1\not{9}\not{9}\not{9}\not{8}\not{0}(78205$
536	———	$1\not{5}\not{6}\not{6}\not{6}\not{6}\not{6}$
———	02	$1\not{5}\not{5}\not{5}\not{5}$
272	2	$1\not{1}\not{1}$
268	———	
———	00	
004		

Jam vero præceptorum ratio dabitur ; et primum quidem liquet,
cur quotientem per partes investigemus.

2 Quæri potest, cur *v. g.* in exemplo supra allato habeatur

6 pro quotiente membri primi per divisorem divisi, nam 67 in 458 centuriis (pro centuriis nimirum habendæ sunt cum duobus locis sinistrorsum ab unitate distent) non sexies, sed sexcenties continetur ? Respondeo, revera, non simpliciter 6, sed 600 scribi in quotiente, duæ enim notæ postmodum inventæ istam sequuntur, atque ita quidem quotienti debitus semper conservatur valor ; nam unicuique notæ tot loci in quotiente, quot membro unde eruebatur, in dividendo postponuntur.

3 Quandoquidem nota quælibet quotientis indicat quoties id, ex quo eruebatur, dividendi membrum divisorem contineat ; æquum est ut ex divisore, in notam proxime inventam ducto, confletur subducendum : tunc nempe aufertur divisor toties ad amussim quoties in dividendo continetur, nisi forsan æquo major aut minor, sit numerus ultimo in quotiente scriptus. De illo quidem errore constabit, si productum tam magnum fuerit, ut subduci nequeat ; de hoc, si e contra productum oriatur tam exiguum, ut peracta subductione residuum divisore majus sit vel ei æquale.

4 Ratio cur tot loci partibus seponantur in quotiente, quot cum iis qui sunt in divisore æquentur locis decimalibus dividendi, ex eo cernitur, quod numerus dividendus sit productum, cujus factores sunt divisor et quotus, adeoque ille tot habeat locos decimales quot hi ambo, id quod demonstravimus de multiplicatione agentes.

5 Patet cyfras decimales ad calcem dividendi adjectas ipsius valorem non immutare. Nam integros quod attinet, ii dummodo eodem intervallo supra unitates ascendant, eundem sortiuntur valorem ; decimales vero non nisi præpositis cyfris in inferiorem gradum deprimuntur.

6 Quoniam quotiens exponit seu denominat rationem dividendi ad divisorem, patet proportione illa sive ratione existente eadem, eundem fore quotientem ; sed abjectis cyfris communibus, ratio seu numerorum ad invicem habitudo minime mutatur. Sic *v. g.* 200 est ad 100, vel (quod idem est) 200 toties continet 100, quoties 2 continet 1, quod sane per se manifestum est.

CAP. VI

DE COMPOSITIONE ET RESOLUTIONE QUADRATI

PRODUCTUM ex numero in seipsum ducto, dicitur numerus *quad-ratus*. Numerus autem ex cujus multiplicatione oritur quadratus, nuncupatur *latus* sive *radix quadrata* ; et operatio qua numeri propositi radicem investigamus, dicitur *extractio radicis quadratæ*, cujus intelligendæ causa juvabit genesin ipsius quadrati, partes-que ex quibus componitur, earumque ordinem situmque contem-plari. Veruntamen quoniam in inquirenda rerum cognitione consultius est a simplicissimis et facillimis ordiri, a contem-platione geneseos quadrati, ex radice binomia oriundi, initium capiamus.

Attentius itaque intuendum est, quid fiat ubi numerus duabus notis constans in seipsum ducatur ; et primo quidem mani-festum est, primam a dextra radicis notam in notam supra posi-tam, seipsam nempe, duci ; unde oritur quadratum minoris membri. Deinde vero, eadem nota in sequentem multiplicandi, *i.e.* alteram radicis notam ducta, provenire rectangulum ab utroque radicis membro conflatum constat. Porro peracta multiplicatione totius multiplicandi per primam radicis notam, ad secundam accedimus, qua in primam multiplicandi notam ducta, oritur jam denuo rectangulum duarum radicis binomiæ notarum ; deinde secunda multiplicandi nota, *i.e.* eadem per eandem, multiplicata, dat secundi membri radicis binomiæ quadratum.

Hinc ergo colligimus, quadratum quodvis a radice binomia procreatum constare primo ex quadrato membri minoris ; secundo duplici rectangulo membrorum, tertio quadrato membri majoris.

Proponatur radix binomia, *v.g.* 23 quadranda, juxta ea quæ *cap.* 4. traduntur ; primo duco 3 in 3, unde pro-ducitur 9, quadratum membri minoris. Secundo duco 3 in 2, alteram radicis notam ; prodit 6, rectangulum utriusque notæ. Tertio, ex 2 in 3 ducto oritur jam secunda vice rectangulum membrorum. Quarto, 2 in 2 gignit 4, quadratum membri majoris.

$$
\begin{array}{r}
23 \\
23 \\
\hline
69 \\
46 \\
\end{array}
$$

Progrediamur ad genesin quadrati a radice trimembri ; atque hic, primo quidem, prima radicis nota in integram radicem ducta procreat, primo, primi membri quadratum ; secundo, rectangulum membrorum primi ac secundi ; tertio, rectangulum membrorum primi ac tertii. Secundo, secunda radicis nota multiplicans radicem dat, primo, rectangulum membrorum primi ac secundi ; secundo, quadratum membri secundi ; tertio, rectangulum membrorum secundi ac tertii. Tertio, ex tertia radicis nota in radicem ducta oritur, primo, rectangulum membrorum primi ac tertii ; secundo, rectangulum membrorum secundi ac tertii ; tertio, quadratum tertii membri radicis.

Hinc porro colligimus quadratum quodvis a radice trinomia genitum complecti, primo, quadratum notæ radicis primæ ; secundo, duplex rectangulum notæ primæ in duas reliquas ductæ ; tertio, quadratum duarum reliquarum, *i.e.* bina singularum quadrata et earundem duplex rectangulum, quæ quidem constituere quadratum duarum notarum jam ante ostendimus.

Simili methodo ostendi potest quadratum 4, 5, quotlibet notarum continere, primo, quadratum notæ infimæ ; secundo, duplex rectangulum ex infima in sequentes omnes ducta genitum ; tertio, quadratum notarum omnium sequentium ; quod ipsum (uti ex præmissis manifestum est) continet quadratum notæ a dextris secundæ, duplex rectangulum ejusdem in omnes sequentes ductæ, quadratum notarum omnium sequentium ; quod pariter continet quadratum notæ tertiæ, bina rectangula illius et sequentium harumque quadratum, atque ita porro, usque quoad ventum sit ad quadratum altissimæ radicis notæ.

Inventis tandem partibus ex quibus componitur quadratum, restat ut circa earum ordinem situmque dispiciamus. Si itaque quadratum incipiendo a dextris in biniones partiamur, ex genesi quam supra tradidimus constabit, primum (a sinistris) membrum occupari a quadrato notæ primæ sive altissimæ, simul ac ab ea duplicis rectanguli ex notis prima et secunda in invicem ductis conflati portione, quæ extra primum sequentis binionis locum redundat : secundi locum primum continere dictum duplex rectangulum, atque insuper quicquid quadrati notæ secundæ, excurrat, secundum capere quadratum notæ secundæ, et quod redundat duplicis rectanguli duarum priorum notarum in tertiam ductarum (quoad notam infimam) ad locum primum tertii binionis pertinentis, et sic deinceps. *v.g.* in exemplo apposito, membrum primum 10 continet 9 quadratum notæ primæ 3, simul ac 1 qua 12 (duplex rectangulum notæ 3 in sequentem 2 ductæ) locum

$$
\begin{array}{r}
321 \\
321 \\
\hline
321 \\
642 \\
963 \\
\hline
10\cdot30\cdot41
\end{array}
$$

primum secundi membri transcendit. Primus locus secundi binionis capit 2 (duplicis rectanguli notarum 3 et 2 reliquum), atque etiam id quod extra locum proxime sequentem redundat, &c.

Perspecta jam compositione quadrati, ad ejusdem analysin accedamus. Proponatur itaque numerus quivis (*e.g.* 103041), unde elicienda sit radix quadrata. Hunc incipiens a dextris, in biniones (si par sit locorum numerus, alioqui membrum ultimum ex unica constabit nota) distinguo. Quæro dein quadratum maximum in (10) membro versus lævam primo contentum, cujus radix (3) est nota prima radicis indagandæ, ipsum autem quadratum (9) a membro (10) subduco. Ex residuo (1) adjecta (3) nota prima sequentis membri confit dividendus (13), quem divido per notam inventam duplicatam (*i.e.* 6), quotiens (2) erit nota radicalis secunda ; qua primo in divisorem, deinde in seipsam ducta, productisque in unam summam collectis, ita tamen ut posterius uno loco dextrorsum promoveatur (*e.g.* ^{12} 4) habeo numerum subducendum (124), hunc aufero ex dividendo (13) aucto (0) nota reliqua secundi membri : residuo (6) adjicio (4) notam primam tertii binionis, ut fiat novus dividendus (64), qui divisus per (64) duplum radicis hactenus

$$103041(321$$
$$9$$
$$\overline{}$$
$$)13{\cdot}0$$
$$124$$
$$\overline{}$$
$$64)641$$
$$\overline{}$$
$$641$$
$$\overline{}$$
$$000$$

inventæ dat (1) notam tertiam radicis indagandæ ; hac tum in divisorem tum in seipsam ducta, factisque ut supra simul aggregatis, summam (641) subduco a dividendo (64) aucto accessione notæ alterius membri tertii : eadem plane methodo pergendum quantumvis producatur operatio.

Si quid post ultimam subductionem superfuerit, id tibi indicio sit, numerum propositum non fuisse quadratum ; verumtamen adjectis resolvendo cyfris decimalibus operatio extendi poterit quousque lubet.

Numerus locorum decimalium, si qui fuerint, in resolvendo bipartitus indicabit, quot ponendi sunt in radice, cujus ratio cernitur ex *cap.* 4.

Ratio operandi abunde patet ex præmissis. Nam *e.g.* adhibui (6) duplum notæ pro divisore, propterea quod ex tradita quadrati compositione, duplex rectangulum notæ illius (3) in sequentem (2) ductæ dividendum complecti rescissem, eoque adeo diviso per duplum factoris unius (3) confactorem ejus (2) *h.e.* notam proximam radicis innotescere. Similiter, subducendum conflavi ex duplici rectangulo quotientis et divisoris, simul ac quotientis quadrato in unum, ea qua dictum est ratione, collectis, quia bina illa rectangula et quadratum eo ordine in residuo et membro sequente, ex quibus fiebat subductio, contineri deprehenderam, atque ita quidem potestatis resolutio ex ipsius compositione facili admodum negotio deducitur.

CAP. VII

DE COMPOSITIONE ET RESOLUTIONE CUBI

RADIX in quadratum ducta procreat cubum. Ut sternamus viam ad analysin cubi, a compositione potestatis (quemadmodum in capite præcedenti factum) sumendum est initium. In productione igitur cubi a radice binomia primum radicis membrum offendit, primo, suiipsius quadratum, unde cubus notæ primæ; secundo, duplex rectangulum membrorum, unde duplex solidum quadrati notæ primæ in alteram ducti; tertio, quadratum membri alterius, unde solidum ex nota prima et quadrato secundæ genitum. Similiter, facta multiplicatione per membrum secundum oritur primo, solidum notæ secundæ et quadrati primæ; secundo, duplex solidum notæ primæ et quadrati secundæ; tertio, cubus membri secundi.

Continet ergo cubus a radice binomia procreatus singulorum membrorum cubos et 6 solida, nimirum 3 facta ex quadrato membri utriusvis in alterum ducto.

Hinc ratiocinio ad analogiam capitis præcedentis protracto, constabit, si (ut quadratum in biniones, ita) cubus a quantavis radice genitus, in terniones distribuatur, ternionem seu membrum a sinistris primum continere cubum notæ sinistrorsum primæ, simul ac redundantiam (si quæ sit) 3 solidorum quadrati ejusdem in secundam ducti; locum primum secundi capere dicta solida et redundantiam 3 solidorum quadrati notæ secundæ in primam, locum secundum eadem 3 solida et redundantiam cubi notæ secundæ; tertium occupari a dicto cubo, simul ac redundantia 3 solidorum, ex quadrato notarum præcedentium in tertiam ducto genitorum: locum primum tertii membri solida ultimo memorata obtinere, et sic deinceps. Hinc facile derivabimus methodum eliciendæ radicis cubicæ, quæ est ut sequitur.

Incipiendo a dextris resolvendum (80621568) in terniones (præter membrum postremum quod minus esse potest) punctis interpositis distribuo. Dein cubum maximum (64) in (80) primo versus sinistram membro contentum subduco, scriptaque illius radice (4) in notam primam radicis quæsitæ, residuo (16) adscribo (6) notam proximam resolvendi, unde confit dividendum (166) quod divido per (48) triplum quadrati notæ inventæ: quotiens (3) est nota secunda radicis, hanc duco, primo in divisorem; secundo, ipsius quadratum in triplum notæ primæ; postremo, ipsam in seipsam bis. Producta ea lege aggregata, ut secundum a primo, tertium a secundo, uno loco dextrorsum ponatur,

$$\left\{ \begin{array}{c} 144 \\ 108 \\ 27 \end{array} \right\}$$ subduco a dividendo aucto accessione duarum notarum

reliquarum membri secundi. Ad eundem modum, utut prolixa sit operatio, numerum dividendum semper
praestat residuum, adjuncta prima sequentis   80·621·568(432
membri nota : divisorem vero, triplum   64
quadrati notarum radicis hactenus inven-   ————
tarum : et subducendum, nota ultimo re-   48)166·21
perta in divisorem ducta, ejusdem quad-   15507
ratum in triplum notarum praecedentium ;   5547)1114568
postremo illius cubus, ea qua diximus ra-   1114568
tione aggregati, constituent.   ————

Si numerus resolvendus non sit cubus,   0000000
quod superest, adjectis locis decimalibus, in
infinitum exhauriri potest.

Radici assignanda est pars tertia locorum decimalium resolvendi.

N.B. Operationes syntheticæ examinari possunt per analyticas, et vicissim analyticæ per syntheticas : adeoque si numero alterutro ex summa duorum subducto, restet alter, recte peracta est additio ; et vice versa, extra dubium ponitur subductio, quoties aggregatum subducti et residui æquatur numero majori dato. Similiter, si quotiens in divisorem, aut radix in seipsam ducta procreet dividendum, aut resolvendum, id tibi indicio sit, in divisionem aut resolutionem nullum repsisse vitium.

ARITHMETICÆ

PARS SECUNDA

CAP. I

QUID SINT FRACTIONES

Scripto divisore infra dividendum, ductaque linea intermedia, divisionem utcunque designari, jam ante [1] monuimus. Hujusmodi autem quotientes dicuntur numeri fracti seu fractiones, propterea quod numerus superior, qui dicitur etiam numerator, dividitur seu frangitur in partes ab inferiore denominatas, qui proinde dicitur denominator : *e.g.* in hac fractione $\frac{2}{4}$ 2 est dividendus seu numerator, 4 divisor seu denominator ; ipsa autem fractio indicat quotientem qui oritur ex divisis 2 per 4, *h.e.* quadrantem duarum rerum quarumvis, vel duos quadrantes unius ; nempe idem sonant.

N.B. Patet numeros qui partes decimales denotant, quique vulgo fractiones decimales audiunt, subscripto nominatore, per modum fractionum vulgarium exprimi posse. *E.g.*, 25 valent $\frac{25}{100}$; ,004 valent $\frac{4}{1000}$ &c. id quod faciamus oportet, aut saltem factum intelligamus, quotiescunque eæ in fractiones vulgares aut vicissim hæ in illas reducendæ sint, aut aliam quamvis operationem, utrosque fractos, vulgares et decimales ex æquo respicientem, fieri contingat.

[1] Cap. v, p. i.

CAP. II

DE ADDITIONE ET SUBDUCTIONE FRACTIONUM

1 Si fractiones, quarum summa aut differentia quæritur, eundem habent nominatorem, sumatur summa aut differentia numeratorum, cui subscriptus communis nominator quæsitum dabit.

2 Si non sunt ejusdem nominis, ad idem reducantur, nominatores dati in se invicem ducti dabunt novum nominatorem ; cujusque autem fractionis numerator, in nominatores reliquarum ductus, dabit numeratorem novæ fractionis datæ æqualis. Dein cum novis fractionibus operandum ut supra.

3 Si integer fractioni addendus sit, aut ab ea subducendus, vel vice versa, is ad fractionem datæ cognominem reducatur ; nempe illi in nominatorem datum ducto idem nominator subscribendus est.

Additio	$\frac{1}{5}$ ad $\frac{2}{5}$ sum. $\frac{3}{5}$
Subductio	$\frac{1}{5}$ a $\frac{2}{5}$ resid. $\frac{1}{5}$
Additio	$\frac{2}{3}$ ad $\frac{3}{4}$, *i.e.* $\frac{8}{12}$ ad $\frac{9}{12}$ sum. $\frac{17}{12}$
Subductio	$\frac{2}{3}$ a $\frac{3}{4}$, *i.e.* $\frac{8}{12}$ ex $\frac{9}{12}$ resid. $\frac{1}{12}$
Additio	3 ad $\frac{5}{8}$, *i.e.* $\frac{24}{8}$ ad $\frac{5}{8}$ sum. $\frac{29}{8}$
Subductio	$\frac{5}{8}$ ex. 3 *i.e.* $\frac{24}{8}$ resid. $\frac{19}{8}$

Primo, Dicendum est, cur fractiones, antequam operemur, ad idem nomen reducamus ; atque id quidem propterea fit, quod numeri res heterogeneas numerantes in unum colligi, aut ab invicem subduci nequeant. *E.g.* Si velim addere tres denarios duobus solidis, summa non erit 5 sol. aut 5 den. neque enim illa prius haberi potest quam res numeratas ad idem genus reducam, adhibendo loco duorum solidorum 24 denarios, quibus si addam 3 den. oritur aggregatum 27 den. pari ratione 2 partes tertias et 3 quartas una colligens, non scribo 5 partes, tertias aut quartas ;

sed earum loco usurpo 8 duodecimas et 9 duodecimas, quarum summa est 17 duodecimæ.

Secundo, Ostendam quod fractiones post reductionem idem valeant ac prius, *e.g.* quod $\frac{2}{3}$ æquentur $\frac{8}{12}$: siquidem uterque nominator et numerator per eundem numerum (*v.g.* 4) multiplicantur, omnis autem fractio exprimit rationem numeratoris, seu dividendi, ad nominatorem, seu divisorem ; proinde dummodo ratio illa eadem manet, fractio eundem retinet valorem, sed ducto utroque rationis termino in unum eundemque numerum, certum est rationem non mutari : *e.g.* si dimidium rei cujusvis sit dimidii alterius rei duplum, erit et totum illud totius hujuis duplum ; quod quidem tam liquido patet, ut demonstratione non indigeat.

Tertio, Integer ad fractionem reductus non mutat valorem, nam si 2 numerorum rectangulum per unum eorundem dividatur, quotiens erit alter ; sed in reductione integri ad fractum is in nominatorem datum ducitur, et per eundem dividitur igitur quotiens ; *h.e.* fractio valet integrum primo datum.

N.B. Utile nonnunquam erit, fractionem ad datum nomen reducere ; *e.g.* $\frac{2}{6}$ ad alteram, cujus nominator sit 9, quod quidem fit per regulam trium (de qua *vide par* 3. *cap.* 1.) inveniendo numerum, ad quem nominator datus ita se habeat ac fractionis datæ nominator ad ejusdem numeratorem ; is erit numerator fracti cujus datum est nomen, valor autem idem qui prioris ; quippe inter fractionis terminos eadem est utrobique ratio.

CAP. III

DE MULTIPLICATIONE FRACTIONUM

1 Si ducenda sit fractio in fractionem, datarum fractionum numeratores in se invicem ducti, dabunt numeratorem producti ; dati item nominatores procreabunt ejusdem nominatorem.

2 Si multiplicanda sit fractio per integrum, ducatur integer datus in numeratorem fractionis, eodem manente nominatore.

3 Si in factore alterutro, vel utroque occurrant integri, aut fractiones heterogeneæ, ei claritatis causa una colligi poterunt.

EXEMPLA MULTIPLICATIONIS

Multiplic.	$\frac{2}{3}$ per $\frac{5}{8}$ pro. $\frac{10}{24}$	$\frac{4}{7}$ per 2 prod. $\frac{8}{7}$
Multiplic.	2 & $\frac{3}{5}$ per $\frac{1}{2}$ & $\frac{2}{3}$ *i.e.* $1\frac{3}{5}$ per $\frac{7}{6}$	

1 Manifestum est quotientem eadem proportione augeri, qua dividendum : *E.g.* si 2 continetur ter in 6, continebitur bis ter in bis 6 ; liquet insuper eundem eadem proportione minui, qua crescit divisor. *E.g.* si numerus 3 continetur quater in 12, continebuntur bis 3 duntaxat bis in 12 : igitur cum ut multiplicem $\frac{2}{3}$ per $\frac{5}{8}$, augenda sit fractio $\frac{2}{3}$ ratione quintupla, quoniam per 5, et minuenda ratione octupla, quoniam non simpliciter per 5, sed solummodo ejus partem octavam multiplicatur ; duco dividendum 2 in 5, et divisorem 3 in 8.

2 Quod ad regulam secundam, constat bis 4 res quasvis æquari 8 rebus ejusdem denominationis, quæcunque demum sit illa.

CAP. IV

DE DIVISIONE FRACTIONUM

1 FRACTIO per integrum dividitur, ducendo integrum datum in nominatorem fractionis datæ.

2 Si fractio per fractionem dividenda sit, numerator divisoris ductus in nominatorem dividendi dabit nominatorem quotientis ; et ejusdem nominator ductus in numeratorem dividendi dabit numeratorem quotientis.

3 Quotiescunque admiscentur integri aut fractiones diversi nominis, facilius operabere si membra utriusque, tum dividendi tum divisoris in binas summas colligantur.

EXEMPLA DIVISIONIS

Div. | $\frac{3}{4}$ per 2, quot. $\frac{3}{8}$ |

Div. $\frac{4}{9}$ per $\frac{2}{5}$, quot. $\frac{20}{18}$

Div. $2\frac{1}{3} + \frac{3}{2}$ per $3\frac{2}{5}$, *i.e.* $\frac{23}{6}$ per $\frac{17}{5}$

1° Quantum ad primam regulam, ex capite præcedenti constat, fractionem eadem proportione minui seu dividi, qua multiplicatur nominator.

2° Postquam dividens fractionem unam per aliam, *e.g.* $\frac{4}{9}$ per $\frac{2}{5}$, duxi nominatorem 9 in 2, fractio $\frac{4}{18}$ dicit tantum quoties 2 continetur in dividendo ; illius vero quintuplum indicabit quoties pars quinta numeri 2 ibidem continetur ; quapropter quotientem primum $\frac{4}{18}$ duco in 5, inde fit $\frac{20}{18}$.

N.B. Si fractiones datæ sunt homogeneæ, brevius est et concinnius dividere numeratorem dividendi per numeratorem divisoris, quotiescunque illum hic metitur. Sic divisis $\frac{6}{8}$ per $\frac{3}{8}$ quotiens erit 2, quæcunque enim numerantur 6 bis continent 3.

2 Si extrahenda sit radix e fractione data, radix nominatoris radici numeratoris subscripta constituet fractionem quæ erit radix quæsita. *E.g.* $\frac{2}{3}$ est radix quadrata fractionis $\frac{4}{9}$, et cubica fractionis $\frac{8}{27}$, nam ex iis quæ de multiplicatione diximus patet, $\frac{2}{3}$ in $\frac{2}{3}$ producere $\frac{4}{9}$, et $\frac{2}{3}$ in $\frac{4}{9}$ dare $\frac{8}{27}$.

CAP. V

DE REDUCTIONE FRACTIONUM AD MINIMOS TERMINOS

1 QUONIAM fractionum quæ ex minimis terminis constant valor clarius agnoscitur, utile est fractionis terminos, quoties id fieri potest, per communem aliquam mensuram dividere. Quanto autem major fuerit communis iste divisor, tanto minores erunt quotientes seu termini fractionis datæ æqualis. Oportet itaque, datis duobus numeris, intelligere methodum inveniendi maximam eorum communem mensuram, *i.e.* divisorem maximum qui datos dividat absque residuo, qui est ut sequitur.

2 Divide majorem e datis per minorem, et divisorem per divisionis residuum, et si quod denuo supersit residuum, per illud residuum prius, *i.e.* ultimum divisorem, dividas ; atque ita porro, donec veneris ad divisorem qui dividendum suum exhauriat sive metiatur, is est maxima datorum communis mensura.

E.g. Proponantur 9 et 15. Divido 15 per 9, restant 6. Divido 9 per 6, restant 3 : porro divisis 6 per 3, restat nihil. Ergo 3 est maxima communis mensura datorum numerorum 9 et 15, quod sic ostendo.

(*a*) 3 metitur 6, at (*b*) 6 metitur 9 demptis 3 ; igitur 3 metitur 9 demptis 3 ; sed 3 metitur seipsum, metitur ergo integrum 9, atque (*c*) 9 metitur 15 demptis 6, ergo 3 metitur 15 demptis 6, metitur vero 6 ; igitur metitur integrum numerum 15. Hinc patet 3 esse propositorum 9 et 15 communem mensuram. Superest ut ostendam eandem esse maximam. Si negas, esto alia quæpiam major, puta 5 ; jam quoniam (*d*) 5 metitur 9, (*e*) 9 vero metitur 15 demptis 6, liquet 5 metiri 15 demptis 6 ; sed et integrum (15) (ex hypothesi) metitur, igitur metitur 6 ; 6 autem metitur 9 demptis 3, ergo 5 metitur 9 demptis 3. Quoniam igitur 5 metitur et integrum 9, et 9 demptis 3, metietur ipsum 3, *h.e.* (*f*) numerum minorem ; quod est absurdum.

Inventa maxima communi mensura, patet fractionem $\frac{9}{15}$ deprimi posse ad hanc $\frac{3}{5}$, quam priori æqualem esse sic ostendo. Omnis fractio denotat quotientem numeratoris divisi per nominatorem, in divisione autem, quotiens dicit rationem dividendi ad divisorem, dum igitur ratio eadem manet, erit et quotiens seu fractio eadem. Porro rationem non mutari, terminis ejus pariter divisis, liquido constat ; *e.g.* si res quælibet sit alterius rei dupla,

(*a*) *per const.*   (*b*) *per const.*   (*c*) *per const.*   (*d*) *per hyp.*   (*e*) *per const.*   (*f*) *per hyp.*

vel tripla, erit et dimidium illius, dimidii hujus, duplum vel triplum, &c.

Qui fractiones per integros dividere et multiplicare novit, is in fractionibus (ut vocant) fractionum ad simplices reducendis nullam difficultatem experietur. Nam *v.g.* hæc fractio fractionis $\frac{3}{4}$ de $\frac{2}{5}$ ecquid aliud est quam pars quarta fractionis $\frac{2}{5}$ triplicata, sive $\frac{2}{20}$ ducta in integrum 3? Similiter ductis in invicem tam numeratoribus quam nominatoribus, fractio fractionis fractionis, &c. ad integrum reducitur. Hæc cum tam clara sint et per se manifesta, mirum profecto per quantas ambages, quam operosam theorematum, citationum, et specierum supellectilem a nonnullis demonstrantur, dicam, an obscurantur?

ARITHMETICÆ

PARS TERTIA

CAP. I

DE REGULA PROPORTIONIS

Regula proportionalis dicitur, qua, datis tribus numeris, invenitur quartus proportionalis. Illius quidem usus frequens est et eximius, unde nuncupatur *regula aurea*. Dicitur etiam *regula trium*, ob 3 terminos datos. Porro quartum directe proportionalem invenies, multiplicando terminum secundum per tertium, et productum per primum dividendo : *E.g.* si ut 2 ad 6, ita se habeat 4 ad quæsitum, duc 4 in 6, et productum 24 divide per 2, quotiens 12 erit quartus proportionalis quæsitus. Quod sic demonstro :

In quatuor proportionalibus, productum extremorum æquatur producto terminorum intermediorum. Nam propterea quod numeri sint proportionales, *h.e.* eandem habeant inter se rationem, ratio vero per divisionem cognoscatur, diviso termino secundo per primum, et quarto per tertium, idem proveniet quotiens ; qui (ex natura divisionis) ductus in terminum primum, producet secundum, et in tertium, producet quartum. Jam, si ducamus terminum primum in quartum, vel (quod idem est) in tertium et quotientem continue, et terminum tertium in secundum, vel (quod idem est) in primum et quotientem continue, patet producta fore æqualia, nam iidem sunt utrobique factores. Sed ex natura multiplicationis et divisionis constat, diviso producto per unum e factoribus, quotientem esse alterum. Igitur, si dividam productum duorum terminorum intermediorum (6 et 4) per primum (2), quotiens (12) exhibebit quartum proportionalem quæsitum.

Quæstio 1 Viator tribus horis conficit quindecim milliaria ; quot conficiet novem horarum spatio ? *Resp.* 45 ; patet enim ex quæstione, ut 3 ad 15, ita 9 esse ad quæsitum : *i.e.* 3 : 15 : : 9 : ergo 135, productum ex 9 in 15, divisum per 3, dabit quæsitum, *viz.* 45.

Quæst. 2 Si 2 operarii 4 diebus merentur 2*s*. 5 quantam mercedem merebuntur 7 diebus? *h.e.* ut 2 in 4 ad 2, ita 5 in 7 ad quæsitum : sive 8 : 2 : : 35 : ? Unde invenitur quæsita merces, *viz*. 8*s*. 6*d*.

Quæst. 3 Tres mercatores, inita societate, lucrifaciunt 100*l*. expendebat autem primus 5*l*. secundus 8*l*. tertius 10*l*. Quæritur quantum lucri singulis seorsim contigit? summa impensarum est 23*l*. Dic itaque, ut 23 ad 5, ita 100 ad quæsitum : numerus proveniens indicabit quantum primo de communi lucro debetur ; æquum nempe est, ut quam proportionem habet cujusque impensa ad summam impensarum, eandem habeat ipsius lucrum ad summam lucrorum. Porro, ad eundem modum, dicendo 23 : 8 : : 100 : ? et 23 : 10 : : 100 : ? cæterorum lucra innotescent.

Proportio composita inversa in simplices facillime resolvitur. *V.g.* 2 homines expendunt, 5, 6 diebus : 30 quot diebus expendent 8 homines? Dic primo 2 : 5 : : 8 : ? invenies 20 ; dic igitur denuo 20 : 6 : 30 : ? et habebis quæsitum. Qua vero ratione terminus quæsitus simul et semel per regulam satis intricatam innotescat, explicare superfluum duco.

Quæst. 4 Quatuor fistulæ implent cisternam 12 horis ; quot horis implebitur illa, ab 8 ejusdem magnitudinis? Dicendum 8 : 4 : : 12 : ? Proinde 4 in 12, *h.e.* 48, divisa per 8, exhibent quæsitum, *viz*. 6. Neque in hoc casu, ubi invertitur proportio ulla est nova difficultas, nam terminis rite dispositis, semper habebimus bina æqualia rectangula, quorum unius notum est utrumque latus, alterum vero conflatur ex noto termino in ignotum ducto ; quare dividendo productum illud prius per notum latus, seu factorem hujus, proveniet terminus ignotus. Quo autem ordine disponendi sint termini, ex ipsa quæstione palam fiet.

CAP. II

DE ALLIGATIONE

REGULA *alligationis simplicis* dicitur, qua, propositis duabus rebus diversi pretii aut ponderis, &c. invenitur tertium quoddam genus, ex datis ita compositum, ut illius pretium vel pondus, &c. æquetur dato cuidam pretio, vel ponderi, &c. inter proposita intermedio. *E.g.* Pollex cubicus auri pendit uncias (18), pollex cubicus argenti uncias (12). Quæritur pollex cubicus metalli cujusdam ex utroque mixti qui pendat 16 uncias ; in quo problemate, pondus intermedium 16 superat argenti pondus per 4, et superatur ab auri pondere per 2. Jam, si capiamus $\frac{2}{6}$ cubi argentei, et $\frac{4}{6}$ cubi aurei, patet eas una conflatas dare pollicem cubicum ; quippe $\frac{2}{6}$ et $\frac{4}{6}$ æquantur unitati. Quin patet etiam metalli hujusce mixti pondus æquari dato intermedio 16 ; nam argenti, quod levius est per 4, accepimus 2 partes ; igitur defectus est 2 in 4 ; auri vero, quod gravius est per 2, accepimus 4 partes ; adeoque excessus est 4 in 2, *i.e.* æqualis defectui ; qui proinde se mutuo tollunt.

Hinc oritur regula pro alligatione rerum duarum. Fractio quæ nominatur a summa differentiarum, et numeratur a defectu minoris infra medium indicat quantitatem majoris sumendam ; et vicissim quæ eundem habens nominatorem, numeratur ab excessu majoris supra medium, indicat quantitatem minoris sumendam.

Quæst. Sunt duo genera argenti, uncia purioris valet 7, vilioris 4, quæruntur 3 unciæ argenti, quæ valeant singulæ 5 ? Resol. constat ex regula, si accipiam $\frac{2}{3}$ unciæ vilioris, et $\frac{1}{3}$ unciæ purioris argenti, haberi unam unciam mixti quæsiti ; hæc triplicata solvit quæstionem.

Quod si res alligandæ sint plures duabus, dicitur *alligatio composita*. *E.g.* sunt quinque vini genera, vis massici est 1, chii 3, falerni 5, cæcubi 7, corcyræi 9 : volo mixtum cujus vis sit 4. Mixti æqualiter ex chio et massico, vis erit 2 : nimirum dimidium summæ datarum 1 et 3, uti per se patet. Similiter, mixti æqualiter ex falerno cæcubo et corcyræo, vis erit 7, *i.e.* $\frac{1}{3}$ numeri 21, seu summæ virium misturam hancce componentium. 2 et 7 alligo cum vi intermedia data, *viz.* 4, defectus est 2, excessus 3, summa differentiarum 5 ; igitur sumendæ sunt $\frac{3}{5}$ misturæ prioris, $\frac{2}{5}$ posterioris ; porro divisis $\frac{3}{5}$ per 2, quotiens indicat quantum singulorum, chii et massici, accipiendum sit. Similiter $\frac{2}{5}$ divisæ per 3 dicent quantum falerni, &c. mixturæ quæsitæ inesse debet. Proinde $\frac{3}{10}$ massici, $\frac{3}{10}$ chii, $\frac{2}{15}$ falerni, $\frac{2}{15}$ cæcubi, $\frac{2}{15}$ corcyræi dabunt quæsitum.

Hinc cernimus, quomodo alligatio composita ad simplicem reducatur. Nimirum pondera, pretia, magnitudines, aut quæcunque demum sunt alliganda, in binas colligantur summas quæ dividendæ sunt, utraque, per numerum terminorum qui ipsam constituunt. Quotientes juxta regulam alligationis simplicis alligentur cum termino intermedio ; quæ proveniunt fractiones, divisæ singulæ per numerum rerum, summam ad quam spectant ingredientium, indigitabunt quantitatem ex singulis capiendam. Demonstratio patet ex dictis.

N.B. In alligatione plurium rerum quæstio quævis innumeras admittit solutiones, idque ob duplicem rationem ; nam primo termini deficientes cum excedentibus diversimode colligi possunt ; unde varii prodibunt quotientes, cum dato termino intermedio alligandi. Cavendum tamen est ne dicti quotientes sint simul majores, aut simul minores medio, quod si eveniat, patet quæsitum esse impossibile. Secundo, unum eundemque terminum licet sæpius repetere ; unde illius portio augebitur, reliquorum vero portiones minuentur.

Libet in studiosorum gratiam hic exhibere solutionem celebris illius problematis, ad Archimedem ab Hierone propositi.

Quæst. Ex conflatis auro et argento fit corona : quæritur quantum ei insit auri, quantum argenti ? coronam interim violari non sinit tyrannus. *Respon.* Parentur binæ massæ, una auri, altera argenti, quarum utraque sit ejusdem ponderis ac corona. Quibus paratis, patet problema, alia forma, sic proponi posse : Datis *v.g.* libra auri, et libra argenti, invenire libram metalli ex utroque compositi, quæ sit datæ intermediæ molis ; igitur inquirendæ sunt massarum et coronæ magnitudines. Quoniam vero coronæ soliditas geometrice determinari nequeat, opus est stratagemate. Singulæ ergo vasi aqua pleno seorsim immergantur, mensuretur autem quantitas aquæ ad cujusque immersionem profluentis quam immersæ moli magnitudine æqualem esse constat ; immerso utique auro, aqua exundans sit 5, argento 9, corona 6. Huc igitur redit quæstio ; datis libra auri cujus magnitudo est 5, et libra argenti cujus magnitudo est 9, quæritur quantum ex singulis capere oporteat, ut habeamus libram metalli cujus magnitudo sit 6 : proinde alligatis 9 et 5 cum magnitudine intermedia 6, innotescet quantitas auri, *viz.* $\frac{3}{4}$ lib, et $\frac{1}{4}$ lib. quantitas argenti, coronæ immisti.

Hinc patet, quam non difficile sit problema, ob cujus solutionem notum illud εὕρηκα ingeminavit olim Archimedes.

CAP. III

DE PROGRESSIONE ARITHMETICA ET GEOMETRICA,
ET DE LOGARITHMIS

Progressio Arithmetica dicitur series numerorum, eadem communi differentia crescentium vel decrescentium. *E.g.* In hac serie 1. 4. 7. 10. 13. 16. 19. 22. 25, 3 est communis excessus, quo terminus secundus excedit primum, tertius secundum, quartus tertium, et sic deinceps : et in hac altera decrescentium serie, 15. 13. 11. 9. 7. 5. 3. 1, 2 est communis defectus, quo terminus quilibet a præcedenti deficit.

Jam ex ipso serierum harumce intuitu et quam præmisimus definitione, manifestum est, unumquemque terminum continere minorem extremum, simul ac communem differentiam, multiplicatam per numerum locorum quibus ab eodem distat. *E.g.* In prima serie terminus quintus 13 constat ex minore extremo 1, et communi differentia 3, ducta in 4, *i.e.* numerum locorum quibus a minimo extremo distat. Hinc dato minore extremo, et communi differentia, terminus quivis, *e.g.* a minimo undecimus exclusive, facile inveniri potest, ducendo differentiam 3 in 11, et productum 33 minori extremo 1 addendo. Idem invenitur, datis majore extremo, differentia communi, et numero locorum quibus terminus quæsitus a maximo sejungitur, ducendo communem differentiam in numerum locorum datum, et productum e majore extremo auferendo. Patet etiam, qua ratione datis termino quolibet, ejusdem indice, et communi differentia, terminus primus assignetur ; et quomodo ex datis termino quovis, illius indice et minore extremo, communis differentia itemque ex datis termino, differentia, et minore extremo, termini index eruatur. Quin et illud etiam patet, *viz.* dimidium summæ duorum terminorum æquari medio proportionali arithmetico. *E.g.* 7 et 13 faciunt 20, cujus dimidium 10 est terminus inter datos medius (*vide seriem primam*). Hæc et alia bene multa theoremata ac problemata, eorumque solutiones, ex ipsa progressionis arithmeticæ natura facile quisquam deduxerit, præsertim si logistica speciosa utatur. Quapropter ea exercitii causa tyronibus relinquo.

Progressio Geometrica vocatur series numerorum, eadem continua ratione crescentium vel decrescentium. *E.g.* 3. 6. 12. 24. 48. 96. sunt in progressione geometrica, cujus ratio communis est dupla, nimirum terminus quisque duplus est præcedentis.

Similiter numeri hujus decrescentis seriei, 81. 27. 9. 3. 1. progrediuntur ratione subtripla, *i.e.* terminus quilibet præcedentis subtriplus est sive $\frac{1}{3}$.

Ubi observandum est, terminum quemvis conflari ex potestate communis rationis, ipsi cognomine, in terminum primum ducta. *E.g.* In serie prima, 48, terminus exclusive quartus, producitur ex 16, potestate quarta numeri 2 (*i.e.* quæ generatur ex 2 ter in seipsum ducto, siquidem ipsa radix dicitur potestas prima) per terminum primum 3 multiplicata. Quamobrem ea quæ de progressione arithmetica diximus etiam hic locum habent, si pro additione et subductione multiplicationem et divisionem, pro multiplicatione et divisione involutionem et evolutionem, sive radicum [1] extractionem adhibeamus. *E.g.* Quemadmodum in progressione arithmetica summa extremorum bisecta dat medium arithmeticum, ita in progressione geometrica medius proportionalis est radix producti extremorum. Adeoque theoremata et problemata quod spectat, iis, cum illa ex nuda serierum contemplatione facillime eruantur, ulterius deducendis non immorabimur.

At vero, unum est progressionis geometricæ theorema, ex quo olim derivata fuit, et etiamnum dependet nobilis logarithmorum scientia, quodque adeo hic visum est explicare.

In progressione geometrica cujus principium est unitas, rectangulum duorum quorumlibet terminorum æquatur termino ejusdem progressionis, qui pro indice habet summam indicum factorum. *E.g.* Si sequentis seriei ducamus terminum secundum $\begin{cases} 1.\ 2.\ 4.\ 8.\ 16.\ 32.\ 64. \\ 0.\ 1.\ 2.\ 3.\ 4.\ 5.\ 6. \end{cases}$ 2 in quartum 8, productum 16 est terminus quintus, cujus index 4 æquatur indicibus secundi et quarti una collectis.

Ratio manifesta est, nam quælibet potestas, in aliam quamcunque ejusdem radicis ducta, procreat tertiam, cujus dimensiones tot sunt, quot fuere in utraque potestate generante. Sed in progressione geometrica, cujus terminus primus sit unitas, patet reliquos omnes subsequentes esse potestates ex communi ratione genitas, quarum singulæ tot habeant dimensiones, quot locis ab unitate distant.

Igitur si infinitæ progressioni geometricæ adscriberetur indi-

---

[1] *N.B.* Quomodo potestatum quarumvis radices extrahantur, lector diligens, juxta methodum quam secuti sumus de quadrato et cubo eorumque radicibus agentes, investigare poterit.

cum series itidem infinita, ad obtinendum duorum terminorum rectangulum haud necesse foret unum per alterum multiplicare ; oporteret solummodo, indicibus una collectis, quærere indicem qui aggregato æquetur, is sibi adscriptum ostenderet rectangulum quæsitum.   Similiter, si dividendus sit unus terminus per alium, differentia indicum, si extrahenda sit radix quadrata aut cubica, $\frac{1}{2}$ aut $\frac{1}{3}$ indicis, quæsitum quotum, vel radicem, indigitaret.

Hinc patet, difficiliores arithmeticæ operationes insigni compendio exerceri posse, si conderentur tabulæ, in quibus numeri naturali ordine collocati habeant singuli indicem a latere respondentem ;   tunc quippe multiplicatio, sola additione ;   divisio, subductione ;   extractio radicum, bisectione vel trisectione indicum, peragerentur.   Sed indices illos, sive logarithmos, numeris accommodare ;   *hoc opus, hic labor est*—in quo exantlando plurimi desudarunt mathematici.

Primi quidem tabularum conditores hac fere methodo usi sunt.   Numeris 1. 10. 100. 1000, &c. in progressione decupla existentibus, logarithmos assignarunt 0.0000000, 1.0000000. 2.0000000. 3.0000000, &c.   Deinde ut numeri alicujus, *v.g.* 4, inter 1 et 10 intermedii, logarithmum invenirent, adjectis utrique septem cyfris, inter 1.0000000, et 10.0000000, medium proportionalem quæsiere ;   qui si minor esset quam 4, inter ipsum et 10.0000000, si vero major, inter eum et 1.0000000, medius proportionalis indagandus erat :   porro inter hunc (si minor esset quam 4) et proxime majorem, sin major, et proxime minorem, denuo quærebant medium proportionalem ;   et sic deinceps, usque dum ventum fuisset ad numerum, non nisi insensibili particula, puta $\frac{1}{10000000}$, a proposito 4 differentem.   Hujus autem logarithmus obtinebatur, inveniendo medium arithmeticum inter logarithmos numerorum 1 et 10, et alium inter ipsum et logarithmum denarii, &c.   Jam si bipartiatur logarithmus numeri 4, habebitur logarithmus binarii, idem duplicatus dat logarithmum numeri 16 ;   et si logarithmo quaternionis addatur logarithmus binarii, summa erit logarithmus octonarii.   Simili methodo, ex uno logarithmo numeri 4 alii innumeri inveniri possunt.

Ad eundem modum, cum cæteris numeris inter unitatem et decadem intermediis aptati essent logarithmi, alios quamplurimos eorum summæ, differentiæ, &c. suppeditarunt.   Sed de his satis, neque enim omnia quæ ad logarithmos spectant tradere statuimus ; id duntaxat propositum fuit, eorum naturam, usum, et inventionem quadantenus exponere.

Miscellanea Mathematica

Sive cogitata nonnulla de radicibus
surdis, de æstu aeris, de cono æquilatero et cylindro eidem sphæræ
circumscriptis, de ludo algebraico ;
& parænetica quædam ad studium
matheseos, præsertim algebræ

The Text

EGREGIO ADOLESCENTI

D. SAMUELI MOLYNEUX,[1]

IN ACADEMIA DUBLINIENSI SOCIORUM COMMENSALI, FILIO
VIRI CLARISSIMI GULIELMI MOLYNEUX,[1] PAUCIS
ABHINC ANNIS ACERBO, TAM PATRIÆ QUAM
REI LITERARIÆ, FATO DENATI.

EGREGIE ADOLESCENS,

Tanta fuit patris tui, dum viveret, apud eruditos existimatio, ut me rem iis pergratam facturum arbitrer, si filium, sui acuminis ac solertiæ hæredem, ipsum reliquisse palam faciam. Fatendum quidem est, patruum tuum, virum doctrina juxta ac humanitate insigni, tale aliquid jam pridem [2] fecisse. Viderat nimirum vir clarissimus, eam esse tui necdum adolescentis indolem, ut te olim paterna pressurum vestigia verisimile judicaret. Cujus tanti viri auctoritas apud me usque eo valuit, ut deinceps magnam de te spem conceperim. Nunc autem, cum ipse studiorum tuorum conscius, te saniori philosophiæ et mathesi operam strenue navantem cernam ; quum spinas quibus obsepta videtur mathesis, quæque alios quamplurimos ab ejus studio deterrere solent, te e contra ad alacrius pergendum stimulare ; quum denique ad industriam illam et sciendi ardorem præclaram ingenii vim sentiam

---

[1] [Samuel Molyneux, 1689-1728, was a politician with scientific interests, like his father William. He graduated B.A. in Trinity College in 1708, and therefore the teaching that Berkeley gave him must have been private tuition (" *studiorum tuorum conscius* "), not in official tutorship. Molyneux became secretary to George, Prince of Wales, and presented Berkeley to the Prince and Princess, and when his sermons on Passive Obedience were misrepresented as Jacobite, Molyneux produced a copy of the work, and proved to the Prince that it was the work of a loyalist. Molyneux became F.R.S., Lord of the Admiralty, and M.P. in both the British and the Irish (for Dublin University) Parliaments.—Ed.]

[2] Vide epistolam Thomæ Molyneux, M.D. ad Episcopum Clogherensem, *Philosoph. Transact.* No. 282.

accedere ; exundantem nequeo cohibere lætitiam quin in orbem literatum effluat, teque ex præcipuis (si modo Deus vitam largiatur et salutem) ineuntis sæculi ornamentis fore, certissimo sane augurio prænuntiem.   Proinde, sequentibus quantuliscunque ad te delatis, ansam hancce tecum publice colloquendi arripere gestiebam ; cum ut ipse proprio cedam affectui, tum ut tu, expectatione de te coorta, tanquam vinculo quodam, alioqui non ingrato, illi rerum pulcherrimarum studio devinciare.

MISCELLANEA MATHEMATICA

DE RADICIBUS SURDIS

ID mihi olim in mentem venit, ut putarem praxin algebraicam factum iri nonnihil faciliorem, si ablegato signo radicali, alia quæpiam excogitaretur potestatum imperfectarum radices computandi methodus, quæ ab usitata in reliquis operationum forma minus abhorreret. Nimirum quemadmodum in arithmetica longe facilius tractantur fractiones a vulgaribus ad decimales reductæ, quia tunc notæ cujusque loco nominatoris vicem obeunte, altera sui parte truncantur, similique forma ac integri descriptæ, eandemque cum iis seriem constituentes, iisdem itidem legibus subjiciuntur ; sic si ex logistica etiam speciosa ablegaretur nota ista radicalis [$\sqrt{\ }$] quæ, ut nominator inter fractiones et integros, operationum diversitatem inter radices surdas ac rationales inducit, praxis proculdubio minus intricata evaderet.

Quidni itaque radices quascunque surdas, perinde ac rationales, per nudas duntaxat literas designemus, *v.g.* pro $\sqrt{b}$ substituto *c* vel *d* ? Quippe surdis ad hunc modum designatis, nihil intererit inter eas ac potestatum perfectarum radices ; additio, subductio, multiplicatio, &c. ad eundem modum utrobique peragentur. Sed objicere in promptu est, vel magis quam signum radicale, species hac ratione multiplicatas calculum divexare. Siquidem cum nulla sit affinitas seu connexio inter *b* et *c*, adeoque una ex altera agnosci nequeat ; videtur illius radix aptius designari per $\sqrt{b}$, cujus statim ac cernitur innotescit significatio. *Respondeo*, huic malo mederi posse, si *v.g.* Græcum alphabetum ad designandas radices introducamus, scribendo β pro $\sqrt{b}$, δ pro $\sqrt{d}$, &c. Quo pacto non tam ipsæ literæ quam characteres variabuntur, et nota quævis substituta in tantum referet primitivam, ut scrupulo non sit locus.

Quantitatis ex aliarum multiplicatione aut divisione conflatæ radix designabitur per earundem radices similiter multiplicatas seu divisas. *E.g.*

$$\sqrt{bc} = \beta\kappa, \text{ et} \sqrt{\frac{bdm}{e}} = \frac{\beta\delta\mu}{\epsilon}.$$

Si vero proponatur quantitas multinomia, seu constans ex pluribus membris (in quibus nulla sit quantitas ignota) signis $+$ aut $-$ inter se connexis : Designetur horum aggregatum (quod et alias quidem sæpe fit) per unicam aliquam literam. *E.g.* fiat $a + b - c = g$ cujus radix est γ.

Quæris autem quid fiat ubi ignotæ quantitates notis connectantur ; sit *v.g.* potestas imperfecta $f + x$: nam si utamur ϕ et ξ partium nempe potestatis radicibus, ex iis nequit determinari radix totius ? Quidni igitur exæquemus potestatem datam imperfectam alteri cuidam perfectæ, *viz.* $f + x = ff + 2f\xi + \xi\xi$, vel $fff + 3ff\xi + 3f\xi\xi + \xi\xi\xi$, &c. ? Tunc enim erit $f + \xi = \sqrt[2]{f + x}$ vel $\sqrt[3]{f + x}$, &c.

Sed illud prætermissum est, qua ratione radicis genus dignoscatur ; utrum scilicet sit quadratica, aut cubica, aut biquadratica. Num itaque quadraticis linquendi sunt characteres Græci, reliquisque deinceps alii itidem assignandi ? An potius manente eodem charactere, puncto supra notato radicem quadratam, binis cubicam, tribus biquadraticam, atque ita porro indigitemus : *e.g.* $\dot{a}$ significet radicem quadraticam quantitatis per a designatæ, $\ddot{a}$ radicem cubicam, $\dddot{a}$ biquadraticam, &c. ? quo quidem modo fluxiones primæ, secundæ, tertiæ, &c. designantur. Seu denique id satis ducamus quod per retrogressum innotescat radicis denominatio ? Quippe inter operandum nihil interest cujus generis sit radix aliqua, quandoquidem omnes absque signo radicali notatæ, iisdem subsint legibus, et ad eundem modum tractentur.

Cruda quidem sunt hæc et imperfecta, quamque nullius sint pretii ut a me proponuntur, sat cerno. Tu autem, *clarissime adolescens*, cui nec otium deest nec ingenium, ex hocce sterquilinio boni aliquid fortasse extraxeris. Cæterum haud scio, an ea quæ disseruimus tyronibus (reliquos ista flocci facturos scio) quadantenus usui esse possint ; eorumque ope disquisitionis analyticæ filum nonnunquam enoduletur eliminatis, cum ipso signo radicali, operationibus quæ illud comitantur heterogeneis. Utut id sit, mihi visus sum iis ex parte adhibitis, vulgarem *de surdis* doctrinam, brevius et clarius quam ab ullo quod sciam factum est, posse explicare. Proinde rem ipsam aggredior.

Radices surdæ dicuntur esse commensurabiles, cum earum ad invicem ratio per numeros rationales exprimi possit, quod si fieri nequeat, incommensurabiles appellantur. Porro si propositis duabus radicibus surdis, quærere oporteat, utrum sint commensurabiles necne : Inveniatur exponens rationis existentis inter potestates quibus præfigitur signum radicale ; hic si sit potestas perfecta, habens eundem indicem ac radices propositæ, erunt illæ commensurabiles : Sin minus, incommensurabiles censendæ sunt. *E.g.* Sint radices propositæ $\sqrt[2]{24}$ et $\sqrt[2]{54}$. $\frac{4}{9}$ fractio quadrata exponit rationem potestatis unius 24 ad alteram 54 ; adeoque radices sunt commensurabiles, *viz.* $\sqrt[2]{24}$: $\sqrt[2]{54}$: : 2 : 3. Proponatur denuo $\sqrt[3]{320}$ et $\sqrt[3]{135}$: ratio numeri 320 ad 135 exponitur per $\frac{64}{27}$, cubum nempe perfectum, cujus radix $\frac{4}{3}$ indicat rationem radicis unius $\sqrt[3]{320}$ ad reliquam $\sqrt[3]{135}$. Demonstratio manifesta est, siquidem norunt omnes radices quadratas esse in ratione subduplicata, cubicas in subtriplicata, biquadraticas in subquadruplicata, et sic deinceps potestatum respectivarum.

Quod si radices sint heterogeneæ quarum exploranda est ratio, ad idem genus reducantur, involvendo numeros signo radicali affixos, singulos juxta indicem radicis alterius ; quibus sic involutis præfigenda erit nota radicalis cum indice ex indicibus primo datis in se mutuo ductis conflato. *E.g.* Sint radices surdæ heterogeneæ $\sqrt[2]{5}$ et $\sqrt[3]{11}$. Cubatis 5, et quadratis 11, proveniunt 125 et 121 : His præfixum signum radicale cum indice 6 præstat radices homogeneas $\sqrt[6]{125}$ et $\sqrt[6]{121}$. Hujus operationis ut cernatur ratio, designemus $\sqrt[2]{5}$ per speciem quamvis simplicem puta b, et $\sqrt[3]{11}$ per c ; eritique $\sqrt[2]{bb} = \sqrt[2]{5}$, et $\sqrt[3]{ccc} = \sqrt[3]{11}$, et $\sqrt[6]{bbbbbb} = \sqrt[6]{125}$, et $\sqrt[6]{cccccc} = \sqrt[6]{121}$. Ubi porro patet quod $\sqrt[6]{bbbbbb} = \sqrt[2]{bb}$ et $\sqrt[6]{cccccc} = \sqrt[3]{ccc}$.

Additionem quod attinet radicum surdarum ; illa, si sint commensurabiles, fit præfigendo summam terminorum rationis signo radicali, cui suffigendus est communis divisor cujus ope dictæ rationis termini innotuerunt. *E.g.* $\sqrt[2]{24} + \sqrt[2]{54} = 5\sqrt[2]{6}$. Nam ex antedictis, et iis quæ sequuntur de multiplicatione,

$$\sqrt[2]{24} = 2\sqrt[2]{6}, \text{ et } \sqrt[2]{54} = 3\sqrt[2]{6}.$$

Ad eundem modum fit subductio, nisi quod differentia terminorum exponentis signo radicali præfigatur. Si addendæ sunt aut subducendæ radices surdæ incommensurabiles, mediantibus signis $+$ aut $-$ connectantur. *E.g.* $\sqrt{6} + \sqrt{3}$ et $\sqrt{6} - \sqrt{3}$ sunt summa et differentia radicum numerorum 6 et 3 ; quo quidem modo surdis adduntur aut subducuntur etiam numeri rationales.

Si radix surda per aliam homogeneam multiplicanda sit ; rectangulo potestatum præponatur nota radicalis, simulque index communis. *E.g.*

$$\sqrt[2]{3} \times \sqrt[2]{7} = \sqrt[2]{21} \text{ et } \sqrt[3]{g} \times \sqrt[3]{x} = \sqrt[3]{gx}.$$

Ad cujus praxeos demonstrationem, designentur radices numerorum 3 et 7 per b et d, ut sit $bb = 3$ et $dd = 7$, et liquido constabit, quod $\sqrt[2]{bb\ dd} = bd$, *i.e.* radix quadrata producti æquatur producto radicum quadratarum. Idem ad eundem modum ostendi potest de aliis quibuscunque radicibus, cubicis, biquadraticis, &c. Radices heterogeneæ, priusquam multiplicentur, ad homogeneas reducendæ sunt. Si numerus rationalis in surdum ducendus sit, elevetur ille ad potestatem datæ imperfectæ cognominem, cui præfigatur nota radicalis, unaque ejusdem potestatis index. Cætera ut prius. *E.g.*

$$5 \times \sqrt[3]{4} = \sqrt[3]{125} \times \sqrt[3]{4} = \sqrt[3]{500}.$$

Vel brevius sic, $5 \sqrt[3]{4}$; et generaliter

$$b \times \sqrt[a]{c} = \sqrt[a]{b^a c} \text{ vel } b \sqrt[a]{c}.$$

Divisionem quod attinet, quoties dividendus et divisor sunt ambo radices surdæ, ablata (si qua sit) heterogeneitate, nota radicalis cum proprio indice quotienti potestatum præfixa, quotum quæsitum exhibebit. *E.g.*

$$\sqrt[2]{7} \div \sqrt[2]{3} = \sqrt[2]{\tfrac{7}{3}} = \sqrt[2]{2\tfrac{1}{3}}.$$

Si vero ex duobus alteruter duntaxat numerus seu species signo radicali afficitur : reliquus, juxta indicem radicis datæ involutus, notæ radicali suffigatur ; deinde ut prius. *E.g.*

$$\sqrt[3]{96} \div 4 = \sqrt[3]{96} \div \sqrt[3]{64} = \sqrt[3]{\tfrac{96}{64}} = \sqrt[3]{\tfrac{3}{2}}.$$

Vel sine præparatione $\sqrt[3]{\dfrac{96}{4}}$. Et generaliter

$$\sqrt[a]{c} \div b = \dfrac{\sqrt[a]{c}}{b^a} \text{ vel } \dfrac{\sqrt[a]{c}}{b}.$$

Hæc, velut præcedentia, facillime demonstrantur.

DE ÆSTU AERIS

Non ita pridem incidi in librum cui titulus, *De Imperio Solis et Lunæ in Corpora humana*, authore viro cl. M.D. et S.R.S. Qui sane quantus sit, et quantulus sim ipse, non ignoro. Sed ut libere dicam quod sentio ; sententiam ejus *De Æstu Aeris*, quam ibidem explicatam dat, utpote celeberrimi Newtoni principiis innixam, ambabus ulnis amplexus sum. Verumtamen haud scio, an author ingeniosus phænomenon quorundam isthuc pertinentium causas tam recte assecutus sit. Quam vero justa sit dubitandi ratio, tu, cujus perspectum habeo acumen, optime judicabis.

Tribuit vir cl. altiorem aeris circa æquinoctia tumorem figuræ sphæroidali terræ ; differentiam insuper inter aeris intumescentiam, quæ a luna meridionali, et illam quæ a luna (ut ita loquar) antimeridionali in sphæra obliqua excitatur, eidem causæ acceptam refert. Ego vero neutrius istorum phænomenon explicationem ab oblata sphæroide petendam duco. Propterea quod, primo, quamvis sententia quæ massam aereo-terrestrem ea esse figura contendit, rationibus tam physicis quam mathematicis comprobetur, et nonnullis item phænomenis pulchre respondeat ; non tamen apud omnes usque adeo obtinet, ut nulli veteris, vel etiam oppositæ sententiæ fautores, iique non minimæ notæ viri, hodie reperiantur. Et sane memini, D. Chardellou, astronomiæ peritissimum, abhinc plus minus sesquianno, mihi indicasse, sibi ex observationibus astronomicis axem terræ diametro æquatoris compertum esse longiorem : Adeoque terram esse quidem sphæroidem, sed qualem vult Burnetius,[1] ad polos assurgentem, prope æquatorem vero humiliorem. Attamen quod ad me attinet, mallem quidem viri clarissimi observationes potius in dubium vocare, quam argumentis quæ terram esse oblatam demonstrant obviam ire. Nihilominus, quoniam sententia ista non omnibus æque arridet, illam tanquam principium ad phænomenon ullum explicandum adhiberi nollem, nisi res aliter commode explicari nequeat. Sed secundo, tantum abest quod supradictorum effectuum explicatio sphæroidalem terræ figuram necessario poscat, ut vix ullam inde lucis particulam mutuari videatur : id quod, appositis quæ in hanc rem scribit vir clarissimus, ostendere conabor. ' *Altius (inquit) solito se attollit aer circa duo æquinoctia, quoniam cum æquinoctialis linea illi globi terrestris circulo adversa respondeat qui diametrum habet maximam, utrumque sidus dum in illa versatur terræ est vicinius.*' De Imp. Sol. et Lun. p. 9. Jam vero, utrum vicinior iste luminarium

---

[1] [Thomas Burnet, 1635–1715, author of *Sacred Theory of the Earth*, 1681.—Ed.]

situs par sit attollendo aeri in cumulum solito sensibiliter altiorem, merito ambigi potest. Etenim tantilla est differentia inter axem

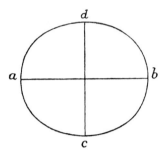

transversum et conjugatum ellipseos, cujus volutione gignitur sphærois terrestris, ut illa ad sphæram quamproxime accedat. Verum ut accuratius rem prosequamur, designet *a c b d* sectionem per polos massæ aereoterrestris, in qua sit *d c* axis, *a b* diameter æquatoris. Jam inito calculo, deprehendi vim lunæ attractricem in *b* vel *a* non esse $\frac{1}{4000}$ sui parte fortiorem quam foret in *c* vel *d*, si illa polo alterutri directe immineret, et proinde differentiunculam istam effectui ulli sensibili edendo imparem omnino esse. Considerandum etiam, lunam ab æquatore nunquam tertia parte arcus *b d* distare, dictamque proinde quantulamcunque differentiam adhuc valde minuendam esse. Quod autem de luna diximus, id de sole, cum multis vicibus longius absit, adhuc magis constabit.

Verum quidem est D. Mead alias insuper causas æstus prope æquinoctia altioris attulisse ; *viz.* ' *agitationem fluidi sphæroidis in majori orbe se revolventis majorem, præterea vim centrifugam effectum habentem eo loci longe maximum.*' Quod ad primam, etsi illa prima fronte nonnihil præ se ferre visa sit, fatendum tamen est, me non omnino percipere, quomodo aliquid inde ad distinctam rei propositæ explicationem faciens colligi possit. Quod ad secundam, constat sane vim centrifugam prope æquatorem esse longe maximam, et propterea massam aereo-terrestrem figuram oblatæ sphæroidis induisse ; quid vero aliud hinc sequatur non intelligo.

Verum etiamsi concedamus aerem, propter causas a clarissimo viro allatas, circa æquinoctia ad æquatorem supra modum tumefieri ; non tamen inde apparet, quamobrem apud nos, qui tam procul ab æquatore degimus, tum temporis altius solito attollatur ; quinimo contrarium sequi videtur. Sequenti pagina sic scribit D. Mead. ' *Ut finem tandem faciam, in iisdem parallelis ubi lunæ declinatio est, illum cæli polum versus qui altissimus insurgit, validissima est attractio, cum illa ad ejus loci meridianum verticem accedit, minima vero, ubi pervenit ad meridianum loci oppositi ; quod contra contingit in parallelis his adversis. Causa est in sphæroide terræ ætherisque figura.*' Ego vero causam non esse in terræ et ambientis ætheris figura propterea puto, quod posita terra vel perfecte spherica, vel etiam oblonga, idem certe eveniret, uti infra patebit.

Restat ut harum rerum explicationem ipse aggrediar, siquidem eo præsertim nomine, suspecta mihi fuit ratio a sphæroidali terræ figura deducta, quod, nulla ipsius habita ratione, res tota clarissime simul ac facillime exponi posse videbatur.

Newtonus, Operis sui Physico-Mathematici, lib. iii. prop. 24. ubi æstuum marinorum phenomena explicat, hæc habet : ' *Pendet etiam effectus utriusque luminaris ex ipsius declinatione seu distantia ab æquatore. Nam si luminare in polo constitueretur, traheret illud singulas aquæ partes constanter, absque actionis intensione et remissione, adeoque nullam motus reciprocationem cieret. Igitur luminaria recedendo ab æquatore polum versus effectus suos gradatim amittent, et propterea minores ciebunt æstus in syzygiis solstitialibus quam in æquinoctialibus.*' Atqui non alia causa videtur quærenda ullius phænomeni æstus aerei, quam quæ ad similem effectum in æstu marino excitandum sufficiat. Sed ut id quod a viro per totum orbem longe celeberrimo breviter adeoque subobscure traditum est, uberius exponam. Sit in priore figura *a d c b* meridianus, et *a b* axis massæ aereoterrestris ; sol autem et luna in polo constitui concipiantur. Manifestum est, quamvis massæ aereæ partem, puta *d*, durante circumvolutione diurna, eandem semper distantiam a luminaribus tueri, adeoque vi ubique æquali in eorum corpora trahi. Proinde aer non uno tempore attollitur, alio deprimitur, sed per totum diem in eadem hæret altitudine. Verum secundo, in eadem figura repræsentet *a c b d* æquatorem aut parallelum quemvis, luminaria interim in plano æquinoctiali existant ; quo tempore manifestum est, tum ipsum æquatorem, tum singulos parallelos, ellipticam induere figuram. Manifestum etiam est, aerem qui nunc *a*, apicem axis transversi, obtinet, adeoque altissimus insurgit, post sex horas, *c*, extremum axis conjugati, ubi humillimus de-
primetur, occupatum ire, maxi-
mamque proinde motus reciprocationem cieri. Ut igitur rem omnem
simul absolvam, gibbos sphæroidis
æstuosæ triplici ratione locari con-
cipiamus : vel in polis, vel in
æquatore, vel in locis intermediis.
In primo casu, esset planum rota-
tionis diurnæ ad axem sphæroidis
perpendiculare, adeoque circulus ;

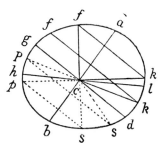

unde nullus foret æstus : in secundo, esset ad eundem parallelum, adeoque ellipsis, inter cujus axes maxima sit differentia ; unde maximi forent æstus : In tertio, quo magis ad situm perpendicularem accederet, eo circulo vicinius esset, adeoque minores forent æstus.

Reliquum est ut demonstrem, differentiam quæ est in sphæra obliqua inter æstum quemvis et subsequentem, ubi luna extra æquatorem vagatur, terra posita vel oblata, vel ad amussim sphærica, vel etiam oblonga, perinde causatum iri. Sit $a\,b$ axis mundi, $g\,d$ æquator, k locus quivis, $f\,k$ loci parallelus, $h\,l$ axis sphæroidis æstuosæ ob actionem, potissimum, lunæ utrinque tumentis. Luna autem prope l constituatur. Demonstrandum est $c\,k$ altitudinem aeris, luna prope loci meridianum existente, majorem esse $c\,f$, aeris altitudine, ubi luna meridianum loci opposite transierit. Ducatur $p\,s$ parallelus priori ex adverso respondens, et producantur $c\,k,\,c\,f$ ad p et s. Per constructionem arcus $p\,h$ æqualis est arcui $k\,l$; ergo arcus $f\,h$ major est arcu $k\,l$; ergo propter ellipsin recta $f\,s$ minor est recta $k\,p$, et $f\,c$ minor $k\,c$. Q.e.d.

DE CONO ÆQUILATERO ET CYLINDRO, EIDEM SPHÆRÆ CIRCUMSCRIPTIS

LEMMA

LATUS trianguli æquilateri est ad diametrum inscripti circuli ut $\sqrt{3}$ ad 1; et perpendicularis ex angulo quovis ad latus oppositum demissa, est ad eandem, ut 3 ad 2.

Hæc cuivis, algebram et geometriam utcunque callenti, facile constabunt.

PROBLEMA

Invenire rationem quæ existit inter Cylindrum et Conum æquilaterum eidem Sphæræ circumscriptos.

Ponamus diametrum et peripheriam basis cylindri esse singulas, unitatem. Eruntque per lemma, diameter basis coni ejusdemque peripheria singulæ $\sqrt{3}$. Proinde $1 \times \frac{1}{4} = \frac{1}{4} =$ bas. cylindri; et $\frac{1}{2} =$ summæ basium. Et $\sqrt{3} \times \frac{1}{4}\sqrt{3} = \frac{3}{4} =$ bas. coni, et superficies cylindri seu quadruplum baseos $= 1$. Et superficies simplex coni $= \frac{3}{2} = \dfrac{\sqrt{6}}{4} \times \sqrt{6}$. Nam $\sqrt{\frac{3}{2}}$ (h.e. media proportionalis inter $\sqrt{3}$ latus coni, et basis radium seu $\sqrt{\frac{3}{4}}$) est radius circuli æqualis superficiei conicæ. Et per præcedentia $1 + \frac{1}{2} = \frac{3}{2} =$ sup. tot. cylindri, et $\frac{3}{2} + \frac{3}{4} = \frac{9}{4} =$ sup. tot. coni. Porro per hypothesin et lemma, axis cylindri est 1, et coni $\frac{3}{2}$. Soliditas autem cylindri $= \frac{1}{4} \times 1 = \frac{1}{4}$, et soliditas coni $= \frac{3}{4} \times \frac{1}{2} = \frac{3}{8}$. Hinc, comparatis inter se homogeneis, eruitur sequens.

THEOREMA

Inter Conum æquilaterum et Cylindrum eidem Sphæræ circumscriptos, eadem obtinet ratio, sesquialtera, quoad superficies
totas, superficies simplices, soliditates, altitudines, et bases.

Duobus abhinc annis Theorema illud non sine admiratione
aliqua inveni. Nec tamen propriam ingenii vim aut sagacitatem
ullam, quippe in re tam facili, sed quod Tacquetus, notissimus
matheseos Professor, tantopere gloriatus sit, de invento cui impar
non sit tyro, id demum admiratus sum. Nempe is invenerat
partem aliquam Theorematis præfati, *viz.* quod *conus æquilaterus
sit cylindri, eidem sphæræ circumscripti, soliditate et superficie tota ses-
quialter ; quodque adeo continuata esset ratio* inter conum æquilaterum,
cylindrum, et sphæram. Hæc est ipsa illa propositio, ad quam
spectat schema, quod præfati authoris tractatus *De Theorematis ex
Archimede selectis*, in ipsa fronte, una cum epigraphe inscriptum
præfert. Quin etiam videas quæ dicat Jesuita in præfatione, in
scholio ad prop. 32, et sub finem propositionis 44^{tae} ejusdem tractatus. Ubi Theorema hocce tanquam illustre aliquod inventum,
et Archimedæorum æmulum ostentat. Idem quod Tacquetus,
etiam Cl. Wallisius in additionibus et emendationibus ad cap. 81
algebræ suæ, a D. Caswello ope Arithmetices Infinitorum demonstratum exhibet. Quod ipsum, quoad alteram ejus partem, facit
D. Dechales in libro suo de Indivisibilium Methodo, prop. 20.
Sed tam ipsa indivisibilium methodus, quam quæ in ea fundatur
arithmetica infinitorum, a nonnullis minus Geometricæ censentur.

Integrum autem Theorema a nemine, quod sciam, antehac
demonstratum fuit. Attamen si verum est quod opinatur Tacquetus : *Idcirco Archimedi inter alia tam multa et præclara inventa,
illud quo cylindrum inscriptæ sphæræ soliditate et superficie sesquialterum
esse demonstrat, præ reliquis placuisse : quod corporum, et superficierum
corpora ipsa continentium, eadem esset atque una rationalis proportio.* Si,
inquam, hoc in causa fuit, cur is cylindrum sphæræ circum-
scriptum tumulo insculptum voluit, quid tandem faceret senex
ille Siculus, si unam eandemque rationalem proportionem bina
corpora quintuplici respectu intercedere deprehendisset ? Illud
tamen quam facile ex ejus inventis profluat, modo vidimus.

Simili fere methodo ac nos illud omnia Tacqueti Theoremata
Archimedæis subjuncta, adde et centum istiusmodi alia si cui
operæ pretium videbitur, haud difficile erit invenire et demonstrare.

DE LUDO ALGEBRAICO

Sub idem tempus quo Theorema illud, Ludum etiam Algebraicum inveni. Quippe cum vidissem e familiaribus meis nonnullos, per dimidios ferme dies, scacchorum ludo gnaviter incumbentes, acre eorum studium in re nihili admiratus, rogavi quidnam esset quod tantopere laborarent? Illi porro pergratum animi exercitium renuntiant. Hoc ego mecum reputans, mirabar quamobrem tam pauci ad mathesin, utilissimam sane scientiam eandemque jucundissimam, animum applicarent. An quod difficilis sit? Sed multi et ingenio valent, nec laborem in nugis fastidiunt ullum. An potius, quod gratissimum animi exercitium non sit? Sed quænam, quæso, est illa ars, aut disciplina, aut quodcunque demum opus, quod omnem animi facultatem, solertiam, acumen, sagacitatem pulchrius exerceat? Sed ludus est mathesis? Nihilo secius jucunda : eo tamen si venisset nomine, tunc forsan lepidi isti homunciones, qui tempus ludendo terunt, ad ejus studium se protinus accingerent. Subiit adhæc sapientissimi viri Johannis Lockii, in re non multum absimili, consilium. Sequentem proinde lusum ad praxin algebræ exercendam, rudi fateor Minerva, excogitavi, sed qualis adolescenti, aliis præsertim studiis occupato, facile spero condonabitur.

Problemata algebraica immediate constituunt æquationes datæ, quæ in quæstionibus determinatis quantitates quæsitas numero exæquant. Quælibet autem æquatio duobus constat membris æqualitatis signo connexis, in quorum utroque considerandæ veniunt ; primo, species, utrum scilicet quantitates datas aut quæsitas designent ; deinde, signa quibus connectuntur. Efficere itaque ut hæc omnia ad constituendas quæstiones sorte obveniant, ludumque tam ex quæstionum formatione, quam ex earundem resolutione, concinnare operam damus.

In asserculo, qualis ad dominarum aut scacchorum lusum vulgo adhiberi solet, depingatur circulus quadrato inscriptus, reliquaque omnia quæ in apposito Schemate [1] continentur : Nisi quod loco circellorum nigrantium facienda sint foramina. Quibus peractis, habebimus Tabulam Lusoriam. Parandus insuper est stylus tenuis e ligno, qui aliquo ex dictis foraminibus infigatur. Reliquum est ut horum usum exponamus.

---

[1] [In two copies in the Library of Trinity College, Dublin, the *Tabula Lusoria* faces this section (p. 72) on an enlarged page ; in the third copy (oo g 55) it is absent.—Ed.]

Ut vides, operationum logisticarum symbola ad latera et angulos quadrati scribuntur : Porro latera prioribus, anguli vero posterioribus, æquationum membris signa impertiunt. Circulus autem inscriptus a sedecim cuspidibus in totidem partes æquales dispescitur, ita ut tres cuspides ad latus et angulum quemvis spectent, sed aliæ directe, aliæ oblique : Quæ oblique latus aliquod aut angulum respiciunt, eæ angulo et lateri communes sunt ; quæ vero directe latus aliquod intuentur, eæ ad angulum nullum pertinent, sed ad utrosque adjacentes pariter referuntur. Et vicissim, quæ angulum aliquem directe intuentur, eæ ad latus nullum pertinent, sed ad utraque adjacentia pariter referri censendæ sunt.

In formanda itaque quæstione, primo observanda est cuspis quam stylus respicit, latusque et angulum ad quos pertineat ; horum signa notentur, quippe quæ, ut diximus, species utriusque

TABULA LUSORIA

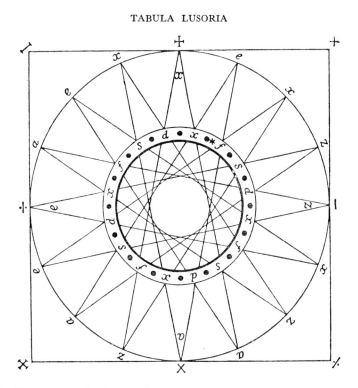

cujuslibet æquationis membri connectent. Dein, stylo literæ ad prædictam cuspidem scriptæ imposito, numera 1, eoque inde juxta rectæ lineæ ductum translato (ut faciunt astrologi, nominum quibus feriæ appellantur rationem assignantes) ad literam oppositam, numera 2. Tunc ad alteram lineæ, tanquam continuata esset per annulum intermedium, extremitatem pergens, numera 3 ; et sic deinceps, donec litera primæ cuspidi adjacens recurrat. Hinc recta descendens ad cuspidem in convexitate interioris circuli terminatam, foramine alterutro adjacenti infige stylum.

Numerus ultimo numeratus indicabit, quot quantitates quæsitæ, vel (quod idem est) quot æquationes datæ fuerint in quæstione. Harum membra priora, quantitates ignotæ alternatim sumptæ et signo laterali connexæ, posteriora, quantitates cognitæ vel incognitæ (prout determinarit litera ad cuspidem internam scripta) quæsitis signo angulari alligatæ, constituent. Porro *d* adhibendas quantitatum cognitarum species diversas, *s* unam solummodo, *f* figuras numerales 2, 3, 4, &c., *x* quantitates quæsitas repetendas esse indicat. Notandum autem, in cujusque æquationis membro posteriore non alias poni quantitates ignotas, quam quæ in primo membro sequentis æquationis reperiantur. Dicta exemplis clarescent.

Ponamus itaque stylum occupare foramen stellula insignitum, cuspisque quam respicit pertinebit ad latus cujus signum est +, et ad angulum cujus signum est ×, quæ signa in charta noto, laterale a sinistris sive primum deinde angulare. Porro *e* ad cuspidem scribitur, ad quam numero 1 ; inde (liberum autem est e duabus lineis utriusvis ductum sequi) sinistrorsum pergens offendo *a*, ad quam numero 2 ; hinc transiens ad *z* numero 3 ; inde autem transversim eunti denuo obversatur *e*, litera primæ cuspidi apposita, ad quam numerans 4, recta descendo ad cuspidem interiorem litera *d* insignitam. Erunt igitur quatuor quantitates quæsitæ in quæstione, quæ signo laterali +, alternatim connexæ, constituent prima æquationum datarum membra. Posteriora vero fient ex quantitatibus ignotis et notis (propter *d*) diversis per signum angulare, nimirum ×, conjunctis. Ad hunc modum.

$$a + e = yb \qquad a = ?$$
$$e + y = zc \qquad e = ?$$
$$y + z = ad \qquad y = ?$$
$$z + a = ef \qquad z = ?$$

Quod si ponamus stylum foramine præcedenti infixum esse, quo pacto + laterale directe intuebitur, lineæque sinistræ ductum sequamur, provenient tres quantitates investigandæ, et cuspis interior habebit literam f. Unde numerus æquationum datarum et priorum earundem membrorum signa, itemque posteriorum species determinantur. Sed quoniam in hoc casu cuspis indifferenter se habet respectu duorum angulorum adjacentium, idcirco eorum signa per vices usurpanda sunt : secundum quas conditiones hujusmodi struatur quæstio.

$$a + e = 2y \qquad\qquad a = ?$$
$$e + y = 3 - a \qquad\qquad e = ?$$
$$y + a = 4e \qquad\qquad y = ?$$

Posito autem stylum sequenti foramine infigi, cuspis stylaris in $\times$ angulare dirigetur, signaque lateralia $+$ et $-$ pariter respiciet. Proinde, si fert animus dextram inire semitam, juxta leges præmissas sequens prodibit quæstio :

$$a + e = ey \qquad\qquad a = ?$$
$$e - y = ay \qquad\qquad e = ?$$
$$y + a = ae \qquad\qquad y = ?$$

[1] Notandum autem primo, quod varietatem aliquam in signorum et specierum combinationibus præscriptæ leges admittant. Unde fit, quod cuspide semitaque determinatis, diversæ oriantur quæstiones.

Secundo, quod etsi ad primæ literæ recursum sistendum esse supra statuimus, lex tamen illa pro cujusvis arbitrio mutari possit : Ita ut progrediamur donec singulæ, a, e, z, x, obversentur, vel aliqua ex iis bis, vel ad aliam quamcunque metam ; sed ad lusum properamus.

Primum itaque e lusoribus aliquis ad methodum jam traditam quæstionem sibi formet. Quod et cæteris deinceps iisdem legibus faciendum est. Porro formatis singulorum quæstionibus, ad ejus quæ sorte obtigit solutionem se quisque accingat. Faciat dein unusquisque fractionem, cujus numerator sit numerus quantitatum in suo problemate quæsitarum, et nominator, numerus graduum sive æquationum quas, dum solveretur quæstio, chartis mandabat. Penes quem maxima sit fractio, is vincat.

Proinde, siquando fugitivæ quantitates inhiantem eluserint algebristam, is omni victoriæ spe excidisse censendus est. Neque id prorsus injuria, siquidem potius eligentis culpa quam infortunio accidat quæstionem esse indeterminatam.

Quotiescunque inter ludendum deveniatur ad æquationem

[1] *Vide Appendicem.*

affectam supra ordinem quadraticum, nihil opus erit exegesi num-
erosa aut constructione per parabolam, sufficit si radix incognita
mutata specie pro cognita habeatur.

Peractis omnium quæstionum solutionibus, quisque proximi
opus percurrat ; ad quod Pellii margines[1] conducant.

Quæ pignora et mulctas spectant, quisquam ad libitum com-
miniscatur : hæc enim aliis permitto.

Problemata quod spectat, illa quidem difficilia non sunt,
alioqui inepta forent ad lusum ; sed ea tamen, quorum solutio
in ingens lusorum commodum cesserit, dum rectum tramitem inire
student, dum longos consequentiarum nexus animo recolunt,
integramque analyseos seriem brevissimo conceptu claudere
laborant.

Permitte jam, adolescens optime, ut alios paulisper alloquar ;
tibi enim, quem ipsa trahit difficultas, nihil opus hortatore. Vos,
adolescentes academici, compello, quibus inest sagacitas, mentis-
que vigor et acumen ; tristem vero in musæo solitudinem, duram-
que eorum qui vulgo audiunt *Pumps*, vitam aversamini, satius inter
congerrones, per jocum et lusum, ingenium prodere ducentes.
Videtis quam merus lusus sit algebra, et sors locum habet, et
scientia, quidni igitur ad tabulam lusoriam accedatis ? Neque
enim, quod in chartis, scacchis, dominis, &c. usu venit, ut dum
alii ludunt, alii oscitanter adstent, hic etiam metuatis. Nam
quotcunque ludendi incesserit libido, iis omnibus ludere simul
ac studere, adde et nonnullis, lucelli aliquid corradere fas est.
Ast aliquem audire mihi videor in hujusmodi verba erumpentem.
Itane vero nos decipi posse putas ? Non ii sumus, quos ad
difficillimam artem sudore multo addiscendum, oblata lusus specie,
inescare liceat. Respondeo, algebram eatenus esse difficilem
quantum ad lusum requiritur : quod si tollas omnem difficultatem, tollitur simul recreatio omnis ac voluptas. Siquidem ludi
omnes totidem sunt artes et scientiæ : Nec aliud est inter cæteros
et hunc nostrum discrimen, quam quod illi præsens solummodo
oblectamentum spectent ; ex hoc vero, præter jucundissimum
laborem, alii etiam iique uberrimi fructus percipiantur. Tantum
autem abest quod hoc in lusus detrimentum cedat, ut is idcirco
omnibus numeris absolutus jure habeatur, juxta tritum illud
poetæ ;

'Omne tulit punctum qui miscuit utile dulci.'

[1] [John Pell (1611–85), mathematician, ' remembered chiefly by his invention
of the sign ÷ for division and of a mode of marginally registering the successive
steps in the reduction of equations.' *Dict. Nat. Biog.*—Ed.]

Sed quinam sunt illi quos prædicas fructus? Hos ut enu-
merem, universa, quaqua patet, mathesis, artesque omnes ac
scientias, quas rem militarem, civilem, et philosophicam promo-
ventes complectitur, perlustrandæ forent. Quippe per hasce
omnes diffunditur mirifica algebræ vis. Eadem apud omnes ars
magna, mirabilis, supremus cognitionis humanæ apex, universæ
matheseos nucleus et clavis, imo apud nonneminem scientiarum
omnium fundamentum audit. Et sane quam difficile esset
algebræ limites assignare, philosophiam naturalem et medicinam
jamdudum invasit, inque dies dissitissima quæque argumenta
aggreditur. Ut alia taceam, in Actis Philosoph. No. 257, de
certitudine testimoniorum et traditionum humanarum algebraica
extant theoremata. Et pro certo statuendum est, ubicunque datur
magis ac minus, ubicunque ratio aliqua aut proportio invenitur,
ibi locum habere algebram.

Verum dixerit fortasse aliquis, se nec mathesin ipsam, nec res
mathematice tractatas morari. Ut lubet : Demus hoc volun-
tati cujuspiam, demus ignorantiæ : Nimirum ex ignorantia
rerum præclarissimarum,[1] *quæque vos a barbaris distinguunt*, con-
temptum proficisci affirmare ausim. Estne vero quisquam qui
ingenium sagax, intellectum capacem, judicium acre parvi faciat?
Siquis usque adeo rationis expers inveniatur, is demum mathesin
spernat, quæ quanti sit momenti ad optimos quosque mentis habitus comparandos, apud omnes in confesso est.

Verulamius alicubi, in iis quæ de Augmentis Scientiarum
conscripsit, analogiam quandam inter pilæ palmariæ lusum et
mathesin notat.[2] Nempe quemadmodum per illum ultra volup-
tatem quæ primum intenditur, alia eaque potiora consequamur,
viz. corporis agilitatem et robur, promptumque oculorum motum:
Sic disciplinæ mathematicæ, præter fines ac usus singulis proprios,
illud etiam collaterale habent, quod mentem a sensibus abstra-
hant, ingeniumque acuant et figant. Idem hoc tam olim veteres,
quam hodie e modernis cordatiores quique agnoscunt. Quod
vero recentiorum algebra ad ingenium formandum imprimis
conducat, inter alios ostendunt, Cartesius, et prolixe Male-
branchius De Inquirenda Veritate, lib. vi. part .1. cap. 5. et part. 2.

---

[1] Vide *Tentamen Anglicum de Hortis Epicuri*, a Gulielmo Temple, Equite
Aurato, conscriptum.
[2] [" So that as tennis is a game of no use in itself, but of great use in respect
it maketh a quick eye and a body ready to put itself into all postures : so in the
mathematics, that use which is collateral and intervenient is no less worthy
than that which is principal and intended." Bacon, *Advancement of Learning*,
Book II, viii. 2—Ed.]

cap. 8. alibique passim. Et regulæ quidem quas hic in quæstionum solutione observandas tradit, lib. vi. part. 2. cap. 1. quæque tam sunt eximiæ, ut meliores angelum non fuisse daturum credat author quidam ingeniosus : illæ, inquam, regulæ angelicæ ex algebra desumi videntur. At quid alios memorem, cum vir omni laude major, Johannes Lockius, qui singulos intellectus humani defectus, eorumque remedia, siquis alius, optime callebat, cum universæ matheseos, tum præsertim algebræ studium, omnibus supra plebem positis, tanquam rem infiniti usus vehementer commendat ? Vide inter Opera ejus Posthuma, pag. 30, 31, 32, &c. Tractatus de Regimine Intellectus : Opus exiguum quidem illud et imperfectum, sed quod vastis et elaboratis aliorum voluminibus jure quisquam prætulerit. At vero author magni nominis ad disciplinas mathematicas acrem nimis meditationem, quæque homini generoso et voluptatibus studenti minus conveniat, requiri putat. *Respondeo*, suadente Lockio, frustra opponi dissidentis Santevremontii [1] judicium. Deinde hic ineptus matheseos judex merito habeatur, quippe qui, uti ex ejus vita et scriptis plusquam verisimile est, eam vix a limine salutarat. Si vero cortex durus videatur et exsuccus, quid mirum ? Sed ut dicam quod res est ; præstat singulos rem ipsam expertos propria sequi judicia. Nec est cur quis ingentes difficultates sibi fingat, eo quod vox algebra nescio quid asperum sonat et horrificum ; artem enim, quantum ad ludum nostrum requiritur, intra breve unius mensis spatium facile quisquam perdiscat.

Exposita demum lusus et consilii nostri ratione, lectorem mathematicum, ut tenues istas studiorum meorum primitias candide accipiat, rogo, potiora forsan posthac daturus. Impræsentiarum autem me alia distinent studia quæ, arida satis et jejuna, suavissimam mathesin exceperunt. Tu interim, Clarissime Adolescens, hanc nugarum rhapsodiam, tanquam aliquod mei erga te amoris symbolum, cape, et vale.

---

[1] [Saint-Evremond, 1613–1703, French soldier, poet, essayist, and politician ; he had to leave France for political reasons and settled in England ; he was buried in Westminster Abbey.—Ed.]

APPENDIX

Ut mentem nostram quilibet plenissime assequatur : Visum est sequentibus paginis omnem in quæstionibus combinationum et specierum varietatem quam præfatæ ludendi conditiones patiantur oculis subjicere.

Notandum autem : Primo, quod sequentes formulæ, quoad modos combinandi et quantitatum species, non item omnes quoad numerum æquationum datarum, ad cuspides respectivas pertinent. Sæpe enim plures quam tres quantitates investigandæ erunt.

Secundo, quod ut omnes quæstionum formulæ haberi possint, metæ diversæ, prout fieri posse supra monuimus, statuendæ sunt. Alioqui duæ tantum ex quatuor classibus ad cuspidem quamcunque pertinebunt.

Primam dico cuspidem quæ in + laterale dirigitur, secundam huic a dextris proximam, atque ita porro.

AD LECTOREM

Ista adolescentiæ nostræ, obiter tantum proprioque marte ad quantulamcunque matheseos scientiam olim enitentis, conamina in lucem protrusisse sero aliquoties pœnituit. Quin et pœniteret etiamnum, nisi quod hinc nobile par Ingeniorum, in spem nascentis sæculi succrescentium, una propalandi enascatur occasio. Neque enim nos aliunde Rempublicam Literariam demereri gloriamur. Atque hæc quidem ad temeritatis etc. censuram, ut et invidiam, si quam mihi forte conflaverim, amoliendum dicta intelligantur.

Cuspis prima

$$a+e = b \times e\ e-b\ b \times y\ y-b\ e \times b\ b-e\ y \times b\ b-y$$
$$s\quad e+y = b-y\ y \times b\ b-a\ a \times b\ y-b\ b \times y\ a-b\ b \times a$$
$$y+a = b \times a\ a-b\ b \times e\ e-b\ a \times b\ b-a\ e \times b\ b-e$$

$$a+e = b \times e\ e-b\ b \times y\ y-b\ e \times b\ b-e\ y \times b\ b-y$$
$$d\quad e+y = c-y\ y \times c\ c-a\ a \times c\ y-c\ c \times y\ a-c\ c \times a$$
$$y+a = d \times a\ a-d\ d \times e\ e-d\ a \times d\ d-a\ e \times d\ d-e$$

$$a+e = 2 \times e\ e-2\ 2 \times y\ y-2\ e \times 2\ 2-e\ y \times 2\ 2-y$$
$$f\quad e+y = 3-y\ y \times 3\ 3-a\ a \times 3\ y-3\ 3 \times y\ a-3\ 3 \times a$$
$$y+a = 4 \times a\ a-4\ 4 \times e\ e-4\ a \times 4\ 4-a\ e \times 4\ 4-e$$

$$a+e = e \times y\ e-y\ e \times y\ y-e$$
$$x\quad e+y = y-a\ y \times a\ a-y\ a \times y$$
$$y+a = a+e\ a-e\ a \times e\ e-a$$

Cuspis secunda

$$a+e = b \times e\ b \times y$$
$$s\quad e+y = b \times y\ b \times a$$
$$y+a = b \times a\ b \times e$$

$$a+e = b \times e\ b \times y$$
$$d\quad e+y = c \times y\ c \times a$$
$$y+a = d \times a\ d \times e$$

$$a+e = 2 \times e\ 2 \times y$$
$$f\quad e+y = 3 \times y\ 3 \times a$$
$$y+a = 4 \times a\ 4 \times e$$

$$a+e = e \times y$$
$$x\quad e+y = y \times a$$
$$y+a = a \times e$$

Cuspis tertia

$$a + e \quad a - e \ = \ e \times b \ y \times b$$
$$s \quad e - y \quad e + y \ = \ y \times b \ a \times b$$
$$y + a \quad y - a \ = \ a \times b \ e \times b$$

$$a + e \quad a - e \ = \ e \times b \ y \times b$$
$$d \quad e - y \quad e + y \ = \ y \times c \ a \times c$$
$$y + a \quad y - a \ = \ a \times d \ e \times d$$

$$a + e \quad a - e \ = \ e \times 2 \ y \times 2$$
$$f \quad e - y \quad e + y \ = \ y \times 3 \ a \times 3$$
$$y + a \quad y - a \ = \ a \times 4 \ e \times 4$$

$$a + e \quad a - e \ = \ e \times y$$
$$x \quad e - y \quad e + y \ = \ y \times a$$
$$y + a \quad y - a \ = \ a \times e$$

Cuspis quarta

$$a - e \ = \ b \times e \ b \times y$$
$$s \quad e - y \ = \ b \times y \ b \times a$$
$$y - a \ = \ b \times a \ b \times e$$

$$a - e \ = \ b \times e \ b \times y$$
$$d \quad e - y \ = \ c \times y \ c \times a$$
$$y - a \ = \ d \times a \ d \times e$$

$$a - e \ = \ 2 \times e \ 2 \times y$$
$$f \quad e - y \ = \ 3 \times y \ 3 \times a$$
$$y - a \ = \ 4 \times a \ 4 \times e$$

$$a - e \ = \ e \times y$$
$$x \quad e - y \ = \ y \times a$$
$$y - a \ = \ a \times e$$

Cuspis quinta

$$a-e \;=\; e\times b \; b\div e \; y\times b \; b\div y \; b\times e \; e\div b \; b\times y \; y\div b$$
$$s \quad e-y \;=\; y\div b \; b\times y \; a\div b \; b\times a \; b\div y \; y\times b \; b\div a \; a\times b$$
$$y-a \;=\; a\times b \; b\div a \; e\times b \; b\div e \; b\times a \; a\div b \; b\times e \; e\div b$$

$$a-e \;=\; e\times b \; b\div e \; y\times b \; b\div y \; b\times e \; e\div b \; b\times y \; y\div b$$
$$d \quad e-y \;=\; y\div c \; c\times y \; a\div c \; c\div a \; c\div y \; y\times c \; c\div a \; a\times c$$
$$y-a \;=\; a\times d \; d\div a \; e\times d \; d\div e \; d\times a \; a\div d \; d\times e \; e\div d$$

$$a-e \;=\; e\times 2 \; 2\div e \; y\times 2 \; 2\div y \; 2\times e \; e\div b \; 2\times y \; y\div 2$$
$$f \quad e-y \;=\; y\div 3 \; 3\times y \; a\div 3 \; 3\times a \; 3\div y \; y\times c \; 3\div a \; a\times 3$$
$$y-a \;=\; a\times 4 \; 4\div a \; e\times 4 \; 4\div e \; 4\times a \; a\div d \; 4\times e \; e\div 4$$

$$a-e \;=\; e\times y \; e\div y \; e\times y \; y\div e$$
$$x \quad e-y \;=\; y\div a \; y\times a \; a\div y \; a\times y$$
$$y-a \;=\; a\times e \; a\div e \; a\times e \; e\div a$$

Cuspis sexta

$$a-e \;=\; b\div e \; b\div y \; e\div b \; y\div b$$
$$s \quad e-y \;=\; b\div y \; b\div a \; y\div b \; a\div b$$
$$y-a \;=\; b\div a \; b\div e \; a\div b \; e\div b$$

$$a-e \;=\; b\div e \; b\div y \; e\div b \; y\div b$$
$$d \quad e-y \;=\; c\div y \; c\div a \; y\div c \; a\div c$$
$$y-a \;=\; d\div a \; d\div e \; a\div d \; e\div d$$

$$a-e \;=\; 2\div e \; 2\div y \; e\div 2 \; y\div 2$$
$$f \quad e-y \;=\; 3\div y \; 3\div a \; y\div 3 \; a\div 3$$
$$y-a \;=\; 4\div a \; 4\div e \; a\div 4 \; e\div 4$$

$$a-e \;=\; e\div y \; y\div e$$
$$x \quad e-y \;=\; y\div a \; a\div y$$
$$y-a \;=\; a\div e \; e\div a$$

Cuspis septima

$$s \quad \begin{array}{l} a-e \ \ a \times e \ = \ e \div b \ \ b \div e \ \ y \div b \ \ b \div y \\ e \times y \ \ e-y \ = \ y \div b \ \ b \div y \ \ a \div b \ \ b \div a \\ y-a \ \ y \times a \ = \ a \div b \ \ b \div a \ \ e \div b \ \ b \div e \end{array}$$

$$d \quad \begin{array}{l} a-e \ \ a \times e \ = \ e \div b \ \ b \div e \ \ y \div b \ \ b \div y \\ e \times y \ \ e-y \ = \ y \div c \ \ c \div y \ \ a \div c \ \ c \div a \\ y-a \ \ y \times a \ = \ a \div d \ \ d \div a \ \ e \div d \ \ d \div e \end{array}$$

$$f \quad \begin{array}{l} a-e \ \ a \times e \ = \ e \div 2 \ \ 2 \div e \ \ y \div 2 \ \ 2 \div y \\ e+y \ \ e-y \ = \ y \div 3 \ \ 3 \div y \ \ a \div 3 \ \ 3 \div a \\ y-a \ \ y \times a \ = \ a \div 4 \ \ 4 \div a \ \ e \div 4 \ \ 4 \div e \end{array}$$

$$x \quad \begin{array}{l} a-e \ \ a \times e \ = \ e \div y \ \ y \div e \\ e \times y \ \ e-y \ = \ y \div a \ \ a \div y \\ y-a \ \ y \times a \ = \ a \div e \ \ e \div a \end{array}$$

Cuspis octava

$$s \quad \begin{array}{l} a \times e \ = \ e \div b \ \ b \div e \ \ y \div b \ \ b \div y \\ e \times y \ = \ y \div b \ \ b \div y \ \ a \div b \ \ b \div a \\ y \times a \ = \ a \div b \ \ b \div a \ \ e \div b \ \ b \div e \end{array}$$

$$d \quad \begin{array}{l} a \times e \ = \ e \div b \ \ b \div e \ \ y \div b \ \ b \div y \\ e \times y \ = \ y \div c \ \ c \div y \ \ a \div c \ \ c \div a \\ y \times a \ = \ a \div d \ \ d \div a \ \ e \div d \ \ d \div e \end{array}$$

$$f \quad \begin{array}{l} a \times e \ = \ e \div 2 \ \ 2 \div e \ \ y \div 2 \ \ 2 \div y \\ e \times y \ = \ y \div 3 \ \ 3 \div y \ \ a \div 3 \ \ 3 \div a \\ y \times a \ = \ a \div 4 \ \ 4 \div a \ \ e \div 4 \ \ 4 \div e \end{array}$$

$$x \quad \begin{array}{l} a \times e \ = \ e \div y \ \ y \div e \\ e \times y \ = \ y \div a \ \ a \div y \\ y \times a \ = \ a \div e \ \ e \div a \end{array}$$

Cuspis nona

$$a \times e \;=\; b+e \;\; e \div b \;\; b+y \;\; y \div b \;\; e+b \;\; b \div e \;\; y+b \;\; b \div y$$
$$s \quad e \times y \;=\; b+y \;\; y+b \;\; b \div a \;\; a+b \;\; y \div b \;\; b+y \;\; a \div b \;\; b+a$$
$$y \times a \;=\; b+a \;\; a \div b \;\; b+e \;\; e \div b \;\; a+b \;\; b \div a \;\; e+b \;\; b \div e$$

$$a \times e \;=\; b+e \;\; e \div b \;\; b+y \;\; y \div b \;\; e+b \;\; b \div e \;\; y+b \;\; b \div y$$
$$d \quad e \times y \;=\; c \div y \;\; y+c \;\; c \div a \;\; a+c \;\; y \div c \;\; c+y \;\; a \div c \;\; c+a$$
$$y \times a \;=\; d+a \;\; a \div d \;\; d+e \;\; e \div d \;\; a+d \;\; d \div a \;\; e+d \;\; d \div e$$

$$a \times e \;=\; 2+e \;\; e \div 2 \;\; 2+y \;\; y \div 2 \;\; e+2 \;\; 2 \div e \;\; y+2 \;\; 2 \div y$$
$$f \quad e \times y \;=\; 3 \div y \;\; y+3 \;\; 3 \div a \;\; a+3 \;\; y \div 3 \;\; 3+y \;\; a \div 3 \;\; 3+a$$
$$y \times a \;=\; 4+a \;\; a \div 4 \;\; 4+e \;\; e \div 4 \;\; a+4 \;\; 4 \div a \;\; e+4 \;\; 4 \div e$$

$$a \times e \;=\; e+y \;\; e \div y \;\; e+y \;\; y \div e$$
$$x \quad e \times y \;=\; y \div a \;\; y+a \;\; a \div y \;\; a+y$$
$$y \times a \;=\; a+e \;\; a \div e \;\; a+e \;\; e \div a$$

Cuspis decima

$$a \times e \;=\; e+b \;\; y+b$$
$$s \quad e \times y \;=\; y+b \;\; a+b$$
$$y \times a \;=\; a+b \;\; e+b$$

$$a \times e \;=\; e+b \;\; y+b$$
$$d \quad e \times y \;=\; y+c \;\; a+c$$
$$y \times a \;=\; a+d \;\; e+d$$

$$a \times e \;=\; e+2 \;\; y+2$$
$$f \quad e \times y \;=\; y+3 \;\; a+3$$
$$y \times a \;=\; a+4 \;\; e+4$$

$$a \times e \;=\; e+y$$
$$x \quad e \times y \;=\; y+a$$
$$y \times a \;=\; a+e$$

Cuspis undecima

$$a \times e \quad a \div e \;=\; e + b \quad y + b$$
$$s \quad e \div y \quad e \times y \;=\; y + b \quad a + b$$
$$y \times a \quad y \div a \;=\; a + b \quad e + b$$

$$a \times e \quad a \div e \;=\; e + b \quad y + b$$
$$d \quad e \div y \quad e \times y \;=\; y + c \quad a + c$$
$$y \times a \quad y \div a \;=\; a + d \quad e + d$$

$$a \times e \quad a \div e \;=\; e + 2 \quad y + 2$$
$$f \quad e \div y \quad e \times y \;=\; y + 3 \quad a + 3$$
$$y \times a \quad y \div a \;=\; a + 4 \quad e + 4$$

$$a \times e \quad a \div e \;=\; e + y$$
$$f \quad e \div y \quad e \times y \;=\; y + a$$
$$y \times a \quad y \div a \;=\; a + e$$

Cuspis duodecima

$$a \div e \;=\; b + e \quad b + y$$
$$s \quad e \div y \;=\; b + y \quad b + a$$
$$y \div a \;=\; b + a \quad b + e$$

$$a \div e \;=\; b + e \quad b + y$$
$$d \quad e \div y \;=\; c + y \quad c + a$$
$$y \div a \;=\; d + a \quad d + e$$

$$a \div e \;=\; 2 + e \quad 2 + y$$
$$f \quad e \div y \;=\; 3 + y \quad 3 + a$$
$$y \div a \;=\; 4 + e \quad 4 + e$$

$$a \div e \;=\; e + y$$
$$x \quad e \div y \;=\; y + a$$
$$y \div a \;=\; a + e$$

Cuspis decima tertia

$$a \div e = e + b \; b - e \; y + b \; b - y \; b + e \; e - b \; b + y \; y - b$$
$$s \quad e \div y = y - b \; b + y \; a - b \; b + a \; b - y \; y + b \; b - a \; a + b$$
$$y \div a = a + b \; b - a \; e + b \; b - e \; b + a \; a - b \; b + e \; e - b$$

$$a \div e = e + b \; b - e \; y + b \; b - y \; b + e \; e - b \; b + y \; y - b$$
$$d \quad e \div y = y - c \; c + y \; a - c \; c + a \; c - y \; y + c \; c - a \; a + c$$
$$y \div a = a + d \; d - a \; e + d \; d - e \; d + a \; a - d \; d + e \; e - d$$

$$a \div e = e + 2 \; 2 - e \; y + 2 \; 2 - y \; 2 + e \; e - 2 \; 2 + y \; y - 2$$
$$x \quad e \div y = y - 3 \; 3 + y \; a - 3 \; 3 + a \; 3 - y \; y + 3 \; 3 - a \; a + 3$$
$$y \div a = a + 4 \; 4 - a \; e + 4 \; 4 - e \; 4 + a \; a - 4 \; 4 + e \; e - 4$$

$$a \div e = e + y \; e - y \; e + y \; y - e$$
$$x \quad e \div y = y - a \; y + a \; a - y \; a + y$$
$$y \div a = a + e \; a - e \; a + e \; e - a$$

Cuspis decima quarta

$$a \div e = b - e \; b - y \; e - b \; y - b$$
$$s \quad e \div y = b - y \; b - a \; y - b \; a - b$$
$$y \div a = b - a \; b - e \; a - b \; e - b$$

$$a \div e = b - e \; b - y \; e - b \; y - b$$
$$d \quad e \div y = c - y \; c - a \; y - c \; a - c$$
$$y \div a = d - a \; d - e \; a - d \; e - d$$

$$a \div e = 2 - e \; 2 - y \; e - 2 \; y - 2$$
$$f \quad e \div y = 3 - y \; 3 - a \; y - 3 \; a - 3$$
$$y \div a = 4 - a \; 4 - e \; a - 4 \; e - 4$$

$$a \div e = e - y \; y - e$$
$$x \quad e \div y = y - a \; a - y$$
$$y \div a = a - e \; e - a$$

Cuspis decima quinta

$$s \quad \begin{aligned} a \div e \;\; a+e &= e-b \;\; y-b \;\; b-e \;\; b-y \\ e+y \;\; e\div y &= y-b \;\; a-b \;\; b-y \;\; b-a \\ y\div a \;\; y+a &= a-b \;\; e-b \;\; b-a \;\; b-e \end{aligned}$$

$$d \quad \begin{aligned} a \div e \;\; a+e &= e-b \;\; y-b \;\; b-e \;\; b-y \\ e+y \;\; e\div y &= y-c \;\; a-c \;\; c-y \;\; c-a \\ y\div a \;\; y+a &= a-d \;\; e-d \;\; d-a \;\; d-e \end{aligned}$$

$$f \quad \begin{aligned} a \div e \;\; a+e &= e-2 \;\; y-2 \;\; 2-e \;\; 2-y \\ e+y \;\; e\div y &= y-3 \;\; a-3 \;\; 3-y \;\; 3-a \\ y\div a \;\; y+a &= a-4 \;\; e-4 \;\; 4-a \;\; 4-a \end{aligned}$$

$$x \quad \begin{aligned} a \div e \;\; a+e &= e-y \;\; y-e \\ e+y \;\; e\div y &= y-a \;\; a-y \\ y\div a \;\; y+a &= a-e \;\; e-a \end{aligned}$$

Cuspis decima sexta

$$s \quad \begin{aligned} a+e &= e-b \;\; y-b \;\; b-e \;\; b-y \\ e+y &= y-b \;\; a-b \;\; b-y \;\; b-a \\ y+a &= a-b \;\; e-b \;\; b-a \;\; b-e \end{aligned}$$

$$d \quad \begin{aligned} a+e &= e-b \;\; y-b \;\; b-e \;\; b-y \\ e+y &= y-c \;\; a-c \;\; c-y \;\; c-a \\ y+a &= a-d \;\; e-d \;\; d-a \;\; d-e \end{aligned}$$

$$f \quad \begin{aligned} a+e &= e-2 \;\; y-2 \;\; 2-e \;\; 2-y \\ e+y &= y-3 \;\; a-3 \;\; 3-y \;\; 3-a \\ y+a &= a-4 \;\; e-4 \;\; 4-a \;\; 4-e \end{aligned}$$

$$x \quad \begin{aligned} a+e &= e-y \;\; y-e \\ e+y &= y-a \;\; a-y \\ y+a &= a-e \;\; e-a \end{aligned}$$

N.B. Est et alia varietas in prioribus æquationum membris, ubi signum analyticum reperitur *viz.* si species transponamus.

E.g. in cuspide quarta adhibitis $\begin{Bmatrix} e-a \\ y-e \\ a-y \end{Bmatrix}$ in duodecima $\begin{Bmatrix} e \div a \\ y \div e \\ a \div y \end{Bmatrix}$

duplicabuntur quæstiones.

Ne quis forte putet quæstiones omnes in ludo nostro possibiles a tabulis exhiberi, notandum est illas revera esse innumeras. Nam metæ infinities variari poterunt : ex his vero pendet numerus quantitatum in quovis problemate quæsitarum, qui proinde pro metarum diversitate erit infinite variabilis ; unde quæstiones orientur innumeræ, in quarum tamen singulis non aliæ servandæ sunt methodi pro signis, combinationibus, et speciebus deter-minandis, quam quæ in solis quæstionibus imparis cujusvis præter unitatem numeri quantitatum quæsitarum, atque adeo in tabulis quas apposuimus exhibeantur.

Of Infinites

First printed in 1901

EDITOR'S INTRODUCTION

THIS important little work was left by Berkeley in manuscript, was preserved among the ' Molyneux Papers ' in the library of Trinity College, Dublin, and was found there by Swift Payne Johnston, the Professor of Moral Philosophy, and was published by him in *Hermathena* (vol. xi, 1901) with an introductory note.

The Molyneux Papers are, for the most part, learned documents contributed to the proceedings of the Dublin (Philosophical) Society, which was founded in 1683 by William Molyneux, Irish statesman and friend of John Locke, and revived by his son, Samuel, Berkeley's pupil and friend, in or about 1707. The *Of Infinites* has all the appearance of an essay read before a learned society, and there is little doubt that it was communicated either to the revived Dublin Society or to its counterpart in the College. The MS. consists of three sheets which measure 153 × 203 in millimetres, and it is endorsed, apparently by Samuel Molyneux, ' Of Infinites by Mr. Berkeley.'

Unlike its companion essay on the cave of Dunmore, it bears no date. Fraser dated it 1705 or 1706, styling it ' this slight juvenile fragment ' ; but his judgment may here be set aside. He does not seem to have considered the paper closely in relation to Berkeley's other studies of the period, and he obviously failed to appreciate the pregnant thought behind it.

Its date and its argument must be considered together. The lower limit is fixed by the reference to *Sir* Isaac Newton, who was knighted 16 April 1705, and by the reference to Cheyne's *Philosophical Principles of Natural Religion*, which came out in that year. For an upper limit we should probably be safe in taking 1709, the year in which Samuel Molyneux left Dublin. Its argument, however, fixes the date within much narrower limits. Here is no abstract mathematical problem, accidentally connected with Berkeley's studies. It touches the heart of his philosophy, and is vitally connected with the massive argument for immaterialism, which Berkeley is known to have been shaping in the years 1707–8. For if space be not only infinitely divisible (subjectively), but infinitely divided (objectively), if, that is, it consists of infinitely small parts, then the New Principle, *esse est percipi*, breaks down, and infinitely divisible space may well house infinitely divisible matter. Berkeley must therefore maintain as a pillar of his system that the minimum quantity is a *minimum sensibile* ; for him there can be no infinitesimal parts of a finite line, much less infinitesimals of infinitesimals ; for him those mathematicians who hold the contrary are illicitly passing in thought from the subject dividing to the object divided, or, in Lockian phrase, they are confusing the idea of the infinity of space with the idea of space infinite. That said, it becomes clear that the work, far from being juvenile, or slight, or a fragment, is mature, of crucial importance, and organically one with Berkeley's main philosophical enterprise.

Examine then the details of the piece, and remarkable parallels with the *Commentaries* come to light. Take the series of entries 351–8, duplicated in the companion notebook (415–24), and compare them with the second paragraph of the *Of Infinites*, you will find that point after point, phrase after phrase correspond. It looks as if Berkeley transferred the entries into both notebooks from the article. The authorities quoted in the article, Locke, Wallis, Cheyne, Leibniz, Newton, and Raphson appear in the *Commentaries*, and the precise point of the reference to Newton appears in entry No. 374, ' Sir Isaac owns his book could have been demonstrated on the supposition of indivisibles.' The *Commentaries* were written between June 1707 and the autumn of 1708, and the article must belong to the same period. I would be even more precise, indeed, and assign it to the earlier portion of that period, for it makes use of the two Lockian principles : (*a*) all words stand for ideas, and (*b*) all knowledge is about ideas. Berkeley held those principles as axioms during the earlier portion of the *Commentaries*, and places them at the head of his ' demonstration ' (No. 378, where see my note), but he gave them up before the end. One may, therefore, with confidence assign the *Of Infinites* to the autumn of 1707 or the following winter.

Berkeley's publications which deal with infinitesimals are, first, those few sections (123–32) in the *Principles* which later he styled ' hints to the public,' [1] and then the *Analyst* with its sequels, the *Defence of free-thinking* . . ., and the *Reasons for not replying*. . . . In these publications are discussed Newton's statement that infinitely small quantities are not necessary to his argument, the right to disregard small errors, the ' nothingness ' of the infinitesimal, the Marquis de l'Hospital's book *Analyse des infiniment petits*, and other topics of the *Of Infinites*.

[1] *Analyst*, Sect. 50.

OF INFINITES

Tho' some mathematicians of this last age have made prodigious advances, and open'd divers admirable methods of investigation unknown to the ancients, yet something there is in their principles which occasions much controversy & dispute, to the great scandal of the so much celebrated evidence of Geometry. These disputes and scruples, arising from the use that is made of quantitys infinitely small in the above mentioned methods, I am bold to think they might easily be brought to an end, by the sole consideration of one passage in the incomparable Mr. Locke's treatise of *Humane Understanding*, b. 2. ch. 17, sec. 7, where that authour, handling the subject of infinity with that judgement & clearness wch is so peculiar to him, has these remarkable words :

'I guess we cause great confusion in our thoughts when we joyn infinity to any suppos'd idea of quantity the mind can be thought to have, and so discourse or reason about an infinite quantity, *viz.* an infinite space or an infinite duration. For our idea of infinity being as I think an endless growing idea, but the idea of any quantity the mind has being at that time terminated in that idea, to join infinity to it is to adjust a standing measure to a growing bulk ; &, therefore, I think 'tis not an insignificant subtilty if I say we are carefully to distinguish between the idea of infinity of space and the idea of space infinite.'

Now if what Mr. Locke says were, *mutatis mutandis*, apply'd to quantitys infinitely small, it would, I doubt not, deliver us from that obscurity & confusion wch perplexes otherwise very great improvements of the Modern Analysis. For he that, with Mr. Locke, shall duly weigh the distinction there is betwixt infinity of space & space infinitely great or small, & consider that we have an idea of the former, but none at all of the later, will hardly go beyond his notions to talk of parts infinitely small or *partes infinitesimae* of finite quantitys, & much less of *infinitesimae infinitesimarum*, and so on. This, nevertheless, is very common with writers of fluxions or the differential calculus, &c. They represent, upon paper, infinitesimals of several orders, as if they had ideas in their minds corresponding to those words or signs, or as if it did not include a contradiction that there should be a line infinitely small & yet another infinitely less than it. 'Tis plain to me we ought to use no sign without an idea answering it [1] ; & 'tis as plain that we have no idea of a line infinitely small, nay, 'tis evidently impossible there should be any such thing, for every line, how minute soever, is still divisible into parts less than itself ; therefore there can be no such thing as a line *quavis data minor* or infinitely small.

Further, it plainly follows that an infinitesimal even of the first degree is meerly *nothing*, from wt Dr. Wallis, an approv'd mathematician, writes at the 95th proposition of his *Arithmetic of Infinites*,[2] where he makes the asymptotic space included between the 2 asymptotes and the curve of an hyperbola to be in his stile a *series reciproca primanorum*, so that the first term of the series, *viz.*, the asymptote, arises from the division of 1 by 0. Since, therefore, unity, *i.e.* any finite line divided by 0, gives the asymptote of an hyperbola, *i.e.* a line infinitely long, it necessarily follows that a finite line divided by an infinite gives 0 in the quotient, *i.e.* that the *pars infinitesima* of a finite line is just nothing. For by the nature of division the dividend divided by the quotient gives the divisor. Now a man speaking of lines infinitely small will hardly be suppos'd to mean nothing by them, and if he understands real finite quantitys he runs into inextricable difficultys.

Let us look a little into the controversy between Mr. Nieuentiit [3] and Mr. Leibnitz. Mr. Nieuentiit allows infinitesimals of the first order to be real quantitys, but the *differentiae differentiarum* or infinitesimals of the following orders he takes away making them just so many noughts. This is the same thing as to say the square, cube, or other power of a real positive quantity is equal to nothing ; wch is manifestly absurd.

Again Mr. Nieuentiit lays down this as a self evident axiom, *viz.*, that betwixt two equal quantitys there can be no difference at all, or, which is the same thing, that their difference is equal to nothing. This truth, how plain soever, Mr. Leibnitz sticks not to deny, asserting that not onely those quantitys are equal which have no difference at all, but also those whose difference

---

[1] [Locke's principles that there can be no knowledge where there are no ideas, and that no words should be used without corresponding ideas, were at first accepted as axioms by Berkeley, and they appear as such in the earlier portion of the *Commentaries*. Later in that work they are rejected, for Berkeley came to realize that we know spirit without ideas, and that words often have a purely emotive value. See *PC* 378 with my note *ib.*—Ed.]

[2] [See *Analyst*, Sect. 17 with my note *ib.*—Ed.]

[3] [Bernard Nieuwentyt (1654–1718), Dutch physician, mathematician, and theologian ; mentioned in *Siris*, Sect. 190.—Ed.]

is incomparably small. *Quemadmodum* (says he) *si lineae punctum alterius lineae addas quantitatem non auges.* But if lines are infinitely divisible, I ask how there can be any such thing as a point? Or granting there are points, how can it be thought the same thing to add an indivisible point as to add, for instance, the *differentia* of an ordinate, in a parabola, wch is so far from being a point that it is itself divisible into an infinite number of real quantitys, whereof each can be subdivided *in infinitum*, and so on, according to Mr. Leibnitz. These are difficultys those great men have run into, by applying the idea of infinity to particles of extension exceeding small, but real and still divisible.

More of this dispute may be seen in the *Acta Eruditorum* for the month of July, A.D. 1695, where, if we may believe the French authour of *Analyse des infiniment petits*, Mr. Leibnitz has sufficiently established & vindicated his principles. Tho' 'tis plain he cares not for having 'em call'd in question, and seems afraid that *nimia scrupulositate arti inveniendi obex ponatur*, as if a man could be too scrupulous in Mathematics, or as if the principles of Geometry ought not to be as incontestable as the consequences drawn from them.

There is an argument of Dr. Cheyne's,[1] in the 4th chapter of his *Philosophical Principles of Natural Religion* which seems to make for quantitys infinitely small. His words are as follows:

'The whole abstract geometry depends upon the possibility of infinitely great & small quantitys, & the truths discover'd by methods wch depend upon these suppositions are confirm'd by other methods wch have other foundations.'

To wch I answer that the supposition of quantitys infinitely small is not essential to the great improvements of the Modern Analysis. For Mr. Leibnitz acknowleges his *Calculus differentialis* might be demonstrated *reductione ad absurdum* after the manner of the ancients; & Sir Isaac Newton in a late treatise informs us his method of Fluxions can be made out *a priori* without the supposition of quantitys infinitely small.

I can't but take notice of a passage in Mr. Raphson's[2] treatise

[1] [George Cheyne (1671–1743), a physician of London and Bath, who wrote on fluxions, medicine, and religion (see *Dict. Nat. Biog.*). Berkeley refers to him in his *Commentaries*, Nos. 367, 387, 459, where see my notes.—Ed.]

[2] [Joseph Raphson, F.R.S. His *De spatio reali* . . ., 1697, left a profound impression on Berkeley because of its virtual deification of space. In his letter to Johnson of 24 March 1730 Berkeley speaks of Raphson as a mathematician who 'pretends to find out fifteen of the incommunicable attributes of God in space.' He is mentioned in the *Commentaries*, Nos. 298, 827.—Ed.]

De Spatio Reali seu Ente Infinito, chap. 3. p. 50, where he will have a particle infinitely small to be *quasi extensa*. But wt Mr. Raphson would be thought to mean by *pars continui quasi extensa* I cannot comprehend. I must also crave leave to observe that some modern writers of note make no scruple to talk of a sphere of an infinite radius, or an æquilateral triangle of an infinite side, which notions if thoroughly examin'd may perhaps be found not altogether free from inconsistencys.

Now I am of opinion that all disputes about infinites would cease, & the consideration of quantitys infinitely small no longer perplex Mathematicians, would they but joyn Metaphysics to their Mathematics, and condescend to learn from Mr. Locke what distinction there is betwixt infinity and infinite.

Writings on Natural History

First published, the three letters in 1717, 1747, and 1750;
the Description of the Cave of Dunmore in 1871

EDITOR'S INTRODUCTION

THE FOUR WRITINGS which follow, of very different dates, show Berkeley's lifelong interest in natural history and the physical science of his day. The three letters were published in his lifetime, the first two in the *Philosophical Transactions*, and the third in the *Gentleman's Magazine*. The Description of the Cave of Dunmore was not published by Berkeley. Fraser found it and published it in his edition (1871) of the *Works*, and I give it in the slightly different version found by Professor S. P. Johnston, and not hitherto published.

The observations of the eruption of Vesuvius were made in April, May, and June 1717 when Berkeley was touring Italy with St. George Ashe. He sent them in a letter to his friend, Dr. Arbuthnot, who communicated them to the Royal Society, and they were published in the *Philosophical Transactions* for October 1717. An abbreviated account is given in the *Gentleman's Magazine*, vol. 20, p. 161. Berkeley shows himself a close and courageous observer. The *Transactions* gives his Christian name as Edward instead of George.

Thirty years later (February 1747) the second letter appeared in the *Transactions*. It is addressed to Thomas Prior and is annexed to a communication from Mr. James Simon ' Concerning the petrifactions of Lough Neagh in Ireland.' Simon had sent his paper to the Bishop, asking for comments, and Berkeley has here put together some general observations on petrifaction and similar processes. The last two paragraphs were added from a letter to Dr. J. Fothergill, dated Dublin, 8 August 1746.

The third letter concerns earthquakes, and it was printed in the *Gentleman's Magazine* for April 1750, vol. 20, p. 166. Fraser (*Life and Letters*, p. 317) writes of it, ' The manuscript of which is in Berkeley's writing.' If Fraser means to imply that the MS. is extant, he is, I think, mistaken. The letter was published by Monck Berkeley in his *Literary Relics*, 1789, p. 310. It is noteworthy for Count Tezzani's report of the earthquake at Catania in 1692 ; Berkeley's mention of his own visit to Sicily and of the earthquake at Messina is of interest. Berkeley spent some three months in Sicily in the winter of 1717–18, travelling through most parts of the island, and on 25 February 1718 he wrote to the Sicilian philosopher, Tommaso Campailla, from Messina evidently on the point of returning to Italy.

The Description of the Cave of Dunmore is of interest as being one of the earliest of Berkeley's writings, and because the cave is a remarkable natural feature well worth a visit. Three manuscript copies of the Description exist, which I will call A, B, and C respectively.[1] A and B are under one cover in the Molyneux Papers (I. 4. 19) in the library of Trinity College, Dublin; A consists of pp. 2, 3, 4, 5, 10, and B of pp. 6, 7, 8, 9; the cover bears the endorsement 'by Mr. Berkley, Jan: 10 1705/6.' The third copy C is in one of the two notebooks which form the volume containing the *Philosophical Commentaries*. Fraser printed from C, that being the only copy known at the time. I print from A, which in certain respects is the most interesting of the three copies. Its address and details of phrasing show that it was the actual copy read before 'this illustrious assembly.' A and B originally contained a mention of Berkeley's father, and A alone has the original conclusion of the essay.

His father, William Berkeley of Thomastown, is not elsewhere mentioned in Berkeley's writings, and this mention is of special interest. It occurs in the passage about the human bones found in the cave. All three copies read, 'I remember to have heard *one* tell. . . .' In A and B Berkeley originally wrote *my father* for *one*; the words can still be detected under the erasure, if the MS. be held to the light. It was natural for Berkeley in his address to name the source of his information, but when he came to revise the Description for the records of the Society, he probably thought it more prudent not to implicate his father in any reference to the terrible massacres of 1641.

If my text be collated with Fraser's (Works, vol. iv, p. 75 *ff*) it will be seen that the two descriptions agree in the main, but that Berkeley has added certain passages in C. These are—the howling of the dogs, Fraser, p. 78; the skull drinking bowl, p. 80; the explicit mention of the massacre of the Protestants, p. 80; the story of the gentleman and his servant, p. 82; the revision by Mr. Jackson, p. 82; and the reference to Woodward's *Natural History*, p. 83.

When the details supplied by the three copies are put together,

---

[1] [See my 'Berkeley's Description of the Cave of Dunmore': *Hermathena*, vol. xxi, 1931.—Ed.]

it becomes clear that Berkeley and his Kilkenny school-friends visited the cave on a warm July day in 1699, when Berkeley was fourteen years old, and that he wrote the account some seven years later.   I have on more than one occasion explored the cave, or rather the accessible portions of it (to enter some of the labyrinthine galleries without adequate lighting might be very dangerous), and can testify to the accuracy of Berkeley's description.

Amongst other accounts of the cave may be mentioned an anonymous journal in the Molyneux Papers (I.4.19) which records a visit on 21 November 1709, a letter from Mr. Adam Walker, dated Dublin, 26 April 1771, published in the *Philosophical Transactions* for 1773, p. 16, an account in Tighe's *Statistical Survey of the County of Kilkenny*, p. 107, A. W. Foot's account in the *Journal of the Royal Historical and Archaeological Association of Ireland*, January 1870, p. 65, and a particularly interesting description by E. T. Hardman in the *Proceedings of the Royal Irish Academy*, vol. ii, 1875–7, p. 168.

Writings on Natural History

The Text

THE ERUPTION OF MOUNT VESUVIUS

(Philosophical Transactions, October 1717)

Extract of a letter of Mr. Edw. Berkeley from Naples, giving several curious observations and remarks on the eruptions of fire and smoak from Mount Vesuvio. Communicated by Dr. John Arbuthnot, M.D. and R.S.S.

April 17, 1717. With much difficulty I reached the top of Mount Vesuvius, in which I saw a vast aperture full of smoak, which hindered the seeing its depth and figure. I heard within that horrid gulf certain odd sounds, which seemed to proceed from the belly of the mountain ; a sort of murmuring, sighing, throbbing, churning, dashing (as it were) of waves, and between whiles a noise, like that of thunder or cannon, which was constantly attended with a clattering, like that of tiles falling from the tops of houses on the streets. Sometimes, as the wind changed, the smoak grew thinner, discovering a very ruddy flame, and the jaws of the pan or crater streaked with red and several shades of yellow. After an hour's stay, the smoak, being moved by the wind, gave us short and partial prospects of the great hollow, in the flat bottom of which I could discern two furnaces almost contiguous ; that on the left, seeming about three yards in diameter, glowed with red flame, and threw up red-hot stones with a hideous noise, which, as they fell back, caused the fore-mentioned clattering.

May 8, in the morning, I ascended to the top of Vesuvius a second time, and found a different face of things. The smoak ascending upright gave a full prospect of the crater, which, as I could judge, is about a mile in circumference, and an hundred yards deep. A conical mount had been formed since my last visit, in the middle of the bottom. This mount, I could see, was made of the stones thrown up and fallen back into the crater. In this new hill remained the two mouths or furnaces already mentioned ; that on our left hand was in the vertex of the hill which it had formed round it, and raged more violently than before, throwing up, every three or four minutes, with a dreadful bellowing, a vast number of red-hot stones, sometimes in appearance above a thousand, and at least 300 foot higher than my head as I stood upon the brink. But, there being little or no wind, they fell back perpendicularly into the crater, increasing the conical hill. The other mouth to the right was lower in the side of the same new-formed hill. I could discern it to be filled with red-hot liquid matter, like that in the furnace of a glass-house, which raged and wrought as the waves of the sea, causing a short abrupt noise like what may be imagined to proceed from a sea of quicksilver dashing among uneven rocks. This stuff would sometimes spew over and run down the convex side of the conical hill, and appearing at first red-hot, it changed colour, and hardened as it cooled, shewing the first rudiments of an eruption, or, if I may so say, an eruption in miniature. Had the wind driven in our faces, we had been in no small danger of stifling by the sulphurous smoak, or being knocked on the head by lumps of molten minerals, which we saw had sometimes fallen on the brink of the crater, upon those shots from the gulf at the bottom. But, as the wind was favourable, I had an opportunity to survey this odd scene for above an hour and a half together ; during which it was very observable that all the volleys of smoak, flame, and burning stones, came only out of the hole to our left, while the liquid stuff in the other mouth wrought and overflowed, as hath been already described.

June 5th, after a horrid noise, the mountain was seen at Naples to spew a little out of the crater. The same continued the 6th.

The 7th, nothing was observed till within two hours of night, when it began a hideous bellowing, which continued all that night and the next day till noon, causing the windows, and as some affirm, the very houses in Naples to shake. From that time it spewed vast quantities of molten stuff to the south which streamed down the side of the mountain like a great pot boyling over. This evening I returned from a voyage through Apulia, and was surprised, passing by the north side of the mountain, to see a great quantity of ruddy smoak lie along a huge tract of sky over the river of molten stuff, which was itself out of sight.

The 9th, Vesuvius raged less violently : that night we saw from Naples a column of fire shoot between whiles out of its summit.

The 10th, when we thought all would have been over, the mountain grew very outragious again, roaring and groaning most dreadfully. You cannot form a juster idea of this noise in the most violent fits of it, than by imagining a mixed sound made up of the raging of a tempest, the murmur of a troubled sea, and the roaring of thunder and artillery, confused all together. It was very terrible as we heard it in the further end of Naples, at the distance of above twelve miles. This moved my curiosity to approach the mountain. Three or four of us got into a boat, and were set ashore at *Torre del Greco*, a town situate at the foot of Vesuvius to the south-west, whence we rode four or five miles before we came to the burning river, which was about midnight. The roaring of the volcano grew exceeding loud and horrible as we approached. I observed a mixture of colours in the cloud over the crater, green, yellow, red, and blue ; there was likewise a ruddy dismal light in the air over that tract of land where the burning river flowed ; ashes continually showered on us all the way from the sea-coast : all which circumstances, set off and augmented by the horror and silence of the night, made a scene the most uncommon and astonishing I ever saw ; which grew still more extraordinary as we came nearer the stream. Imagine a vast torrent of liquid fire rolling from the top down the side of the mountain, and with irresistible fury bearing down and con- suming vines, olives, fig-trees, houses, in a word, every thing that stood in its way. This mighty flood divided into different channels, according to the inequalities of the mountain. The largest stream seemed half a mile broad at least, and five miles long. The nature and consistence of these burning torrents hath been described with so much exactness and truth by Borellus in his Latin treatise of Mount Ætna, that I need say nothing of it. I walked so far before my companions up the mountain, along the side of the river of fire, that I was obliged to retire in great haste, the sulphureous stream having surprized me, and almost taken away my breath. During our return, which was about three-a-clock in the morning, we constantly heard the murmur and groaning of the mountain, which between whiles would burst out into louder peals, throwing up huge spouts of fire and burning stones, which falling down again, resembled the stars in our rockets. Sometimes I observed two, at others three, distinct columns of flames, and sometimes one vast one that seemed to fill the whole crater. These burning columns and the fiery stones seemed to be shot 1,000 feet perpendicular above the summit of the volcano.

The 11th, at night, I observed it, from a terrass in Naples, to throw up incessantly a vast body of fire, and great stones to a surprising height.

The 12th, in the morning, it darkened the sun with ashes and smoak, causing a sort of eclipse. Horrid bellowings, this and the foregoing day, were heard at Naples, whither part of the ashes also reached. At night I observed it throw up flame, as on the 11th.

On the 13th, the wind changing, we saw a pillar of black smoak shot upright to a prodigious height. At night I observed the mount cast up fire as before, tho' not so distinctly, because of the smoak.

The 14th, a thick black cloud hid the mountain from Naples.

The 15th, in the morning, the court and walls of our house in Naples were covered with ashes. In the evening flame appeared on the mountain thro' the cloud.

The 16th, the smoak was driven by a westerly wind from the town to the opposite side of the mountain.

The 17th, the smoak appeared much diminished, fat and greasy.

The 18th, the whole appearance ended, the mountain remaining perfectly quiet without any visible smoak or flame. A gentleman of my acquaintance, whose window looked towards Vesuvius, assured me that he observed this night several flashes, as it were of lightening, issue out of the mouth of the volcano. It is not worth while to trouble you with the conjectures I have formed concerning the cause of these phænomena, from what I observed in the Lacus Amsancti, the Solfatara, &c., as well as in Mount Vesuvius. One thing I may venture to say, that I saw the fluid matter rise out of the centre of the bottom of the crater, out of the very middle of the mountain, contrary to what Borellus imagines ; whose method of explaining the eruption of a volcano by an inflexed syphon and the rules of hydrostaticks, is likewise inconsistent with the torrent's flowing down from the very vertex of the mountain. I have not seen the crater since the eruption, but design to visit it again before I leave Naples. I doubt there is nothing in this worth shewing the Society : as to that you will use your discretion.

E. BERKELEY

BERKELEY TO PRIOR ON PETRIFACTIONS

(annexed to a communication from Mr. James Simon
on the petrifactions of Lough Neagh, read before the
Royal Society, February 1747, and printed in the *Philosophical Transactions*, No. 481)

CLOYNE, May 20, 1746

DEAR SIR,

I here send you back the curious dissertation of Mr. Simon,
which I have perused with pleasure ; and tho' variety of avoca-
tions gives me little time for remarks on a subject so much out of
my way, I shall nevertheless venture to give my thoughts briefly
upon it, especially since the author hath been pleased to invite
me to it by a letter.

The author seems to put it out of doubt, that there is a petrifying quality both in the lake and adjacent earth. What he
remarks on the unfrozen spots in the lake is curious, and fur-
nisheth a sufficient answer to those who would deny any petrifying
virtue to be in the water, from experiments not succeeding in
some parts of it ; since nothing but chance could have directed
to the proper places, which probably were those unfrozen parts.

Stones have been thought by some to be organised vegetables,
and to be produced from seed. To me it seems that stones are
vegetables unorganised. Other vegetables are nourished and
grow by a solution of salt attracted into their tubes or vessels.
And stones grow by the accretion of salts, which often shoot into
angular and regular figures. This appears in the formation of
crystals on the Alps : and that stones are formed by the simple
attraction and accretion of salts, appears in the tartar on the
inside of a claret-vessel, and especially in the formation of a stone
in the human body.

The air is in many places impregnated with such salts. I
have seen at Agrigentum in Sicily the pillars of stone in an ancient
temple corroded and consumed by the air, while the shells which
entered into the composition of the stone remained intire and
untouched.

I have elsewhere observed marble to be consumed in the same manner ; and it is common to see softer kinds of stone moulder and dissolve merely by the air acting as a menstruum. Therefore the air may be presumed to contain many such salts, or stony particles.

Air, acting as a menstruum in the cavities of the earth, may become saturated (in like manner as above-ground) with such salts as, ascending in vapours or exhalations, may petrify wood, whether lying in the ground adjacent, or in the bottom of the lake. This is confirmed by the author's own remark on the bath called the Green Pillars in Hungary. The insinuating of such salts into the wood seems also confirmed by the author's having observed minute hexagonal crystals in the woody part of the petrifactions of Lough-Neagh.

A petrifying quality or virtue shews itself in all parts of this terraqueous globe, in water, earth, and sand ; in Tartary, for instance, and Afric, in the bodies of most sorts of animals : it is even known that a child hath been petrified in the mother's womb. Osteocolla grows in the land, and coral in the sea. Grottoes, springs, lakes, and rivers are in many parts remarkable for this same quality. No man therefore can question the possibility of such a thing as petrified wood ; though perhaps the petrifying quality might not be originally in the earth or water, but in the vapour or steam impregnated with saline or stony particles.

Perhaps the petrifaction of wood may receive some light from considering amber, which is dug up in the King of Prussia's dominions.

I have written these hasty lines in no small hurry ; and send them to you not from an opinion that they contain anything worth imparting, but merely in compliance with your and Mr. Simon's request.

[Added from a letter to Dr. J. Fothergill, dated Dublin, 8 August 1746.]

And yet before I have done I must needs add another remark, which may be useful for the better understanding of the nature of stone. In the vulgar definition, it is said to be a fossil incapable of fusion. I have nevertheless known stone to be melted, and when cold to become stone again. Such is that stuff, by the natives called *Sciara*, which runs down in liquid burning torrents from the craters of Mount Ætna, and which, when cold and hard, I have seen hewed and employed at Catania and other places adjacent. It probably contains mineral and metallic particles ;

being a ponderous, hard, grey stone, used for the most part in the basements and coinage of buildings.

Hence it should seem not impossible for stone to be cast or run into the shape of columns, vases, statues, or relievo's ; which experiment may perhaps some time or other be attempted by the curious ; who, following where nature has shewn the way, may (possibly by the aid of certain salts and minerals), arrive at a method for melting and running stone, both to their own profit, and that of the public.

I am, dear Sir,[1]

Your most humble servant,

G. CLOYNE.

---

[1] [John Fothergill (1712–80), noted London physician and scientist, F.R.S. ; keenly interested in botanical gardening.   Six papers of his are published in the *Philosophical Transactions*, including one on the origin of amber (1744), a subject to which Berkeley refers above (p. 252).

I have printed Berkeley's letters to Prior and to Fothergill as they appear in the *Transactions*.   Simon had evidently seen both letters ; for he has a footnote on the letter to Fothergill, confirming ' what the Bishop says.'   The dating from ' Dublin, 8 August 1746 ' is of interest ; for, if correct, it proves a hitherto unknown visit by Berkeley to Dublin.   Earlier in the year (1746) he had mentioned to Gervais that he might visit Dublin to pay his respects to the Lord Lieutenant.   The visit had not been paid by 3 July, and he writes again from Cloyne on 24 August ; but between those two dates there would have been time for a short visit to Dublin.—Ed.]

ON EARTHQUAKES

(In the *Gentleman's Magazine*, April 1750, vol. 20, p. 166)

OBSERVATIONS BY A RT. REV. PRELATE IN IRELAND CONCERNING EARTHQUAKES

Having observed that it hath been offered as a reason to persuade the public that the late shocks felt in and about London were not caused by an earthquake, because the motion was lateral, which it is asserted the motion of an earthquake never is, I take upon me to affirm the contrary. I have myself felt an earthquake at Messina in the year 1718, when the motion was horizontal or lateral. It did no harm in that city, but threw down several houses about a day's journey from thence.

We are not to think the late shocks merely an air-quake (as they call it), on account of signs and changes in the air, such being usually observed to attend earthquakes. There is a correspondence between the subterraneous air and our atmosphere. It is probable that storms or great concussions of the air do often, if not always, owe their origin to vapours or exhalations issuing from below.

I remember to have heard Count Tezzani at Catanea say, that some hours before the memorable earthquake of 1692, which overturned the whole city, he observed a line in the air (proceeding, as he judged, from exhalations poised and suspended in the atmosphere) ; also that he heard a hollow frightful murmur about a minute before the shock. Of 25,000 inhabitants 18,000 absolutely perished, not to mention others who were miserably bruised and wounded. There did not escape so much as one single house. The streets were narrow and the buildings high, so there was no safety in running into the streets ; but on the first tremor (which happened a small space, perhaps a few minutes, before the downfall), they found it the safest way to stand under a door-case, or at the corners of the house.

The Count was dug out of the ruins of his own house, which had overwhelmed above twenty persons, only seven whereof were got out alive. Though he rebuilt his house with stone, yet he ever after lay in a small adjoining apartment made of reeds plastered over. Catanea was rebuilt more regular and beautiful than ever. The houses indeed are lower, and the streets broader than before, for security against future shocks. By their account, the first shock seldom or never doth the mischief, but the *repliches* (as they term them) are most to be dreaded. The earth, I was told, moved up and down like the boiling of a pot, *terra bollente di sotto in sopra*, to use their own expression. This sort of sub-sultive motion is ever accounted the most dangerous.

Pliny in the second book of his natural history, observes that all earthquakes are attended with a great stillness of the air. The same was observed at Catanea. Pliny further observes, that a murmuring noise precedes the earthquake. He also remarks, that there is *signum in coelo, praeceditque motu futuro, aut interdiu, aut paulo post occasum sereno, ceu tenuis linea nubis in longum porrectae spatium* ; which agrees with what was observed by Count Tezzani and others at Catanea. And all these things plainly show the mistake of those who surmise that noises and signs in the air do not belong to or betoken an earthquake, but only an air-quake.

The naturalist above cited, speaking of the earth, saith, that *varie quatitur*, up and down sometimes, at others from side to side. He adds, that the effects are very various : cities, one while demolished, another swallowed up ; sometimes overwhelmed by water, at other times consumed by fire bursting from the earth. One while the gulph remains open and yawning ; another the sides close, not leaving the least trace or sign of the city swallowed up.

Britain is an island ; *maritima autem maxime quatiuntur*, saith Pliny, and in this island are many mineral and sulphureous waters. I see nothing in the natural constitution of London, or the parts adjacent, that should render an earthquake impossible or im-probable. Whether there be any thing in the moral state thereof that should exempt it from that fear, I leave others to judge.

I am your humble servant,

A. B.

A DESCRIPTION
OF THE CAVE OF DUNMORE

(In the Molyneux Papers in the library of Trinity College, Dublin)

MR. PRESIDENT AND GENTLEMEN,

There is one of the raritys of this kingdome wch tho' I judge considerable enough to take place among the rest, yet so it is I neither find it described nor so much as mentioned by those who are curious in enquirys of this nature, I mean the cave of Dunmore. Wherefore having had the curiosity to see it, in defect of a better I present you with my own account of this wonderfull place so far as I shall be able to copy it from wt I remember either to have seen my self or heard from others.

This rarity is distant 4 miles from Kilkenny & 2 from Dunmore his Grace the Duke of Ormond's country house whence it has its name. It's mouth or entrance is situated in a rising ground and affords a very dismal prospect being both wide & deep & all its sides rocky & precipitious save one wch is a slope, part whereof is fashioned into a path & in some places into steps by the frequent descents of those who out of curiosity visit this stupendous cave. This as well as the rest of the sides is overrun with elder and other shrubs wch add to the horrour of the place & make it a suitable habitation for ravens, screech-owls & such like feral birds that dwell in the cavitys of the rocks.

At the foot of this descent by an opening wch resembles a wide arched gate we entered into a vast cavern the bottom whereof is always slabby by reason of the continuall distillation of rock water. Here we bad farewell to day-light plunging into a more than Cimmerian darkness that fills the hollows of this subterranean dungeon into whose more retired apartments we were admitted by 2 passages out of this first cavern ; for having by candlelight spy'd out our way towards the left hand & not without some difficulty clambered over a ruinous heap of huge, unwieldy stones, we saw a farther entrance into the rock but at some distance from the ground ; here nature seemed to have made certain round stones jut out of the wall on purpose to facilitate our ascent.

Having gone thro this narrow passage we were surprised to find our selves in a very vast and spacious hall, the floor [of] wch as well as the sides & roof is rock, tho' in some places it be cleft into very frightful chasms yet for the most part is pretty level & coherent ; the roof is adorned with a multitude of small round pipes as thick as a goose-quill and (if I misremember not) a foot long or thereabouts ; [from margin, they are made of an almost transparent stone and are easily broken.] From each of them there distills a drop of clear water wch congealing at the bottom forms a round, hard, & white stone, the noise of those falling drops being somewhat augmented by the echo of the cave seems to make an agreeable harmony amidst so profound a silence ; the stones (wch I take to be 3 or 4 inches high they all seeming much of a bigness) standing pretty thick in the pavement make it look very odly. Here is likewise an obelisque of a duskish, gray colour & (I think) about 3 or four foot high, the drop wch formed it has ceased so that it receives no farther increment.

This cave in the great variety of its congelations as well as in some other respects seems not a little to resemble one I find described under the name of Les grottes d'Arcy, in a French treatise *de l'origine des fontaines* dedicated to the famous Huygenius & printed at Paris in 1678, but I must own that French cave has much the advantage of ours on account of the art & regularity wch nature has observed in forming its congelations ; or else that authour has infinitly surpassed me in strength of fancy, for after having given a long detail of severall things wch he says are by them represented, he concludes with these words : *enfin l'on y voit les ressemblances de tout ce qu'on peut imaginer, soit d'hommes, d'animaux, de poissons, de fruits,* etc. *i.e.* in short, here you may see the resemblance of wtever you can possibly imagine, men, beasts, fishes, fruits etc. ; now tho' as much be confidently reported & believed of our cave yet to speak ingenuously 'tis more than I could find to be true, but on the contrary am mightily tempted to think it proceeds from strength of imagination, for like as we see the clouds so far comply with the fancy of a child as to resemble trees, horses, men or whatever else he's pleased to think on, so it is no difficult matter for men of a strong imagination to shape the irregular congelations after the model of their fancy ; in short they need only for their diversion conceive on the petrify'd water the impression of their own brain to see men, beasts, fishes, fruits or any thing else they can possibly imagine.

By what has bin already observed it appears the congelations are not all of the same colour, for the colour of the pipes is much like that of alum, the stones formed by their drops are of a white inclining to yellow, and the obelisque I mentioned differs from both. Moreover there is a quantity of this congealed water that by reason of its very white colour and irregular figure at some distance resembles a heap of snow and such at first sight I took it to be much wondering how it could come there. When we approached it with a light it sparkled and cast a lively lustre, and we discovered in its superficies a number of small cavities as you may see in the above cited treatise, p. 279 & 287. But the noblest ornament of this spacious hall is a huge, channeled pillar wch standing in the middle reaches from top to bottom. There is in one side of it a cavity wch from its figure is called the alabastre chair. The congelations wch from this column are of a yellowish colour & as to their shape something like the pipes of an organ ; but organs I find are no rarity in places of this nature, they being to be met with not onely in the caves of Arcy and Antiparos (an isle in the archipelago) but also in one near the firth of Forth in Scotland mentioned by Sir Robert Sibbald in ye Phil. Trans. Num 222. This I look upon to be in all respects by far the greatest pillar I ever saw, & believe its pedestal (wch is of a dark colour & with a glorious sparkling reflects the light of a candle) is as much as three men can well fathom.

I am concerned that I did not take the dimensions both of this lofty pillar & of the other things I endeavoured to describe. I am sorry I cannot furnish this illustrious assembly with an exact account of the length, breadth & height of these subterranean chambers, and have reason to think I have been by this time often censured for using such undetermined expressions as wide, narrow, deep, etc. where something more accurate may be lookt for ; but I have this to offer in my excuse, that wn I visited this place I had no thoughts of satisfying any ones curiosity besides my own, having done it purely for my diversion [1] and by consequence might well be supposed to omit severall things that may be taken notice of by a curious observer & expected in an exact & accurate description wch I am far from

[1] *prima manu*, in the company of some other schoolboys merely out of a childish humour.

pretending this to be. Moreover the vast horrours of this melancholy place had so far filled the capacity of my mind that I was obliged to overlook severall things that demanded a particular regard.

Here it was, I desired one of the company to fire of his gun (wch he brought with him to kill rabbets that we saw in great numbers about the mouth of the cave) : the sound we heard for a considerable time roll thro' the hollows of the earth & at last it could not so properly be said to cease as to go out of our hearing. I have bin told that a noise made in the cave may be heard by one walking in St. Canice's church at Kilkenny, but know no one who ever made the experiment.

Having viewed the wonders of this place & not discovering any further passage, we returned thro the narrow entrance we came in by. By this time some of our company thought they had seen enough and were very impatient to get out of this dreadfull dungeon ; the rest of us went on thro a passage opposite to the former and much of the same wideness that led us into another cave wch appeared every way formidably vast being of a prodigious length and astonishing height, & tho' the intervall of time may have rendered my ideas of severall particulars I there saw dim & imperfect, yet the dismall solitude, the fearfull darkness & vast silence of that stupendous cavern have left lasting impressions in my memory. The bottom is in great part strewed with huge, massive fragments wch seem by the violence of an earthquake to have bin torn from the rock. The roof (as far as we could discern it by reason of the height) seemed to be of a blackish rock, and was destitute of the chrystal pipes above-mentioned ; advancing forward we met with a great white congelation set against the side of the cave wch resembles a pulpit with a canopy over it, and hard by we saw the mold newly turned up at the entrance of a rabbet hole, and I have heard others affirm that very far in this dark and dismal place they have met with fresh rabbet's dung. Now to me it seems difficult to conceive what these little animals can live on, for it passes imagination to think they can find the way in and out of the cave except their eyes be fashioned to see in consummate darkness. Having gone a little farther we were surprised with the agreeable murmur of a rivulet falling through the clefts of the rock, it skims along the side of the cave & may be (as I guess) about 6 foot over ; its water is wonderfully cool & pleasant & so very clear yt where I thought it had scarce bin an inch deep I found my self up to my knees ; this excellent water runs but a little way ere the rock gapes to receive it.

But what is most surprising is that the bottom of this spring is all over spread with dead men's bones & for how deep I cannot tell. 'Tis likewise reported & (if I mistake not) I have discoursed wth some who said they themselves had seen great heaps of dead men's bones piled up in the remote recesses of this cavern. Now wt brought these bones hither there's not the least glimmering of tradition that ever I could hear of to inform us. 'Tis true I remember to have heard one [1] tell how an old Irish man who served for a guide into the cave solved him this problem by saying that in days of yore a certain carnivorous monster dwelling there was wont furiously to lay about him & whoever were unhappy enough to come in his way hurry them for food into that his dreadfull den. But this (methinks) has not the least show of probability ; for in the first place Ireland seems the freest country in the world from such man-slaughtering animals, & again, allowing there was some such pernicious beast, some anamolous [sic] production of this country, then these bones being supposed the relicks of devoured men, one might reasonably expect to find them scattered up & down in all parts of the cave rather than piled up in heaps or gathered together in the water. And here if I may be allowed to publish my conjectures, I think it more probable that in former times this place served the Irish for the same purpose for wch the huge subterraneous vaults of Rome & Naples called catacombs were intended by the ancients, i.e. that it was a repository for their dead ; but still what should move them to deposit the bones we saw in the water I cannot devine. 'Tis likewise very hard to imagine why they should be at the pains to drag the corps thro long & narrow passages that so they may interr it farther in the obscure depths of the cave ; perhaps they thought their deceased friends might enjoy a more undisturbed security in the innermost chambers of this melancholy vault.

Proceeding forward we came to a place so low that our heads almost touched the top ; a little beyond this we were forced to stoop, & soon after to creep on our knees ; here the roof was thick set with the chrystall pipes, but (I think) they had all given over dropping ; they were very brittle and as we crept along we broke them of with our hats which rubed against the roof ; on our left hand we saw a terrible hiatus that by its black & dreadfull looks seemed to penetrate a great way into the bowels

[1] *prima manu*, my father.

of the earth, and here we met with a good quantity of petrify'd water in wch tho' folks may fancy they see the resemblances of a great many things, yet I profess I know not what more fitly to compare it to than the blearings of a candle ; these congelations standing in our way had almost stopt up the passage ; so that we were obliged to return.

I will not deny that there are other passages wch by a diligent search we might have discovered or a guide acquainted with the place have directed us to ; for 'tis generally reported that no one ever went to the end of this cave ; but that being sometimes forced to creep through narrow passages one comes again into great and spacious vaults. I have heard talk of severall persons who are said to have taken these subterraneous journeys ; particularly one, St. Leger, who having provided a box of torches and victuals for himself and his man is said to have travelled 2 or 3 days in the abstruse paths of this horrible cave, and that when his victuals were well nigh spent, and half his torches burnt out, he left his sword standing in the ground and made haste to return ; also I have bin informed that others having gone a great way writ their names on a dead man's skull wch they set up for a monument at their journey's end. But I will not vouch for the truth of these and the like storys I have heard whereof a great many are apparently fabulous.

I have likewise bin told that people are apprehensive of damps in this place, but this, I conceive, is a groundless fear ; indeed in coal-pits where the air impregnated with sulphureous exhalations and pent up in some close hole may get vent by the digging of the collier ; it is not unlikely such things may happen, but here I do not think [three or four illegible words] the like effect. I am sure so far as we went the candles after all burnt very clear the air being exceeding temperate & calm.

I have known some so unreasonable as to doubt whether this cave was not the workmanship of man or giants in old times, notwithstanding that it has all the rudeness & simplicity of nature, & might easily be accounted for without having recourse to art, considering its entrance is in a hill, and the country all around it hilly and uneven, for from the origine of hills and mountains as it is delivered by Descartes and since him by our later theorists, 'tis plain they are hollow and enclose vast caverns wch is farther confirmed from experience and observation.

This is all I have to say concerning the cave of Dunmore. I have every where endeavoured to raise in yr imagination the same ideas I had myself when I saw it as far as I could call to mind at the distance of almost seven years.

log : num. 216
test : num : 257 [1]

EDITOR'S NOTE

In C (the copy in the volume of the *Philosophical Commentaries*) for the last paragraph (' This is all . . . seven years ') is substituted the following :

Soon after I finished the foregoing description of the cave, I had it revised by Mr. William Jackson, a curious and philosophical young gentleman, who was very lately there. He said the account I gave was very agreeable to what he himself had seen, and was pleased to allow it a greater share of exactness than I durst have claimed to it. He had with him an ingenious friend, who designed to have taken the plan and dimensions of the several caverns, and whatever was remarkable in them ; but the uneasiness they felt from a stifling heat hindered them from staying in the cave so long as was requisite for that purpose. This may seem somewhat surprising, especially if it be observed that we on the contrary found it extremely cool and refreshing. Now, in order to account for this alteration, 'tis to be observed those gentlemen felt the heat about the beginning of spring before the influence of the sun was powerful enough to open the pores of the earth, which as yet were close shut by the cold of the preceding winter ; so that those hot streams which are continually sent up by the central heat—for that there is a central heat all agree, though men differ as to its cause, some deriving from an incrusted star, others from the nucleus of a comet sunburnt in its perihelion—remained

[1] [The MS. concludes with this note which has nothing to do directly with the Cave of Dunmore, and is only of interest as a mark of time, connecting that essay with Berkeley's first publication, *Arithmetica and Miscellanea Mathematica*, published early in 1707. If I am not mistaken, it is a note of two references to the *Philosophical Transactions* that Berkeley required for that publication. No. 216 is by E. Halley on logarithms, and No. 257 is on the application of algebra to testimony, and Berkeley refers to No. 257 in his *De ludo algebraico*, and probably needed the other reference for his section on logarithms ; see above, pp. 197 and 219.—Ed.]

pent up in the cavern, not finding room to perspire through the uppermost strata of rock and earth : whereas I was there about a month after the summer solstice, when the solar heat had for a long time and in its full strength dwelt upon the face of the earth, unlocking its pores and thereby yielding a free passage to the ascending streams. Mr. Jackson informed me of another observable [fact] that I had not taken notice of, *viz.* that some of the bones which lay in the water were covered over with a stony crust ; and Mr. Bindon (so was the other gentleman called) told me he met with one that to him seemed petrified throughout.

Before I have done I must crave leave to advertise my reader that where, out of compliance with custom, I use the terms congelation, petrifaction, &c., I would not be understood to think the stones formed of the droppings were made of mere water metamorphosed by any lapidific virtue whatever ; being, as to their origin and consistence, entirely of the learned Dr. Woodward's [1] opinion, as set forth in his *Natural History of the Earth*, pp. 191 and 192, where he takes that kind of stone, by naturalists termed stalactites, to be only a concretion of such stony particles as are borne along with the water in its passage through the rock from whence it distils.

[1] [John Woodward (1665–1728), F.R.S., geologist and professor of Physic, Gresham College, London, author of *Essay toward a natural history of the earth . . .*, London, 1695.—Ed.]

THE END

Printed in Great Britain by
Thomas Nelson (Printers) Ltd, London and Edinburgh